MONASTIC WISDOM SERIES: NUMBER SEVENTY-TWO

THE WAY OF THE HEART

MONASTIC WISDOM SERIES: NUMBER SEVENTY-TWO

The Way of the Heart

The Spiritual Experience of André Louf

Charles Wright
Translated by Brian Kerns, OCSO

Cistercian Publications
cistercianpublications.org

LITURGICAL PRESS
Collegeville, Minnesota
litpress.org

A Cistercian Publications title published by Liturgical Press

Cistercian Publications
Editorial Offices
161 Grosvenor Street
Athens, Ohio 45701
cistercianpublications.org

Translated from Charles Wright, *Le Chemin du Coeur: L'expérience spirituelle d'André Louf (1929–2010)*, © Éditions Salvator, Paris, 2023, by permission from Salvator.

1 2 3 4 5 6 7 8 9

Library of Congress Cataloging-in-Publication Data

Names: Wright, Charles, 1981- author. | Kerns, Brian, translator.
Title: The way of the heart : the spiritual experience of André Louf / Charles Wright ; translated by Brian Kerns, OCSO.
Other titles: Chemin du coeur. English
Description: Athens, Ohio : Cistercian Publications ; Collegeville, Minnesota : Liturgical Press, [2024] | Series: Monastic wisdom series ; number 72 | Translation of: Le chemin du coeur. | Includes bibliographical references. | Summary: "Award-winning French author shares the biography and spiritual journey of Cistercian abbot Dom André Louf. Based on a wide variety of interviews, printed sources, and Dom André Louf's spiritual journal, The Way of the Heart narrates Louf's spiritual journey from his childhood in Flanders through his becoming a monk in a Cistercian monastery, his ten years of retirement as a hermit in a Benedictine monastery in the south of France, and his death. During his career he struggled with conflicting vocational desires-sometimes wishing to serve as a pastor, academic, abbot, or to immerse himself in eremitic contemplation. That struggle is the leading thread through this biography, which portrays a man whose immense gifts pulled him in many directions, while always endeavoring to submit himself to God's will"—Provided by publisher.
Identifiers: LCCN 2024012912 (print) | LCCN 2024012913 (ebook) | ISBN 9780879073350 (trade paperback) | ISBN 9780879073374 (epub) | ISBN 9780879073398 (pdf)
Subjects: LCSH: Louf, André. | Abbots—Belgium—Biography. | BISAC: RELIGION / Monasticism | RELIGION / Christianity / Catholic
Classification: LCC BX4705.L6758 W7513 2024 (print) | LCC BX4705.L6758 (ebook) | DDC 271/.1202 [B]—dc23/eng/20240412
LC record available at https://lccn.loc.gov/2024012912
LC ebook record available at https://lccn.loc.gov/2024012913

For Elvira, Joseph, and Anaïs
For Julie

The Kingdom of God is within you. (Luke 17:21)

The terrible conflicts that divide the world
are the consequences of a general lack of interior life.
(*Amour et silence,* by Dom Jean-Baptiste Porion)

To consent, O Lord, to be your work, to be nothing
more than that: the work that you build with patience,
with the debris of the masterpieces of our dreams.
(*Journal Spirituel*, by André Louf, July 16, 1977)

Contents

Translator's Preface xi

Introduction xiii

Chapter 1 Infancy of a Contemplative 1

Chapter 2 "All Is done, and All Begins" 21

Chapter 3 The Roman Escape 37

Chapter 4 Discovering the Internal Man 47

Chapter 5 The Grace of *Collectanea* 57

Chapter 6 A Solitary Soul 67

Chapter 7 *Habemus Abbatem* 85

Chapter 8 A Flemish *Staretz* 99

Chapter 9 The Exegete of *Aggiornamento* 107

Chapter 10 The Book of Experience 125

Chapter 11 Spiritual Accompaniment 143

Chapter 12 A Carthusian Heart 169

Chapter 13 A Hesychast Abbot 187

Chapter 14 Toward the One Undivided Church 205

Chapter 15 Oracle of the Trappist Order 225

Chapter 16 Renunciation 247

Chapter 17 The Hermit of Saint-Lioba 261

Epilogue 285

Sources 295

General Bibliography 309

Notes of Gratitude 315

Translator's Preface

Reading and translating Charles Wright's biography of André Louf has been a spiritual experience for me. It has taken over four years, but it was worth it. We owe Charles Wright a debt of gratitude for making such a spiritual life available to us, and of course Marsha Dutton and Cistercian Publications for accepting it. The author adopts a very conversational style that makes for readability, although excursions into mystical theology can be problematic, and Louf was conversant especially with the Flemish mystical tradition, not to mention the Syriac. Other than that, the book reads smoothly throughout.

I have tried for a literal translation, but this has not always been possible, perhaps because of the complexity of the subject. Once André's adoption of his father's first name became clear, we have tried to simplify references by using his surname, "Louf," most of the time. For the footnotes we have tried to simplify by incorporating passages originally in footnotes into the main text, especially where they were explanatory or extended the argument of the text. I have reproduced the bibliography at the end as in the original French. I trust Dom André is pleased.

Br. Brian Kerns
Abbey of the Genesee
Piffard, NY 14533

Introduction

The Painter of Interiority

March 2016. Trappist Abbey of Mont-des-Cats. It is 5:15. The bell announces the Office of Vespers. From the four corners of the monastery silent shadows converge in the direction of the church. From a distance we have the impression of a flock of sheep driven home by a shepherd to drink from the watering place.

Some hours earlier a bus driver was alert enough to let me off at the bottom of a hill in a little brick town with an unpronounceable name, like so many in this part of French Flanders. Despite my being a native of Paris (not the best introduction to the northerners), this carnival personage honored me with his sympathy: "When I pick you up in ten days," he declared in escorting me onto the sidewalk, "If you manage to pronounce 'Godewaersvelde' without stumbling over the syllables, I will buy you a beer to drink to the health of the monks, since it is certainly there that you are going, is it not?" I agreed with a smile, then, loaded down like a mule, I climbed by a little path that crossed the potato fields and ended up on top of the hill that was crowned by the graceful shadow cast by the Cistercian abbey. With the red ochre of its bricks and its church capped with small towers in a neo-Gothic style, I thought I was in an English boarding school. The brother guest master took me to my room on the third floor of the guest house with a view of the monks' cemetery, where the one lies to whom I owe my presence here: Fr. André Louf, who was the abbot of this place for thirty-five years, 1963–1997.

The abbey's garden where I am walking before the Office starts is enchanting. Mont-des-Cats' height is 150 meters. It is not Everest, but this is flat country, and the smallest contrast uncovers a vast landscape. On one side is the northern plain that goes from Arras to Ypres, then stretches out toward Gand and Bruges. It is a broad strip of flat land, about which Marguerite Yourcenar, native of the place, had the feeling "of advancing on a bed where the sea had retired for the night."[1] In clear weather we seem to catch a glimpse of the outskirts of Pays-de-Calais and even the belfry of Lille. On the other side of the peak the view reaches all the way to the coast from Ostend to the cape Gris-Nez, with, at the turn of the horizon, the cranes at the port of Dunkirk. It is that side I am viewing, looking towards the Netherlands, which runs into the sea. There it is before me the country as the primitive Flemish painted it on their canvases, full of radiant serenity and simple majesty, with tillage as far as the eye can see, a checkerboard of cut fields like a Cubist painting or like a chaplet of villages connected around churches as slender as needles. Faced with this landscape, completely flat except for bell towers, belfries, and a few birches that lift up their crowns, we can understand why it is here that giants are found; it is a way for these tall northern people not to let themselves be shut in by the absence of a horizon, to take pride in themselves, and to keep raising and elevating their aspirations to the skies.

September 2016. Abbey of Sainte-Lioba, Simiane. The fire of the Provençal sun has eclipsed the intimacy of Flemish light. Here in 1997 André Louf put down his luggage after having laid down his abbatial charge. At the age of sixty-five

1. Marguerite Yourcenar, *Archives du nord* (Paris: Gallimard, 1977), 17.

he would finally hearken to his life's dream and become a hermit, a solitary devoted to silence and continual prayer. With all haste the abbess of the place, his friend Elaié, had transformed the former donkey's stable into a wee little house, hidden from view by high wooden ramparts; it was an ideal space to shelter the last days of the abbot. Here in that hermitage next to the abbey I am writing these lines. Mother Elaié, who still shines at the head of her Benedictine community, proposed that I make a stay here to get a feel for the place, breathe in the atmosphere, and understand the interior things. I settled down in Dom André's office, where he spent hours translating obscure ancient authors, mostly Syrian monks of the seventh century. The window limits the horizon that was his for the space of twelve years. There are some olive trees, lightly shaken by the wind, some pines, some live oaks, the blue sky, and the Royal Pillar, which resembles a rocky tooth lost on top of a crest. Dom André loved this landscape, the velvet color, and its spirituality. I linger for some time in the tiny dark place that served as an oratory for him, and the silence covers me like an overcoat. A stunning density is present there. He kept vigil there for so many hours and sowed so many prayers that prayer seems to stick to the walls and be secreted from their surface.

In the course of a stroll, the crackling of the pine needles under my feet awakened me from my reverie, and I asked myself what place Dom André had taken in my life in six months. I have to say that I had known his name for a long time as a strange sound. At a time when I was discerning in myself a vocation to prayer, I happened upon a documentary film about this place, Simiane, showing him in his hermitage. I remember how surprised I was by the humble joy that radiated from his presence and by the way he spoke about prayer as a leveling or an internal shock. Then, after I became a novice in a monastery, I was confronted with what is modestly called in monastic parlance "self-knowledge"; it is as stirring as it is uncontrollable, this interior world that silence and the absence of distractions awake in us, as if it were a sleeping beast.

In this context I happened upon one of Louf's works that was devoted to ascesis, that is, to the interior combat. Essentially, he wrote in that book, the objective of the monastic life is not to realize ascetic prowess, like an athlete accumulating exploits with the force of his arm to derive honor therefrom; rather, it is to guide the monk to a dilemma, a defeat, a heartbreak, a point of death, or a point of despoilment, where he is confronted by his fragility and gropes about in his poor truth until on his knees he learns that he cannot go on alone. In this way he is reduced to his simplest terms and to his radical poverty, and is then ready to meet the grace of the face-to-face vision that awaits him, precisely at the point of extreme frailty that few accept.[2]

The discovery of these pages, which I intuited to be a transcript of his own path, were a kind of balm for me, a light, as if in them the understanding of the trials in which I was engulfed had been revealed. Although frightening, this crisis was a stage in my human and spiritual growth, aiding me to acquire humility.

Such were the few memories that kept running through my mind when I learned of a USB drive that held the memory of the computer he had used while he was a hermit, from 1998 until his death in 2010, the last twelve years of his numerical existence. This drive, not yet studied by anyone, held part of the archives of Mont-des-Cats. According to my information, the monks were not opposed to its utilization, and my profile, combining certain historical credentials with an intimate knowledge of the monastic world, had reassured them.

So I journeyed to the abbey in March 2016 for a preliminary visit. I still remember the emotions I felt when I inserted

2. André Louf, *La Voie Cistercienne: À l'école de l'amour* (Paris: Desclée de Brouwer, 1980), 86–90.

the drive in my computer. What would I find? Unpublished texts? Anything inadmissible? Correspondence? A spiritual journal? I spent whole nights opening the files of this drive with Word 95, one after the other. They were as poorly arranged as was his cell. Although I dug up certain nuggets, such as a series of unpublished homilies Louf had delivered here at Sainte-Lioba that are the best introduction to his spirituality,[3] the collection was on the whole rather disappointing. Or so it would have been for an editor eager for unpublished material or a journalist anxious for revelations. But I was neither of these, and the essential thing was somewhere else. For me the window opened upon a continent. This drive in fact gave me access to his teaching, scattered among various articles that had been published during the last ten years of his life.

Another important figure of contemporary Christianity, the Jesuit François Varillon, has recounted that his discovery of the novelist Paul Claudel was for him a decisive revelation. Claudel's writings had uncovered for him the deep regions of his being. He even invented an expression to signify this collaboration: such authors are "delegates of expression":[4] "Claudel was a delegate of expression for me; he expressed with the most lyrical and reasonable language what essential being and life are."

In plunging into Louf's articles I had the impression that I had found such a delegate, one who bore the word. His classical language expressed all that I held deep within me, without being able to formulate it, but also all toward which I secretly tended and aspired. Through him I discovered my own aspirations. An appearance of nothing, a quest then took a new turn, a more personal one. The father was now no

3. André Louf, *S'abandonner à l'amour. Méditation à Sainte-Lioba* (Paris: Salvator, 2017).

4. François Varillon, *Traversée d'un croyant* (Paris: Bayard, 2005), 37.

longer simply an object to study. Instead, his life and writings revealed my own self to me. It was as if he had asked the same questions, as if he had struck against the same walls, as if he had fallen into the same ruts before finding the light that shone on every page of his writings and guided me like a beacon in a period of my own life that was cloudy. An old abbot to whom I confided this interior way wrote to me one day, "It belongs to spiritual fatherhood so to anchor the desire for life and happiness that lies deep within every one of us. There is no helpful map for the venture into the desert, because no one is able to discern the topography of these strange places. A guide is essential. You have found one of the best. Do not lose him." In the space of a year Louf had become the guide in the desert of my life. He traced out sure paths for me through the "living life," the beautiful expression of the Flemish mystic Ruusbroec, all of whose works Louf translated into French.

To speak thus is to say that I had not understood one iota of this man, whose teaching exercised a strange spiritual fatherhood beyond the tomb. For more than a year I had lived with him in the light of his radiance. I had spent hours in the library sifting his interminable bibliography to gain understanding of his writings. Plans for conferences and outlines for retreats kept in the archives rendered the movement of his thought familiar to me. I met his family and found the friends of his youth. I even located the Greek interpreter, today a teacher of theology at a retreat in Thessalonica, the one who escorted Louf on his visit to Mount Athos in 1969, where he met all those considered spiritually prominent on the Holy Mountain.

I surveyed most of the places where he had lived, and I wrote to abbots, abbesses, psychologists, Flemish historians, Roman archivists, and Orthodox archimandrites with CV's as long as their beards, but also to simple Christians whose lives had been enlightened by a word spoken by him. I used diplomacy to loosen the tongues of monks who were not inclined to confide. Like bottles in the sea, my letters went out into the whole world, to the Roman Curia, to Finnish hermitages, to French and Italian Carthusians, to English, Dutch, Belgian, American, and Argentinian Trappists. I plowed the four corners of France, and I visited many of the European countries. And as the months passed my determination bore some fruit. Testimony began to flow from everywhere. Like a puzzle, Louf's portrait took shape. Most people delivered the sound of the same bell: meeting this great witness of the Christian contemplative tradition had been one of the graces of their lives.

Then one day, when I could no longer breathe the dust of archives, I noticed three school notebooks negligently placed near a yellow folder. Shaking all over, I opened the first one. At the top of the first page a date was written in close handwriting: "July 20, 1958." Underneath that a short paragraph began thus: "I must try to live in obedience in the present moment and for his grace."[5] I had dug up the treasure coveted by every biographer: the subject's spiritual journal.

The three small notebooks began in 1958, when Louf, still a young monk, was only twenty-seven, and they ended in 1997, at the time when the sixty-eight-year-old abbot had turned in his staff to plunge into the silence of a recluse. Nearly forty years of his existence were recorded in this text of high spiritual and literary quality, a work that I was doubtless the first one to open and that revealed the most intimate possession of any person: his prayer, and his dialogue with God. By the grace of this reading I had access to the holy of holies, to the interior sanctuary where the monk exposed without varnish his doubts, his desires, his contradictions, his suffering, his enthusiasms, and his yearnings.

5. André Louf, *Journal Spirituel* (henceforth JS), July 20, 1958.

The book below proceeds from a long apprenticeship under this great spiritual teacher of the West. Even if his name no longer speaks to the younger generation, Dom Louf was a giant, like those who brightened the carnivals of his youth. During his abbatial tenure his presence brightened the abbey of Mont-des-Cats, leading it to become one of the beacons of Western contemplative life. He was elected abbot during the Second Vatican Council, and he played leading roles in the movement back to the sources of the monastic life, re-interpreting the whole patristic tradition in the light of contemporary anthropology. For more than twenty years he was one of the oracles of the Trappist Order, known for the clarity of his thought, the depth of his viewpoints, and his contemplative sensitivity. His authority was uncontested, his resounding words listened to even by popes, who esteemed his intellectual and spiritual stature. Many of them appealed to Louf, for example confiding delicate missions to him because of his charismatic discernment; John Paul II, because of the quality of Louf's interior life, invited him to compose the meditations for the Way of the Cross at the Coliseum in Rome in 2004.[6] In ecumenical dialogue, where he was considered a goldsmith, he was respected as a spokesman for Latin monasticism.

But Louf's influence radiated well beyond the monastic world and the church. His writings became classics, translated into all the world's languages, and they advanced him as a spiritual teacher for contemporary Christianity. His books seek to inculcate Christian mysticism in contemporary language and ways of thinking; through these books he has awakened many men and women to the awareness of that heaven that everyone has within, sometimes without knowing it. In this he resembled his friend Thomas Merton, writing at the same time across the Atlantic.

6. André Louf, *Chemin de Croix du Colisée* (Namur: Fidélité, 2005).

Faced with such a person I began to doubt and even to feel giddy. He had dived into the deepest water of the spiritual life, where I had hardly wet my feet. How could I expect to examine the states of his soul? The density of his personality was intimidating, not to say overwhelming. On the surface Louf seemed to have attacked all the domains of curiosity: movement of ideas, his final literary creations, and poetry, of which he had published a youthful collection. His was a truly universal mind; he was at the same time theologian, erudite, polyglot, amateur artist, writer, giver of conferences, and music lover—but also a musician, able to play many of the scores of Bach on the piano or organ. And all this did not deter him from political reality, which he observed with almost as much interest as he did an ancient Syrian manuscript from the time when Christianity was emerging from its swaddling clothes. Of men of this quality there are only one or two in a generation.

When I was just about ready to give up, some monks and nuns came to cheer me up. It was high time, they insisted, that light should be shed on this spiritual person, who had, like a poor man, died to general indifference. The reactions of friends also incited me to perseverance. Every time I read them passages from Louf's writings the miracle was repeated: they felt themselves understood, met in their deepest aspirations. How could this man, who could have been their grandfather and who knew nothing about their lives, living out his own life within a cloister, have touched them so deeply? What did his spirituality have that was so special that it could leap over epochs in this way?

If Louf's teaching jumped over seasons and seemed, like that of the saints, unfashionable, there were many reasons. All that he wrote he had first lived. We are not dealing with a theologian of the parlor. Besides, he never composed foursquare systematic treatises. All that is his is illuminated by interior life. Like his teacher, Saint Bernard, he spoke from experience. To use technical language, Louf was a phenomenologist of the spiritual life. He described, as few previous writers have, what happens when a person prays, the experience of one who frees oneself to pray.

One of the great contemporary historians of Christian mysticism has revealed the existence of a spiritual tradition whose beginnings go back perhaps as far as the Desert Fathers. But it really ripened with the Cistercians, then with the Franciscans Duns Scotus and Bonaventure, before the refulgence of Rusbroec and the Devotio Moderna. Its path was also followed by Ignatius of Loyola and the Salesians, until it inspired Charles de Foucauld.[7] André Louf took his place among the heirs of this tradition. For them the queen of the faculties of the soul is not the *intellect*, as it is for the followers of Saint Thomas Aquinas, but what can be called—according to the anthropology going back to Aristotle—the *will*, that is, the faculty of the affections or desires. In this spiritual movement the turning point of the experience of God is less reason than the power of being affected, in the sense that Saint Bernard gives to the word *affectus*. It covers the whole gamut of responses of human sensitivity when it is touched, moved, or shaken by the Holy Spirit, the Master of the interior work. Louf was one of the great teachers of that spiritual sensitivity that is attentive to the vibrations of the breath of God, who like a musician causes the music and dancing of souls.

Like the spirituality of the fathers of the church, Louf's is supported by a dynamic and unifying anthropology. It is with all one's faculties—psychological, affective, bodily, intellectual, and spiritual—that one journeys toward God. So the patristic tradition inspired Louf's therapeutic approach to the spiritual life. He appealed to an encounter with Christ, the physician

7. Dominique Salin, Introduction to Louis Lallement, *Doctrine Spirituelle* (Paris: Desclée de Brouwer, 2011), 21–22.

of souls and bodies, so his teaching proposes a "spiritual medicine"[8] intended to heal the person in his depths.

Louf's vision of the church and of God is thus perfectly in accord with the coordinates of our times: a Christianity placed in the world, stripped of all triumphalism. He flourished long before the coming of Pope Francis, who seems to have drawn his themes and approaches from him. Louf's fervent appeal was for "a church of the poor at the service of the poor." He invited Christians "to a conversion to mercy and to a humble pardoning love."[9]

He expressed this goal in his explanation of monasticism today:

> Monasticism has an exterior face that is unceasingly adjusted from one reform to the next, to the variable imperatives of the epochs that follow one another without ever being the same. But above all, in their interior grace, there is progressive detail in harmony with the spiritual waves awakened by the Spirit in the church. Just as there was a monasticism for the early Christian period, and for the later time of cathedrals and crusades, so also there is already a monasticism for a period that has become secular, and for a church that makes herself a servant and poor, which has distanced herself from all the earthly powers.[10]

He was twenty years ahead. Like all the great spiritual teachers of the twentieth century, he insisted that God hides

8. Jean-Claude Larchet, *Thérapeutique des maladies spirituelles: Introduction à la tradition ascétique de l'église orthodoxe* (Suresnes: Éditions de l'Ancre, 1991), 13.

9. André Louf, "Donnons à Dieu l'occasion de se manifester," *La Croix* 25 Dec. 1999.

10. André Louf, "Saint Benoït, homme de Dieu pour tous les temps," in *Fraternités monastiques de Jérusalem, Saint Benoït aujourd'hui* (Paris: Cerf, 1980), 13–14.

beneath the poor and humble features of Christ. It was the meek and humble heart of Jesus that appealed to Louf. So his name is written in the whole spiritual literature of the late twentieth century, a literature that promotes the image of a discreet, effaced, even feeble God, projected for example by *The Lowest* by Christian Bobin, *The Humble God* by François Varillon, or even the spirituality of Maurice Zundel or Jean Vanier.[11]

But the principal reason for Louf's attraction is found elsewhere; it is related to the fact that this adventurer had explored the soul in every culture. If he ran away to the desert, it was for the sake of the intense experience made available by silence and solitude. He went out basically as a pioneer, to go and meet the great questions of existence through poverty and fundamental human solitude, to unmask every single one of its illusions and myths, and to experience what he called "the very bottom of human existence."[12] That is why we feel unmasked when we open his books. He has pierced the human heart, toured the feelings, and experienced all the emotions. In an epoch of impoverishment of sensitivity, when the smiley image takes the place of internal meteorology, Louf emerges as an impressionist painter able to show all the minute shades of the soul's colors with perfect mastery over nuances.

In one of his novels Antoine Blondin has someone tell his hero, "I have formed the habit of living outside my own doorway. It is too dark inside."[13] Most of us, like him, have

11. For the origin of this theme of the veiling of God, so much a part of the history of the twentieth century (Verdun, Auschwitz, Gulag), see Dominique Salin, Introduction to *L'Abandon à la providence divin* (Paris: Desclée de Brouwer/Bellarmin, 2005), 7–30.

12. André Louf, *À la grâce de Dieu: Entretiens avec Stéphane Delberghe* (Namur: Fidélité, 2002), 99.

13. Antoine Blondin, *Un singe en hiver* (Paris: La Table Rond, 1959), 59.

lost the sense of the interior. We live on the surface of ourselves, indifferent to what is happening in the heart; we live in a world that calls our attention to externals. As soon as the moment arrives to land, to reflect, to clarify events, we throw up our screens, assembled by the continual flow of impressions. At the end of his life, Louf was more and more anxious about this culture of dispersion and distraction. Contemporary humanity was divided, he thought: "At one and the same time people were impelled toward the outside of themselves and toward centers of interest that opened up before their eyes but left them hungry, and then were secretly attracted toward the interior, tormented by a thirst whose meaning they could no longer decipher."[14] Louf himself knew where to find the meaning of this thirst that burns the heart of every person. Years of prayer had refined his spiritual senses. He was a practitioner of the art of interior listening that was on the way to disappearance, and he was counted one of the best formators in the life of the Spirit.

In fact that is the reason that I have written this biography. It is definitely not a pious biography, like those that tamper with the lives of saints to make them harmless, to fix them in plaster, and to offer them as sources of edification.[15] Rather it is a story that traces a journey along crooked lines with its incertitudes and contradictions, bogged down and urged on by questions such as "Can God really fill one's life?" "How can we land on this continent that each one bears within?" "Is it possible to tame the desires that rumble in our hearts and trouble us?" "What good is the spiritual life?" "How can we learn to pray?" "Can anyone become a peaceful person?"

14. André Louf, Preface to Jean-Marie Howe, *Secret of the Heart. Spiritual Being*, Monastic Wisdom series 2 (Kalamazoo, MI: Cistercian Publications, 2005), x–xii.

15. The method owes much to Jean-François Six, "De l'hagiographie à la biographie," *Vie Spirituelle* (Nov.–Dec. 1939): 719–21.

And then, in this world that spins like a crazy top, "are there still some things that don't pass away, or rocks to which we can tie our lives?" "What is the secret of humble love, that love that retains nothing for itself?" "How can we be made free?" What is this mystical life like to which religious are supposed to be committed? Does God really raise up again the broken-hearted through their trials? How does the person so broken behave to be rehabilitated?

The intention is not so much to answer such questions logically, as intellectuals might do privately in their rooms, or to offer the questions as sources of edification. Instead they are posed in the concrete existence of a monk—of one of the greatest monks to whom the twentieth century gave birth. The following chapters form a spiritual treatise on his life.

CHAPTER 1

Infancy of a Contemplative

Although no one can be reduced to his physical descent, nevertheless ancestry poses a dilemma when it is a question of one's total existence. Jaak Louf was the fruit of the union between Elvire Decramer and André Louf. During his youth Louf bore his baptismal name, Jaak, but as required by monastic usage, he later dropped it in favor of the name André.

Originally from western Flanders, Jaak's father André was a teacher of law and a lawyer. He had a taciturn temperament and was very introverted. He never recovered from the death of his mother a few weeks after his birth, and he carried a deep sense of melancholy. Yet he had an inclination toward poetry that his melancholy fostered, publishing several collections praised by Flemish critics. When he sat alone to compose his verses, his wife teased him: "Be quiet. He is conversing with his muse."[1] Tuberculosis, not entirely cured, afflicted him with a handicap, a kind of stiffness in his leg, that from his infancy on caused him to limp. As a result, he had an irrational fear lest his children should contract that illness; he repeatedly asked them to dress warmly and to avoid catching cold.

1. Willy de Smedt, Dom André's brother-in-law, in a conversation with the author.

André Louf the elder met Elvire during his studies at Louvain, and Jaak was born on December 28, 1929, the feast of the Holy Innocents. The following year, 1930, the couple settled at Bruges, where Jaak lived for the whole period of his childhood. The family belonged to the average middle class, but the couple's ancestry was more modest. Jaak's paternal grandfather, Léon, ran a grain concern at Neuve-Église in the region of Ypres at the French border, but his mother's side was still more plebeian: she was a native of Gistel, near Ostend. Louf grew up in a family that was marked by a certain social mobility. From his mother he inherited his warm disposition, his communicative gentleness, and his way of accepting people. To his father, with whom he had a rather restrained relationship, he owed his legal education and his taste for poetry.[2] That is, he had a concern for the right word and for precise thinking, qualities that served him well later on as abbot and architect of the new regulations for monks arising from *aggiornamento*.

The family home in the Rue des Aiguilles in Bruges was a feminine world. Except for his father, Jaak was surrounded by women: his mother, his two beloved sisters, Lieve and Maria, and his godmother, Amilia-Sophie Demeester, who had raised Elvire after her biological mother died when she was still a baby.[3] Even if their parents showed a certain restraint in expressing strong feelings, as was the custom of the time, the children grew up in an environment that was protective and loving. Louf later wrote, "When we accompany people in the path of growth in the monastic life, we can determine how far failures on the level of relationships with parents can sometimes cause immeasurable wounds. It is as though a person had no spinal column to let him stand up, to be 'vertical-

2. Under the pseudonym of Tillo Van Wiek, in 1965 Louf published a collection entitled *Gelouterd Gelaat,* which means "purified countenance."

3. From Lieve Louf, Dom André's sister, in correspondence with the author.

ized.' I think that I have received the gift of internal force that enables me to say who I am and to situate myself."[4]

The only shadow in this picture was the character of Jaak's father, whose self-effacement certainly left a grievous wound, a void in the boy's life. "Of all the things a father gives his son," he later said,

> His word is undoubtedly one of the most essential. It is almost the same as the gift of life. A father who is mute or voiceless would not be prepared to assume his role toward his son. It is not enough for a father to beget and give life. It is necessary for him to take charge of that life, direct it, and give it meaning. It is necessary that he call it by his name. Without this the life of his own son will always remain formless, a mass of infinite possibilities, but undetermined; he will not deliver any one of them, because no father will have freed it in him, giving him a name and an identity. By his words every father begets his son a second time and launches him with confidence on the adventure of existence.[5]

Undoubtedly Jaak waited for these words a long time, and they never came. Is it necessary to seek any other cause for his lack of self-confidence, his need for confirmation, assurance, and love, and the irresolution that he fought against all his life?

The Love of God and the Desire for Learning

Jaak received his formation in private teaching first from nuns,[6] then at the Collège Saint-Louis at Bruges, reputed for

4. André Louf, *À la grâce de Dieu: Entretiens avec Stéphane Delberghe* (Namur: Fidélité, 2002), 14.

5. André Louf, Homily for the sixth Sunday of Easter, Archives of Mont-des-Cats, 1980 (hereafter ADMC).

6. The Sisters of St. Joseph, says Lieve Louf in correspondence with the author.

the quality of its teachers.[7] In later years he would preserve intact the memory of these teachers, whose literary culture and pedagogical quality had given him "a solid formation in humanism, which an initiation in the spiritual life completed with success."[8] With complete loftiness of intelligence and feeling these educators (mostly Jesuits) awoke in him a love for Greek and Latin antiquity and for Flemish and French classical literature. At their side he learned French by reading Racine, La Fontaine, and Corneille. He appreciated the purity of the seventeenth-century French language, including its spiritual writers, with Fenelon at the head, and this literature would remain a faithful attendant all his life.

Additionally, it was by reading these writers that this born psychologist learned to decipher the gamut of feelings. To the great Christian romantics—Mauriac, Claudel, Bernanos—he owed the knowledge of the heart that permitted him partially to compensate for the lack of human experience linked to his entering the monastery at seventeen, when he had the psychological and affective structure of an adolescent. Later he also drew from literary wisdom the inspiration with which to nourish his meditations. To novices who had been hampered by bad parents, he sometimes suggested that they read Mauriac's *Genitrix,* which recounts the control of one mother over her son. In fact, like a stream of water, literature crops up in all his teaching.[9]

7. Adolphe Gesché, *Discours pour la remise du titre de docteur, honoris causa, à André Louf*, Université catholique de Louvain, 2 Feb. 1994.

8. Louf, *À la grâce de Dieu*, 9

9. In one place he quotes Jean Paul Sartre (*Au gré de la grâce: Propos sur la prière* [Paris: Desclée de Brouwer, 1989], 39–41), in another Julien Green (Homily for the twenty-sixth Sunday of Ordinary Time, IMC, 2005), elsewhere a poem of Lamartine ("Salve Regina," *La Vie Spirituelle* 80 [2000]: 340). In a homily on a young brother's taking of the habit he cites Didier Decoin's last novel: *Homélie pour la prise d'habit de David*, ADMC 1997. At the beginning of his monastic life he discovered the "new joy of

Jaak was endowed with a lively intelligence and uncommon memory. He was a brilliant student. With his natural curiosity he browsed in most areas of knowledge. He even knew how to restore those aspects that he had not only stocked, but had also amalgamated and placed under control. He had an above-normal ability to synthesize and express both oral and written thoughts. Among his many aptitudes, that for languages most surprised his teachers. Although born Flemish, he excelled primarily in French. Although he always had his writing in French read over by a native French speaker, for fear of having slipped in some Flemish idiom, he wrote a pure, classical, elegant French.[10] He loved to distraction this French language, that with which he expressed his intimacy in his God.

But his talent for languages made him much more than a Francophone—he would become a veritable polyglot, at home with more than ten living and dead languages: Dutch, English, German, French, Italian, Russian, Greek, Latin, Syriac, Hebrew, Aramaic, with smatterings of Danish and Slavonic, the language used in the Orthodox liturgy. He also had a mastery in Middle Dutch, the dialect in which the mystic Ruusbroec wrote his masterpieces.

Jaak's teachers, however, were not only people endowed with great humanistic and Christian culture, but also prayerful people. Life at school was marked from one end to the other by religious practices. "We were obliged," recalled Louf,

> to participate in the daily Eucharist, as well as Sunday Vespers. It was about this time that I began to appreciate the celebration of the Divine Office. I also impatiently

---

love by having eliminated all self absorption," and at that point Cyrano de Bergerac came to his mind as a figure of a "friendship that is a pure gift of self in self-forgetfulness" (JS March 21, 1960).

10. Willy de Smedt, conversation with the author.

> waited for the yearly retreat, usually preached by one of the Jesuit fathers. There I acquired this taste for the interior life that has never deserted me. I also owe much to my spiritual father, one of the teachers at the high school. He was the one who taught me to pray, not with long discussions, but chiefly by his own powerful example. I can still see him sit down beside me, open his missal, and read such and such a text from the daily Mass, and comment on it, praying with a loud voice. Was there any better school for someone who would later devote himself to a life consecrated to prayer?"[11]

A Chivalrous Spirit

Besides the Greco-Latin humanities, Catholic Action was Louf's other great source of apprenticeship. Jaak's mind was formed in contact with this movement, which arose during the 1920s at the wish of Pope Pius XI as a defense against the rise of atheism and rationalism, which formed a vast front that he deemed able to shake Christianity to its foundations. With the 1922 encyclical letter *Ubi arcano Dei consilio* the Holy Father launched a great counter-offensive, a kind of campaign of reconquest of the masses. Catholic Action was conceived at that point, considered the spearhead of this effort of "moral rearmament."[12] During the years 1940–1950, those of Louf's adolescence, this movement of Catholicism saw its golden age, especially in Flanders, where it was involved with the education of young people. Jaak invested himself therein with all his heart, especially at the center of the Katholieke Studentenaktie (KSA), the Flemish ornament of the Francophone students. He joined the group in 1941, at the age of

11. André Louf, *À la grâce de Dieu*, 9–10.

12. Lieve Gevers, "Apogée et fin d'une époque (1926–1961): L'archevêché sous le cardinal Van Roey," in *L'Archidiocèse de Maline-Bruxelles. 450 ans d'histoire*, 2 vols. (Anvers: Halewijn, 2009), 2:193.

twelve, and he did not leave it until the moment of his entrance into the abbey in 1947, six uninterrupted years.

In 1930, anti-Belgic Flemish nationalism (Flamingantism) began to affect an important portion of these movements, in a singular form.[13] The Katholiek Studentenactie (KSA) had been founded in 1928 by the bishop of Bruges to counter this tendency toward political activism and turn the young people again toward religious and apostolic action, at the same time assuming that they were rooted in Flemish identity, but conceived as an openly cultural affiliation. "There," recalls Louf, "We received an education in a citizenship that rooted us in our double identity, Flemish and Belgian. Without going to extremes, of course. It was a way of entitling us to a legitimate claim to Flemish existence, while taking care that this clearly affirmed difference could become the basis of a new brotherhood."[14]

A little like the Boy Scouts, the movement proposed a total experience to the young people. They received an intellectual, human, and spiritual formation, joining openness to the world with a rootedness in Christian and Flemish history. This openness focused primarily on the mind. The young people were encouraged for example to prepare talks on the great authors of their patrimony. At the same time their curiosity was stimulated by the publication of a monthly review that attracted Christian social attention towards the world. Those on the staff, both lay and religious, wished also to communicate to the young people a sense of service and en-

13. Roger Aubert, "Organisation et caractères des mouvements de jeunesse catholiques en Belgique," in *La "Gioventu cattolica" dopo l'unita, 1868–1968*, ed. Gabriele de Rosa, Politica e Storia 28 (Rome: Ediziones di storia et letteratura, 1972), 309–10; Lieve Gever and Louis Vos, "The Catholic Flemish Student Movement, 1875–1935: Emergence and Decline of a Unique Youth Movement," in Griet Verschelden, et al., *The History of Youth Work in Europe,* 7 vols. (Strasbourg: Éditions du Conseil de l'Europe, 2009), 1:32–34.

14. André Louf, *À la grâce de Dieu*, 12.

gagement for the transformation of the world. But the movement also claimed for itself the terrain of concrete fraternity. Pilgrimages and summer camps regularly gathered them to let them experience a fellowship sealed by rituals inspired by the Boy Scouts: saluting the flag, competition in sports, and long walks in natural surroundings.

This kind of openness went along with an enthusiasm for the romance and chivalry of the Middle Ages, associated with the golden age of the church. The pedagogy of the movement took place during summer camps at old castles in order to inspire the youth through this medieval environment, aiming at transforming them into missionaries, capable of spreading the spirit of the Gospel in the circumstances of their lives. Inspired by the pope's encyclical, KSA's motto—*Vlaanderen Hernieuwen in Christus* ("Restore Flanders to Christ")—placed the emphasis on the apostolate. "A member is expected to be a soldier of Christ," confirms the movement's archivist. The uniform bore the symbol XP, the two Greek letters for Christ. Each member knew by heart the KSA law that belonged to a catechism.[15] Every evening each one was to recite, kneeling, a meter away from the bed in order not to fall asleep during prayer, "Je vous salue Marie," three times, and a "Notre Père."[16]

Once a member reached fifteen, the movement proposed a still more intense experience of faith. In the romantic style

15. "He lives a life of union with Christ; bound by [Christ's] grace he venerates Mary as Queen-Mother; he is a child of the church, faithful to the pope and to the bishop; he wants to be an apostle by his example, his words, and his actions; he serves his people and his homeland by his love and strong fidelity; at school and at home he is joyful and responsible, and he sees a brother in every comrade; he remains faithful to the truth and to his pledged word; he submits his own will to God's; he lives righteously and soberly according to the Flemish tradition of chivalry" (English translation from the French translation of Éric Colenbier).

16. "I greet you, Marie," and "Our Father," that is, the Lord's Prayer (Éric Colenbier, archivist of the Katholiek Studentenactie in the diocese of Bruges, in correspondence with the author).

characteristic of the time, this experience of faith was called an engagement of chivalry; it was a matter of offering of one's whole life to Christ. There was a ceremony of "dubbing" preceded by a night of meditation; "then the knight commits himself to make a daily quarter hour's prayer and have spiritual accompaniment by a priest," as Louf recalls. He made his oath in April 1946 at the age of sixteen. The least we can say is that he kept his promise.

In one of his rare autobiographical writings Louf expressed his debt toward this movement, which was "the occasion of a real human and spiritual growth."[17] Through this commitment he first discovered the whole extent of his potential, especially his talent of leadership, his ability to convince, to have ascendancy over other people, to attract other people, thanks to his words of persuasion. In the presence of these adolescents, thanks to the play-acting that he did at school, Jaak practiced the oratorical art at which he would be a virtuoso once he became abbot. And so this introverted young man freed all his potential for sociability in his contact with the youth movement.

Finally Louf owed to the movement his sharpened interest in the important evolutions taking place in the world. It was during this period that his taste for politics started to grow; it would never leave him. His inclination then favored the Christian Democrats, a conviction shared by many members of his family, but later his choice fell on General de Gaulle, whose elevated vision he admired.

A Son of Bruges

"Every city is a state of soul," wrote the author Rodenbach about Bruges. "She exercises an ascendancy over those who

17. André Louf, *À la grâce de Dieu*, 10–11.

sojourn there."[18] There is no doubt that the Venice of the North formed the imagination of Louf and fashioned his sensitivity and his religious feeling. Bruges is not a city like any other city. This city of art and history invented a style of painting, of architecture, and of mysticism, a whole spiritual language, in fact, which Jaak learned to speak. In the prayer he recited on the eve of his solemn profession in 1954, the young monk counted among his great renunciations the fact that he would never see Bruges again. "By my vow of stability," he wrote, "which ties me to one French monastery, I sacrifice my homeland, my people, my mother tongue, and the whole Dutch culture. I separate myself in a special way from the city of Bruges. You know, O Lord, to what point all that has lived in my heart."[19] When he became abbot and wanted to honor a guest, they made a pilgrimage to the city of his birth, passing the Basilica of the Precious Blood, to which he had a great devotion, and then the Collège Saint-Pierre, where he had been baptized; finally he would linger by the canals and the Beguine Convent, near the ramparts.

Jaak was truly a son of Bruges, and Bruges had transmitted to him a sense of art and its beauty. Following in the footsteps of his father, but especially of his grandfather Léon, a great amateur painter, Jaak spent all his free time browsing in the museums of the city. During this time he sharpened his aesthetic vision, which later earned for him inclusion among the specialists of the world on the primitive Flemish painting style. However, his artistic calling was not confined to painting: it also found expression in music. His paternal grandmother had already performed all Chopin's *Polonaises*, and following her lead, Jaak's father had had a piano installed in his family home. "My sister and I," recalled Lieve, "were not

18. Georges Rodenbach, *Bruges-la-Mort* (1892) (Paris: G. F. Flammarion, 1998), 193.

19. André Louf, Letter detailing the list of renunciations connected to my solemn profession, ADMC, 1 Feb. 1954.

very talented, but Jaak was the favored one, and he had a great deal of talent."[20] At the age of fourteen he performed Beethoven's *Pathétiques* and the greater part of his classics. Also during this period, he practiced his first scales on the organ in the old church, where he went with his sisters, whom he charged with operating the pedals.

The Soul's Landscapes

Although he was a native of Bruges, the elder André Louf had a broad vision of Flanders. Because his family had originated in the western part of the province, he thought of this area less as a distinctly defined territory than as an open spirit, of which the Beguines, the paintings of Memling and of Rogier van der Weyden (also called Rogier de La Pasture), and the piety of Ruusbroec and the *Imitation of Christ* were among the most lovely incarnations.[21] For Dom André the abbey of Mont-des-Cats was inspired by this great spirit. This sense of belonging, which went to the point of hoisting the Flemish lion at the rear end of some of the monastery's vehicles,[22] was for him at once both an anchorage and a legacy.

20. Lieve Louf, correspondence with the author.

21. No doubt he would have recognized it in these words of the poet C.-H. Rocquet: "I am talking about Flanders to designate the country Caesar called Gallic Belgium, the country divided by languages and frontiers that have over time divided into nations—distinct if not adverse—territories, kingdoms, dukedoms, communes, republics, regions, and separate confessions. But in its profundity and its light it is one country, one single spiritual homeland. From the prophets sculpted by Sluter for the Carthusian house of Champmol to the Basilica of the Precious Blood at Bruges, and from the abbey of Mont-des-Cats to the diocese of Saint-Lambert, bishop of Liège, and from the penitents at Furnes to the White March of Brussels yesterday, the land is one and the same: Roman, Latin, Flemish, Germanic, French, and Walloon" (Claude-Henri Rocquet, *Ruysbroeck l'Admirable* [Paris: Salvator, 2014], 57).

22. I have this information from Père Paul Verdeyen, SJ.

The legacy of a certain spirit, of a certain world view, was characterized by the sense of the real, according to the Jesuit Paul Verdeyen, well-known specialist in Flemish mysticism. Contrary to their French neighbors, who retain a liking for clear, distinct ideas, says Verdeyen, the Flemish are no rationalists. "At bottom," he continues,

> They are Germans, scattered and deprived of settled dispositions. That is why the idea of God derived from Aristotle as an unmoved Mover has never taken hold among us, who sense intuitively that such a fixed vision is incompatible with the mystery of the Trinity. With William of Saint-Thierry, a native Flamand, but also with Hadewijch of Anvers, Ruusbroec, and their like, we find a dynamic, open approach to divinity, and hence also to humanity, and that approach infused the young Louf. Distrusting any idea of system, the Flemish soul is distinguished by a kind of openness to the real, on the order of infantile abandon.[23]

An anchorage, then, especially in a landscape. After Bruges, the biological milieu of Dom André's spiritual life, if we may speak thus, was Mont-des-Cats. It was through the particular landscapes of this monastery that the invisible took on form and color in his eyes. Living under one sky is not insignificant: it roots the soul and plants it in a strip of earth, it links it to a geography. Louf was extremely sensitive to spiritual soil, which Julien Gracq called "provinces of the soul."[24] One day, celebrating All Saints in an African monastery, Louf wrote to his brother monks, "I notice that I have a sensitivity for the spiritual climate of this feast, and it lies in the season of autumn, that is, autumn at Mont-des-Cats: the gray sky, the first cold mornings, the fog rising and covering the horizon, the humid wind moving the branches that are already half

23. Paul Verdeyen, conversation with the author.

24. Julien Gracq, *Lettrines* (Paris: José Corti, 1967), 217.

bare, the dead leaves piled up on the walkways of the grotto, and the vague feeling that we will have to spend the long winter alone on the empty hillock. That dismal, wintry plain with winter at its gates makes me think of heaven without much difficulty. It frees up a space inside me where God quickly reveals himself as very near. This is how intensely we have need of the earth in order to find heaven, even an earth so precise. Here on African earth I am completely homeless."[25]

A Loving Clap of Thunder

Why did this gifted young man with the promise of a brilliant career and of a life as part of a couple, for which his profuse tenderness predisposed him, renounce all that for a life without apparent influence, enclosed in the confined space of a monastery? Every human vocation hides a secret, something impossible to explain that makes it unique, in fact the part of one person alone. Louf never really dwelt much on his call, even if on certain rare occasions, especially at someone's taking the habit or at burials, when his homilies had to account for the profound interior life of his monks and nuns, he lifted up a discreet corner of the veil that covered his own path. If we want to draw near to the mystery of his vocation, it is undoubtedly there, between the lines, that we must look.

The evidence imposes itself on these texts. For Louf the religious vocation is a love story, a kind of dance, a tango, in which the two lovers turn each other about, look at each other, draw near, wheel about, and finally fall into each other's arms. Besides, Louf presents Christ in his homilies as having the characteristics of "an eternal impenitent charmer"[26] or "an incorrigible lover."[27] One day, Louf says, this seducer decides

25. André Louf, Letter to the community, ADMC, 31 Oct. 1967.

26. André Louf, Homily for the profession of Sr. Marie, ADMC, date unknown.

27. André Louf, Homily for Trinity Sunday, ADMC, 2005.

to ravish a person's heart. He wins him as a follower, "not at all by means of his external aspect, that of the handsomest of the sons of men," said Louf later, but by a mysterious interior touch that embraces him. His joy suddenly overflows, and, possibly for whole days and weeks, it makes his eyes shine and perfumes his heart."[28] Another time Christ chooses to rest his gaze on someone else, a gaze that wounds without hurting, "a wound of love, the sweetest and most delightful love."[29]

"Only the person who has been touched by such a gaze," Louf continues in this homily, "can really say 'yes' freely, without constraint, even until death." The day of this encounter remains stamped forever in the memory like a sweet remembrance—a *dulcis memoria,* as the ancient fathers said. After that happens, the person's whole existence is transformed: "The Christian who has once recognized Jesus in his life finds that his life is guided by his mysterious presence."[30] That person's only desire then joins that of the psalmist: that the Lord's face whose beauty has subdued him should shine on him again: "Once the retina of our eye has been dazzled by the light of Jesus' face, it remains forever marked by it. It cannot fix itself on anything other than that light. It searches everywhere for it attentively and lovingly. Its life has no longer any other meaning."[31] In the deepest part of oneself the Christian then feels a mysterious urge, an invincible attraction; he feels burned interiorly, as though lifted up and carried away by the love that Jesus bears him, whose powerful tenderness does not leave him alone for a second."[32]

28. André Louf, Homily for the thirteenth Sunday of Ordinary Time, ADMC, 1995.

29. André Louf, Homily for the second Sunday of Ordinary Time, ADMC, 1997.

30. André Louf, Homily for the funeral of Fr. Jerome, ADMC, 1980.

31. André Louf, Homily for the profession of Jacques, ADMC, 1978.

32. André Louf, Homily for the Jubilee of Fr. Maur, ADMC, 1983.

The one who has found this precious pearl, the discovery of which renders all renunciations painless, has from then on one single obsession: to withdraw inside that love, to enclose oneself in it. Louf continues, describing the contemplative life:

> Of this dwelling close to Jesus and with him, and all that it evokes of stability, intimacy, and secrecy, the monastic life in its traditional environment is the sign and sacrament. Solitude, the very site of the monastery hidden in a secret valley, with a certain distance from the succession of external events, the rare departures and contacts—all that has no meaning except that of signifying the enclosure of love; without love all would be completely meaningless. Making a profession of stability in this place and in this community is quite simply a consent to love, devotion to Jesus, making oneself available, even physically, for all that he wills.
>
> It is not easy really to love beyond a little sentimental excitement that will not last, especially if it is a question of loving to the point of giving one's life. But once the source is the love of Christ, and once it is initiated, that source will never stop springing up. And it is not the walls of the enclosure that will check the flow. At the deepest level of the heart, those who have been touched by Jesus' love know that they are at the heart of the church, at the heart of the world, unceasingly spreading his love and pouring out despite themselves the treasures of his grace upon the entire universe.
>
> "At the heart of my mother the church," Thérèse of Lisieux had cried, "I will be love."[33] Every Christian could say the same, but more especially every monk and every nun, whose vocation is precisely that: being touched by love, delivering oneself up to love, overflowing with love,

33. *The Complete Therese of Lisieux*, trans. and ed. Robert J. Edmonson (Brewster, MA: Paraclete Press, 2009), 174.

> and in this way letting God through them pour out his love on the whole world.[34]

That is what led the young Jaak to the decision to leave all things: in his fifteenth year he heard a clap of thunder. The results, however, remained hidden for a very long time.

Birth of a Vocation

Every prayer is contagious. "It is necessary," Louf insisted, "to have seen true believers and true witnesses with one's own eyes in order to be irresistibly led to believe in one's turn."[35] He had of course had the opportunity to grow up in a fervent family, with parents who bore a living faith that was alive and engaging. Indeed, he dedicated his first book to his parents: "To my father and my mother, whom I often saw praying, and from whom I learned to pray."[36] In fact his infancy was encompassed on every side by the Christian religion. Prayer was at the center of his family life, and it gave that life its rhythm and its ritual. Every meal was introduced by a blessing, and every day Jaak accompanied his mother and two sisters to the Eucharist celebrated at the parish church of Saint-Jacques, a few steps from their house. He loved that church with its palpable atmosphere, the light playing on the stained-glass windows, the plaster saints playing hide and seek behind the clouds of incense, the primitive Flemish paintings that showed faces radiant with silence. No doubt it was through his contemplation of these masterpieces that art entered his life. During his vacations at his grandfather's house at Neuve-Église he also prayed the rosary and

34. André Louf, Homily for the Jubilee of Fr. Maur, ADMC, 1983.

35. André Louf, Homily for the bestowal of the diocesan award of merit to Jean Jourdain, ADMC, 1989.

36. André Louf, *Seigneur, apprends-nous à prier* (Brussels: Lumen Vitae, 1972), 7.

the litany of saints. All these rituals played an important role in the birth of his vocation by embedding in his heart "the interior conviction that a person does not bring about his own birth, but he receives it from God."[37]

In his paternal grandfather's house, Louf learned of the existence of monks. Léon's house, where Jaak spent his vacations, is only a few kilometers from Mont-des-Cats. From its garden the monastery's outline can be seen atop a short hill. Léon explained to his grandson that monks lived there, and that they kept silence for the sake of prayer. The young man felt himself a partner of those who led a life of prayer, devoted to perpetual silence. For a long time he felt himself predisposed to solitude and to contemplative inwardness. When his sister entered his room early in the morning, it was not rare for her to find him on his knees at the foot of the bed, having kept vigil the whole night.[38]

But this interior desire did not jeopardize his enjoyment of adolescence. "At this time," he later recalled, "I was impressed by the presence of God in the human heart and in my own heart personally: he was all-powerful but close, present in the heart of my heart."[39] In order to deepen this intimacy, confusedly glimpsed in prayer, he thought about a consecrated life, wholly given to God, but without a clear notion of what that would mean. A religious vocation? Monastic? Priesthood? "I didn't know very much about it," he would recall, "but I was searching; I was on the lookout for anything that could enlighten me."[40]

At that time two images co-existed in his heart, even struggled there. At first the life of a missionary held his attention. His father was involved in an association to aid missions;

37. Louf, *À la grâce de Dieu*, 9.

38. Lieve Louf, correspondence with the author.

39. "Paroles d'ermite: Le père André Louf," documentary, directed by Laurence Chartier (CFRT/KTO), 2009.

40. Louf, *À la gràce de Dieu*, 15.

he had introduced Jaak to many of those warriors who had left to evangelize the world. Their stories of adventure stirred dreams of travel in him. But this apostolic life, toward which his character also inclined him, and the pastoral feeling he discovered with the Katholieke Studentenaktie, did not erase the other image he had glimpsed in his grandfather's house. The life of these monks given over to contemplation attracted him like a lover. After starting to gather information, purchasing books about the Belgian abbeys of Orval, Westmalle, and Saint-Sixte, he ended up talking the idea over with his spiritual director, who accepted his desire simply and seriously. "It was an essential experience for me," Louf later recalled. "He neither encouraged nor discouraged me; instead he made me face my own interior path and invited me to live a deeper life from that time on."[41]

This time of maturing, from age fourteen to sixteen, is highly important. A conflict became rooted in Louf's heart between two different tendencies, both of which he carried inside and struggled with for a long time afterward. A desire for solitude and contemplation occupied him on one side, and an attraction for pastoral action and relationships on the other.[42] The figure of Charles de Foucauld, whom he discovered during this period, seemed to him to reconcile the two contradictory callings. He even thought of joining the first, claustral, version of the Little Brothers of Jesus, which Père René Voillaume had just started at El Abidoh Sidi Cheikh.[43]

41. Louf, *À la gràce de Dieu*, 16.

42. Louf, *À la gràce de Dieu*, 14.

43. Mustapha Ameur Djeradi, "Quand la violence révèle l'espace ksourien," *Cas de El Abiodh Sidi Cheikh. Penser la ville-approches comparatives*, Oct 2008, Khenchela, Algérie, n. 17; 5. See also Sophie de Villeneuve, "Dom Louf et la prière d'abandon," www.croire.com. [I have been unable to locate the article by Sophie de Villeneuve, which the author cites; I have therefore added the article by Mustapha Djeradi. BK]

In May 1945 when chance brought André to the neighborhood of Mont-des-Cats, he and a friend decided to knock on the monastery gate. Having arrived in time for dinner, the two young men were offered a repast by the brother guestmaster, who also showed them a barn where they could spend the night. He proposed that they attend the final Office of the day, Compline. "It was the first time that I had participated in this evening prayer," Louf recalled, "and that I heard the chanting of the *Salve Regina*, that prayer to Mary that closes each day in all the monasteries of our Order."[44] He later described the effect of that experience: "When the monks start singing in the semi-darkness, it is like a 'clap of thunder.' "[45] The call imposed itself like a sudden conviction, evidence: Jaak had the certainty that God was there calling him to that Cistercian monastery. "Nothing could have made me change my mind,"[46] Louf later insisted, despite the fact that he was no more than fifteen years old at the time. "When you live through such an intense event, in an instant it invades the whole field of the conscience. Of course it will suffer the erosion of time, like every one of our periods of light; nevertheless, in a definitive way it marks a radical break. The event will have a 'before' and an 'after.' We do not leave it totally different, perhaps, but we are no longer exactly the same."[47]

Nevertheless, Jaak had gained nothing. On paper everything militated against such a choice. His knowledge of French was still imperfect, he was still young, and even if his parents did not oppose a religious vocation, they hesitated to see their son embrace a life whose usefulness was not obvious, even for the faithful. And then there was his role in Catholic Action, which oriented him toward apostolic life and engagement for the

44. Louf, *À la grâce de Dieu*, 18.

45. André Louf, "Marchons vers notre Pâque intérieur," *Panorama* (April 2002): 26–27.

46. Louf, *À la grâce de Dieu*, 18.

47. Louf, *À la gràce de Dieu*, 19.

sake of others. But as the months passed, Jaak, guided by his spiritual advisor, perceived that prayer had its own fruitfulness and that the contemplative life was not a flight from the world, but a way of acting for the world by intercession: "In choosing the Cistercian way of life, I did not have a sense of fleeing from the world. I was at the time very much involved with Catholic Action, and I experienced my entry [into the monastery] as a direct prolongation of that involvement. I had then, and I still have, the intuition of living this life of prayer for the world."[48] Those monks there on the hill, he wondered: do they not watch over their surroundings?

From then on Louf's vocation of prayer at the heart of the church and of the world would not let him go. "Walking down the old streets of the city where I grew up, which I passionately love, I sensed that I was already invested with the responsibility of interceding for all the people whom I passed," he wrote in an unpublished statement.

After some retreats to confirm his intention, and having taken full account of the sacrifices that monastic life would entail, Jaak announced his decision to his parents. His father took it coldly. He felt that his son was too young, and he thought that it was foolish to bury in a Trappist monastery the numerous talents that Jaak could put at the service of the diocesan church. He would also have preferred that Jaak choose a Belgian abbey. His mother, however, was more favorable: "She accepted my choice simply, perhaps even with secret gladness. Besides, she had to intervene to soothe my father, since after all, my father was never really opposed to my entry," recalled this later abbot of Mont-des-Cats.[49]

48. André Louf, "La Tradition ne regarde pas en arrière," *La Croix* 14 Jan. 1989.

49. Louf, *À la grâce de Dieu*, 20.

CHAPTER 2

"All Is Done, and All Begins"

Externally monastic life is a long tranquil stream, a cradle song by Chopin. For those who live the interior life it is rather like an opera of Wagner or like Niagara Falls.

In October 1947 a young man who cast a slender shadow presented himself at the iron gate of Mont-des-Cats Abbey to become a monk. He did not know that dark storms lay ahead. He was not yet eighteen. "It was foolish to enter so young," he would later say, "but it was a preparation for going through a string of vicissitudes, of chaotic episodes, of torments." We must linger on his monastic youth. Like gold in a crucible, he arrived through the trials of this decisive period at the refinement of his spiritual intuitions.

Impossible Heroism

During the nineteen fifties, life at Mont-des-Cats resembled that of any Trappist house before the Council.[1] The rigor of asceticism was emphasized, along with the toughness of living conditions and the austerity of observances. Before becoming abbot of La Trappe, Dom Marie-Gérard Dubois was a monk of Mont-des Cats. He entered in 1947, the same year as

1. The Second Vatican Council, 1962–1965.

Louf,[2] and he remembers the cold and the lack of privacy inherent and ubiquitous in the dormitories:

> Our cells were like alcoves, all lined up in two aisles, each one two meters long and a meter and a half wide with partitions of plaster board or wood, hardly as high as the head of a standing monk. There was no door; only a simple curtain closed the cell with a number and a name. It let through all the noise of the snorers, who of course always went to sleep first. At the time of my entrance the dormitory was unheated in winter, and it often happened that the holy water fonts installed at the entrances of the cells would freeze, despite the salt sprinkled on the water when it was blessed.[3]

It was still the old regime of penances with the Friday discipline, prostrations in the refectory, and mutual accusations at the Chapter of Faults. The whole life of the monk appeared to be regimented, regulated to the last millimeter, and surrounded by procedures. Dubois continues:

> At the time of my novitiate everything concerning the places where we could go and how we were to move around was legislated. The main cloister led around a square courtyard, and the silence was absolute. One could not walk down the middle, but only along either wall, except when in community walking in a straight line. The usages specified keeping our hoods up in the cloister, in the dormitory, in the refectory, and in the

2. From this point onward this translation refers to him as Louf, leaving *Jaak* to his premonastic life.

3. Marie-Gérard Dubois, *Le Bonheur en Dieu: Souvenirs et réflexions du Père Abbé de La Trappe* (Paris: Robert Laffont, 1995), 78; Dom Marie-Gérard Dubois, *Happiness in God: Memories and Reflections of the Father Abbot of La Trappe*, trans. Georges Hoffmann and Jean Truax, Monastic Wisdom series 58 (Collegeville, MN: Cistercian Publications, 2019), 74.

> cabinets.[4] For someone who has no vocation only one question can arise: do I still have a right to breathe? One was surrounded on every side.[5]

Was Louf comfortable in this environment, which, even if anointed with love, was frightening in its strictness? How did he put up with this regime with its military aspect, bristling with prohibitions, bound by rituals, where poverty, abstinence, and ascesis held such an important place? Both well and poorly. First, he coped with it well because such heroism was in accord with the philosophy with which he had been inoculated in his youth. He had been brought up during an epoch when Christianity was dominated by a voluntarist ascesis and had been imbued with a culture of achievement and safety acquired by one's own strength. So he was not bewildered by the Trappist spirituality of the time, which held rigor as a value and gauged the quality of observances by their own weight of inconvenience and suffering. As he later confirmed,

> Having received—in the family home, at school, and in the movement *Action Catholique,* which I had frequented—an education that emphasized "will power," I was predisposed, as were many of the young militant Christians of my generation, to fall into this trap. At the time militant behavior that was elsewhere inclined to the external was here simply turned around and made internal, but its internal movement had not changed its nature or its orientation. It always thought itself capable of obtaining everything by brute force.[6]

4. French usage calls *cabinets* what English calls "toilets" or "urinals" [BK].

5. Dubois, *Le Bonheur,* 80; Dubois, *Happiness,* 76.

6. André Louf, "Autrement la grâce n'est plus la grâce," in André Louf, Denis Huerre, and Marie-David Girard, *Dieu intime: Paroles des moines* (Paris: Bayard, 2003), 59–60.

During his two years of novitiate, 1947–1949, Louf was victimized by this ideology, which under the cover of devotion flattered his self-love. With sincere generosity he fell into excessive austerities, and in his prowess he added still more. Unreasonable fasting made him as skinny as a rake, and he wore a cloak that was the most patched garment in the wardrobe.[7] With casual visitors he showed off his poverty, exposed it, and secretly boasted of it. When his family was surprised at seeing him wear shoes that did not match, he proudly replied, "That is my monastic poverty."[8]

At the same time Louf put up with this austere regime poorly, because he reached the limits of his resistance, and his health broke completely. In truth, the beginning of his monastic life was torture. Psychologically he kept ruminating, going around in circles, suffering from a sense of suffocation, so that he had trouble returning to the ranks. This anguish soon touched his body. Afflicted with migraine headaches and loss of sleep, he detected the first signs of fatigue. After 1949 more serious ill health arrived. Hyperthyroidism left him exhausted and rendered him uneasy and nervous; it obliged him to tame his novitiate fervor and to live at a more moderate pace for two years, slightly on the margin of the community, "neither sick enough to have the privilege of staying in the infirmary nor on the other hand well enough to follow a Trappist rhythm of daily life."[9]

For Louf, who had made it a point of honor to become a good monk, like one on a postcard, this shock was humiliating. By himself, by the sole force of will, it was impossible, he could not do it: he kept knocking up against his own limita-

7. Frère Guerric Aerden, monk of the Abbey of Westmalle, in correspondence with the author.

8. Willy de Smedt, conversation with the author.

9. André Louf, *À la grâce de Dieu: Entretiens avec Stéphane Delberghe* (Namur: Fidélité, 2002), 61–62.

tions. His idealized image of himself flew away in flashes. But it was a salutary trial, as this experience of his own powerlessness freed him from the myth of "champion monk"[10] that had haunted his imagination. The experience also allowed him to recognize something else: no longer the exaggerated ascesis that he practiced like an athlete, with a puffed-out chest, but the evangelical ascesis of weakness and fragility, revealing the depths of poverty hidden in all persons to allow them to appear before God's mercy.

An Avant-garde Father Master

In the year that Louf entered Mont-des-Cats the abbey numbered about eighty monks. The novices lived slightly apart from the community in order to do their apprenticeship peacefully; to the twelve of them were added the simply professed—the young monks who were bound by temporary vows but had not yet made their solemn vows—so the total number in the novitiate was twenty-five. They were under the authority of a wholly original person, Dom Francis Decroix, master of novices. He was a former lawyer who had entered the monastery at a mature age, and he was a real spiritual guide. Louf owed much to him. He was avant-garde, with bold teaching. Dom Francis would not allow his novices to mechanically obey the rules that encompassed their lives. Instead of seeing observances as attitudes to practice in a servile manner, he invited the novices to reflect upon their meaning, to understand them, and to perform them internally. This approach was revolutionary at the time.

But Dom Francis's boldness went far beyond that. He was strongly attracted by the movement to rediscover the fathers of the church, which had started a decade earlier. The series

10. André Louf, "Autrement la grâce n'est plus la grâce," 65.

Sources Chrétiennes had begun publication in Paris at Les Éditions du Cerf in 1942. Dom Francis introduced his recruits to the ancient monastic sources that were still very little used at the time. He encouraged them to read Cassian and the works of the first Cistercians, especially the sermons of Saint Bernard.[11] Louf breathed in this climate of a return to the sources, only beginning at the time but already amounting to a veritable breath of fresh air.

Initiation into the word of God was not the least of the openings into Louf's mind made by his father master. It is important to remember that during the 1940s, reading the Bible in one's native tongue was hardly possible for the ordinary faithful Catholic. As a youth, the only contact Louf had had with Holy Scripture came from the excerpts that could be found in the pious books used in high school to support what was then called *meditation*, "a kind of reflection of the intellect by some people, edifying thoughts by others," he recalled.[12] One meditated as one performed a duty or an exercise, by repeating formulas and carrying out a protocol completely before ending with a good resolution to preserve ethics. It can be said that when Louf heard Dom Francis speak passionately to him about Holy Scripture, that opened a new world up to him.

In 1950 a book by the theologian Louis Bouyer appeared: *Le sens de la vie monastique*. The father master had this book read to his novices. It contained a phrase that Dom Francis never stopped repeating: "What the *Exercises* are for the Jesuit, methodical prayer for the Sulpician, contemplative prayer for the Carmelite, *lectio divina* should be for the monk."[13] Louf

11. Dubois, *Le Bonheur,* 91; Dubois, *Happiness,* 87.

12. André Louf, "Une expérience de '*lectio divina*,'" *La Vie Spirituelle* 81 (2001): 740, p. 462.

13. Louis Bouyer, *Le sens de la vie monastique* (1950; Paris: Cerf, 2008), 257; *The Meaning of the Monastic Life,* trans. Kathleen Pond (London: Burns and Oates, 1955).

was stamped by this work, which awakened a whole generation of monks to what was essential in their vocation: this slow, patient, and savory approach to the Bible, called *lectio divina,* "not because it is reading that tells us about God, but because it is reading in which God speaks to us."[14]

One father of the church compares the Bible to a letter God sends to his creature. That is exactly what it is. Every morning the monk devotes himself to his *lectio*, and he opens Holy Scripture as if he were preparing to open a love letter, or as if he were going to keep a noble rendezvous. The monk is persuaded that the Spirit breathes in the Scriptures, and by a prayerful reading he attempts a kind of interior rumination, breaking open the shell of the words to find the deepest meaning and to take in a word that is capable of nourishing his personal life and of sowing seeds in his heart.[15]

But Louf was not there yet. He was still locked in the pseudo-rational[16] culture that he had received in his youth. He still had to labor to move from the head to the heart. We can say that it had not yet clicked. But his father master and Bouyer had traced out the way on which he enthusiastically rushed forward. On this road he quickly met Elizabeth of the Trinity. "I found in her," he would confess, "not only an interior spirituality, which has always profoundly attracted me, but also the practice of the Word of God in her inward experience. Hers was an extremely spiritual reading of the

14. André Louf, Homily for the third Sunday of Ordinary Time (ADMC, 2010).

15. In Guigo the Carthusian (from the 12th century), who bestowed on this art born of monastic life the gift of his noble works, this practice is presented as a ladder guiding the monk from his reading to contemplation according to four steps: *lectio*, *meditatio*, *oratio*, and *contemplatio*. "Reading," continues Guigo, "offers substantial nourishment to the monk's mouth; meditation lets him chew and masticate the food; prayer tastes it, and contemplation lets him enjoy its sweetness."

16. Louf, "Une expérience de *lectio divina*," 464.

sacred text that had surprised this soul that it had wounded, and from which had burst an extraordinary experience."[17]

But the decisive break happened in 1953. Louf owed it to the Swiss Protestant theologian Karl Barth, the first volume of whose *Dogmatique* had just been translated. Louf bought it and concealed it from his abbot. In this work Barth invites the reader to prepare for what he calls "the Event of the Word of God." According to Barth, there is in the Word an activity of God that can touch whoever reads it with a disciple's heart, a heart that listens and lets itself be perfected. For Louf this was a revelation. He understood for the first time that this Word is creative, dynamic, and powerful, but is also contemporary. Above all he became conscious that, engrossed in his intellectualism and an insatiable scientific curiosity, he had never yet experienced this event. For him the Bible had remained a sealed book.[18]

Between 1947 and 1953, thanks to the father master who had instilled in him a love for *lectio divina*, Holy Scripture entered Louf's life as the entryway for any authentic spiritual experience.

A New Name; Simple Vow

Despite his delicate health and low morale, and especially the sense of oppression that tormented him, Louf held on, aided by the rhythm of his first years, when there was always something new to discover. Time passed, formation and studies ran their course, and the perspective of the different stages he passed through was made clear. Everything in each stage held his attention and stimulated his desire. On November 21, 1949, he traded the novice's white habit for the black and white of the simply professed. He pronounced his simple

17. Louf, "Une expérience de *lectio divina*," 464.
18. Louf, "Une expérience de *lectio divina*," 467.

vows. The ritual of changing his given name marked this important stage, a first step toward the final commitment. So he became Frère André. Later he told his brothers about his affection for this new identity:

> I feel that this ancient monastic custom of changing a person's name makes a great deal of sense; it is the moment when he enters more deeply into the mystery of his vocation. It is not that I prefer André to Jaak. I would really not know why. André and Jaak were both apostles very close to the Lord. But through the new name of André, my monastic identity becomes little by little part of me, since my spiritual father and my brothers call me that in order to have me in their midst in the bosom of monastic fraternity. This name was my whole new vocation, and through my brothers, especially through my spiritual father, it was the Lord who called me to be near him, for a destiny about which he alone knew the secret.[19]

Having become a simple professed, Louf began his course of studies. The patristic rediscovery that had awakened in the church had not yet affected the theological formation of the young monks. Their course consisted essentially of the study of Saint Thomas Aquinas. For the time being, the fathers remained the gateway of studies, because of the notion that their teaching had not yet reached completion. The *doxa*—the knowledge—of the period maintained that the church had no real theology before Saint Thomas, and that mysticism began with Saint Bernard, as it was explained to Father Placide Deseille, who was at this period a young monk of Bellefontaine:

> The thought of the fathers had remained in the stage of a rough draft. Between them and the great classics of

19. André Louf, Letter to the community, 30 Nov., ADMC, 1970.

> Roman Catholicism, all of them after the twelfth century, there was a whole wall like that which separates childhood and adolescence from the age of maturity. Even Father Urs von Balthasar, who was for all that an expert on patristic thought, judged that "the writings of the fathers were an interior journal of the church at the age of seventeen."[20]

To prepare himself for ordination to the priesthood, Placide was counseled by the father abbot of Bellefontaine to read a treatise on the priesthood. As Deseille recalls, the abbot replied to this monk who preferred to read the works of one of the fathers, " 'But you are not thinking right! You are going to be ordained in three weeks. You have to read something serious about the priesthood. You will always have time to read the fathers later to fill in . . . .' And I went right to a pious book of the nineteenth century, as sentimental in its effusions as it was ratiocinating in its theology."[21] Such was the theology in the monasteries of the period: a rehashing of Thomism and endless cogitating that made no waves.

Pastoral Temptation Returns

Simple profession did not quiet André: a diffuse anxiety and physical distress continued to trouble him. His hyperthyroidism kept forcing him back to inactivity, to a retreat from the rhythm of the common life. Idleness is the enemy of the soul; because of this free time, Louf started to reflect, to ponder, and to scrutinize himself. More and more he doubted his vocation. Was his place really behind the walls of the enclosure? Should he not offer the best of himself rather

20. Placide Deseille, *Étapes d'un pélerinage: Autobiographie spirituelle* (Saint-Laurent-en-Royans: Monastère Saint-Antoine-le-Grand, 2015), 9.
21. Deseille, *Étapes d'un pélerinage.*

as a parish priest and the pastor of a Christian community? The old desire to consecrate himself to an apostolic service awoke and would no longer leave him in peace.

From 1949 to 1952, the greater part of the time under temporary vows, Louf was haunted by the thought of the pastoral influence that he could have. At the end of 1952, which marked the normal end of his temporary vows, the abbot of Mont-des-Cats, Dom Achille Nivesse, judging that Louf was immature, decided to delay his final commitment. He proposed that Louf discern his call further by undertaking a provisional service as the abbey's guestmaster. Dom Achille was a person endowed with a great openness of spirit and a sure sense of discernment. He had perceived Louf as a brilliant, promising monk, but at the same time as a young person who was sensitive and peculiar, whose way would never be absolutely clear. Without Dom Achille's patience and understanding, it is not clear whether Louf would have persevered, as he himself later admitted, speaking of Dom Achille as that "father thanks to whom I was able to continue."[22]

After Louf had spent three months at the guest house, Dom Achille asked him to take up the common life again, the life of solitude for God, and to declare his intention whether or not to lead that life. With this act of ordinary procedure Louf's attraction to pastoral activity was slightly cooled, especially because of two particular texts. The first was a message once addressed by Pope Pius XI to the Carthusians: "Those who consecrate themselves to prayer and penance in a hidden life do much more for the advancement of the kingdom of God than those who consecrate themselves to it by their labors."[23] The other came from Cassian's *Conferences*: "The objective of every religious person, and his highest perfection, consists

22. André Louf, "First meeting as abbot with the nuns of Belval," ADMC, 6 Feb. 1963.

23. Louf, *À la grâce de Dieu*, 22–23.

in perseverance in prayer and in preserving, as far as human frailty allows, peace of soul and purity of heart. That is the so-precious good toward which all the efforts of our body and all the aspirations of our spirit should tend."[24]

Louf has recounted the vivid impression this latter statement had upon him: "I heard it for the first time when I was still a young professed monk, and it entered my heart and my inward parts like an arrow; it moved me deeply and has remained fixed in me until this day. It seemed to me that it had found my very reason for being."[25] In the words *peace of soul* and *purity of heart* he revealed his desire for a purely contemplative life—a hesychast life, from the Greek noun *hesychia*, which signifies repose, peace, and quiet. For Louf it referred to monks who consecrate themselves exclusively to the solitary life, one of continual prayer. The spiritual orientation of this stream of tradition goes back to the beginning of monasticism, that is, to the Desert Fathers and their apophthegmata. It is, as Pierre Adnès has explained, essentially contemplative:

> Hesychasm in fact places human perfection in union with God through continual prayer. What is amazing is the way it insists on solitude, retreat, and anchoritism. Practicing hesychia belongs to the monk established in the desert, living on mountains and in caves, or at least inhabiting an isolated cell. But material solitude is not enough. In his search for God the hesychast has a more dangerous enemy than the noisy society of men and the distractions that society produces: dissipation of the heart.[26]

24. Jean Cassien, *Conférences*, Sources Chrétiennes 2 (Paris: Cerf, 1958), 40.

25. André Louf, "Homily for Jean-Paul's receiving the habit," ADMC, 1982.

26. Pierre Adnès, "La méthode hésychast," *Studia Missionalia* 25 (1976): 279–80.

In the summer of 1953, with his mind torn between the desire for interior life and the persistent attraction for pastoral service, Louf could no longer choose. Doubt paralyzed him. Dom Achille was still patient and again put off the solemn profession, proposing that Louf rest from community life by pursuing studies at Louvain. That September Louf undertook an academic semester at the Catholic University of Louvain, beginning with the study of historical criticism with Professor Lucien Cerfaux, a specialist in Pauline theology.[27] This was Louf's first encounter with academic exegesis, and he was enchanted by it, as well as by life among students, surrounded by friends on his own Flemish terrain. However, his sojourn there was of short duration, as he was recalled to the abbey in December. After four happy months, he left Louvain with a heavy heart. Doubt again assailed him. He felt that he could have succeeded in a university career. On the evening before his departure for Mont-des-Cats he wrote from Louvain, "It really makes me very sad. The city, the faculty, the country, the mother tongue. But I am a monk. I chose a monastic life."[28]

"A Holy Gesture by a Sinner"

Louf made the great leap two months later. On February 2, 1954, Candlemas Day, he made his solemn profession. He later wrote that his final commitment was a "holy gesture by a sinner."[29] He was twenty-four. The evening before he had composed his act of consecration to God, a beautiful and

27. Adolphe Gesché, *Discours pour la remise du titre de docteur*, honoris causa, à André Louf, Catholic University of Louvain, Feb. 2, 1994.

28. André Louf, Notes written on a loose sheet falling out of his journal, ADMC, 21 Dec. 1953.

29. André Louf, Letter detailing the list of renunciations, ADMC, 1 Feb. 1954.

simple text in which his nuptial espousal and loving spirituality already blooms:

> Christ Jesus, I thank you for the great grace of monastic consecration. You have loved me with a love that I would not suspect. I ask you most earnestly with all the intensity of my heart to "seize" me ever more and more. I consecrate all my intelligence to you, and I give up that spiritual pride that your grace resists. I agree to spend my whole monastic life in the humblest and least interesting chores. I consecrate to you the dynamism and the spiritual power you put in my heart. I completely consecrate my whole body, which I loved and was proud of. You know to what extent I desired to make it express a great noble love. I give you my hands: they will no longer be enclosed in anyone else's hands; I give you my head: it will no longer rest on any shoulder; I give you my breast, which no other human being will embrace. I give you everything, and I will try with your grace, humbly but firmly, with meek stubbornness, to give you all that to tell you that I am responding to your choice by choosing you in my turn.
>
> I love you, Christ Jesus. I thank you for having made my heart equal to the measure of this solitude where I should meet you all alone, because with all that, it is my own heart that I am giving you. I deliver it to you today completely, without holding anything back, in order that you may make it a living sacrament of your church. I consecrate to you all the tenderness that you have put in my heart, in order that the apparent uselessness of such a capacity to love may serve the cause of your greater love, because it is love and the sacrifice of the cross that have given birth to the church and made her grow. Now, Christ Jesus, all is done, and all begins. I am a monk for all eternity, committed after and along with so many others to realize your kingdom in the increasing search for your face. My will, my body, and my heart will never

> serve anyone else; my hands and my intelligence will work no more, except for the work of the communion of saints, where love is the only efficacious work.[30]

So Louf writes, "All is done, and all begins," well knowing that the hardest part is ahead of him. In another document, also written on the eve of his profession, he adds the list "of the little renunciations implied by my profession to prove to myself that I have taken into account quite clearly all the sacrifices to which I give my consent."[31] Three principal renunciations stand out from this catalogue, renunciations that would form the structure of his monastic life. The first concerns pastoral activity: "I take into account in a very pointed way that I normally sacrifice all pastoral activity. I accept the suffering that entails, and I even foresee that it may be very painful. With your strength, Lord, and your light, I hope to be able to make it bear fruit in love." The second has to do with chastity and human affectivity: "This solitude of the heart will represent for me a real martyrdom; there is no doubt about it." "I consecrate to you all the delicate tenderness with which I would have wanted to surround human beings, as a gift that will prove my will to love you alone." The third has to do with self-love: "My temperament is very little monastic. It lets me keep certain external faults that will hardly edify those around me. Can I say in advance that I am one of those people about whom it will never be said, 'There is a monk!'? Perhaps so. But that, O Lord, will change nothing in my immovable resolution to be a true monk, and before you alone I accept this humbling situation, which will often be very painful to my self-love." The questions of pastoral

30. André Louf, Act of Consecration, ADMC, 1 Feb. 1954.

31. Louf, Letter detailing the list of renunciations. [Although the author refers to "another document," he here cites the original list of renunciations.]

outreach, of chaste love, and of vanity and attracting the attention of others: at the outset of his monastic life he posed these three questions, which would, in the future, form his spiritual combat.

CHAPTER 3

The Roman Escape

September 1955. Despite his personal reservations, Louf has just been ordained a priest,[1] by order of the abbot. At this period most choir monks were ordained. In addition, he had completed the course of theology guaranteed by the abbey. He then left for Rome along with another brother of Mont-des-Cats, Marie-Gérard Dubois. Dom Achille had ascertained the abilities of these two monks, so he sent them to refine their biblical formation with the notion of making them future professors of Holy Scripture for the course of studies at Mont-des-Cats. Louf was twenty-five, and this escape from the monastic environment delighted him, all the more because at the time Rome was stirred by the effervescence of preparation for the Second Vatican Council. It was a boiling city, full of riches to be discovered.

"The Earthly Garment of the Word"

At Rome the two monks stayed at the Generalate, where the abbot general, the head of the world's Trappists, along

1. The bishop of Xiwanzi, Msgr. Leon-Jean-Marie de Smedt, presided at his ordination, which took place on July 19, 1955. [The French text identifies Msgr. De Smedt as a bishop of Bruges. BK]

with the monks who formed his council, resided. The young brothers found there the milieu of a monastery with the usual observances, but without an enclosure, since they scattered every day to attend the universities of the eternal city to pursue their studies.

Located on the Via Icilio on the Aventine Hill, the Order's house was a little Babel with the noise of various languages. From all the countries of the world Cistercian abbeys sent their monks to be formed. "There was in that place a real spirit of diversity," one brother remembers. "We Americans were excited to be in Rome, and we were surprised by the linguistic mastery possessed by most Europeans, especially the Dutch and the Belgians. I remember Dom André as a young man. He was calm and worked very quickly. He spoke excellent English, even though he stayed mostly with his brothers from the north."[2] Americans, Dutch, Australians, and representatives of various African monasteries all bore witness to the formidable expansion of the Order; they lived together in a mixing of mentalities and cultures that opened Louf's mind to the sensitivities of other people.

During the university year 1955–1956 Louf followed a course in theology at the Gregorian Pontifical University in order to perform a feat of strength, impossible today, by obtaining a license in theology in one year, the open sesame to enter the Pontifical Biblical Institute. The intellectual level of the Gregorian Institute was disappointing at that period. "I found there," he recalled, "that Holy Scripture had been reduced to an arsenal of apologetic arguments, weapons to confuse adversaries."[3] Dom Dubois doesn't disagree: "As the period required, the courses exercised memory more than

2. Fr. Casimir Bernas, former abbot of the Abbey of the Holy Trinity in Huntsville, Utah, in correspondence with the author.

3. André Louf, "Une expérience de *Lectio Divina*," *La Vie Spirituelle* 81 (2001): 740, p. 472.

reflection. The final examination for the license, completely in Latin, required us to know a hundred theological theses and to be able to defend them—that is, essentially to memorize the 'authorities' that backed up one side or the other."[4]

The next university year, with his theology license in his pocket, Louf discovered the Biblical Institute. The requirements there were a much greater source of stimulation. The Institute had been founded by the Jesuits in 1909, and it had valiantly become one of the bastions of scientific exegesis, resisting the assaults of the anti-modernists, that is, all those, still quite influential, who refused to submit the Bible to critical study. During the 1950s the Institute was in full bloom. The number of students exploded, and the new rector, Fr. Ernest Vogt, had engineered a profound renewal of the group of professors to emphasize the university level of the teaching dispensed. Prominent among these young recruits, who were destined to dominate scientific exegesis as the years passed, were Fathers Augustin Bea, Maximilian Zerwick, Stanislaus Lyonnet, and Luis Alonso Schökel.[5]

Guided by these masters, for two years Louf explored what he called "the earthly garment of the Word."[6] He began a rigorous study, both historical and literary, of the Old and New Testaments. He plunged into the companion sciences of the Bible (archaeology, geography, history), but above all he made his honey from the ancient languages—Hebrew, Aramaic, and especially Syriac, just discovered at the time—which

4. Marie-Gérard Dubois, *Le Bonheur en Dieu: Souvenirs et réflexions du Père Abbé de La Trappe* (Paris: Robert Laffont, 1995), 107; Marie-Gérard Dubois, *Happiness in God: Memories and Reflections of the Father Abbot of La Trappe,* trans. Georges Hoffmann and Jean Truax, Monastic Wisdom series 58 (Collegeville, MN: Cistercian Publications, 2019), 104.

5. Maurice Gilbert, *L'Institut Biblique Pontifical: Un siècle d'histoire (1909–2009)* (Rome: Éditions Bibliques Pontificales, 2009), 180–81.

6. Louf, "Une expérience de *Lectio Divina*," 472.

he learned with a facility that disconcerted his companions.[7] In June 1957 he received his bachelor's degree in Holy Scripture with his work on Ezekiel. The following year he obtained a license, crowned by a remarkable thesis: "The Scapegoat as a Figure of the Passion of Christ."[8] In order to construct the framework for this study he had appealed to the Jesuit Father Lyonnet for help. Lyonnet was a specialist in the Pauline letters and was to participate in preparing an edition of the Bible de Jérusalem. He was also Louf's spiritual father. At the beginning of the Second Vatican Council he was one of the scapegoats of those who opposed scientific exegesis. Dismissed from teaching for a time, he returned to favor during the discussions on *Dei Verbum.*[9] His recommendations were then willingly heard by the council fathers, and the Constitution promulgated in 1965, which began a new era of exegesis, owed him a great deal.[10] While Père Lyonnet was initiating Louf in the Ignatian pedagogy of discernment, he suggested to him a possible harmony between scientific rigor and the spirit of faith, even though Louf still had trouble reconciling the two points of view.

The Light of the Fathers

After its beginning in the 1940s, a vigorous biblical, patristic, liturgical, and theological renewal had been quickening

7. Frère Étienne Goutigny, former prior of Dombes, in correspondence with the author.

8. I thank Carol Valentino, the general secretary of the Biblical Institute, for having furnished me with this information and having communicated the *Acta Pontificii Instituti Biblici* for the years 1956–1958, which list the courses and professors at the Institute when Louf was studying there.

9. *Dei Verbum* is the title of the Second Vatican Council's Dogmatic Constitution on Divine Revelation; it is one of the Council's core documents.

10. Gilbert, *L'Institut Biblique Pontifical*, 463.

every part of the church. New horizons were traced and new roads opened up. A whole generation responded enthusiastically. At Rome the desire for renewal especially permeated the atmosphere. Louf breathed in long drafts of this air and shared it with his brothers, notably with Placide Deseille.[11]

An intellectual friendship between Deseille and Louf was grounded in their common attraction to the sources of monasticism, the Christian East, and the fathers of the undivided church of the first millennium. At the time, through his Syriac studies, Louf discovered both Isaac of Nineveh and, with one thing leading to another, the writings of ancient monasticism. He was awestruck at the thought of the fathers and their unifying anthropology that integrated all the human powers, including the body itself, and formed a hierarchy of those powers around that internal summit called *heart* or *noûs*, and their corresponding view that the place of God was in humankind.[12] Louf had been raised with the notion that the divine will was forcefully crucifying, that like a victim of the sword of Damocles, one was bound to end up sooner or later tasting its painful sharpness. But now he was receiving a kind of illumination. Far from the painful sacrificial approach, those ancient authors revealed to him that faith is an expansion of all being.

The fathers were for Louf an opening for light in a gray sky. Nursed by Thomistic philosophy, Louf, Deseille, and that whole generation suddenly glimpsed a new theological approach, another way of using reason, another world. It was with the help of an architectural metaphor that Deseille later described the opening up that he and his friends represented:

11. Archimandrite Placide Deseille, hegumen of the monastery of Saint-Antoine-Le-Grand, correspondence with the author.

12. He developed this anthropology in "Y at-il une attitude de prière propre au moine?" *Collectanea Cisterciensia* 33 (1971): 41–56.

> I could not help but admire the coherence and harmony of the Thomist theological synthesis. But it evoked for me the Gothic architecture of its time: genial, yes, but with its required material too rigorously impregnated by reason. The scholastic method seemed to me exposed by its very nature to the danger of reducing the mysteries of God to whatever the reason could understand by separating it in its definitions or by putting it into syllogisms. On the other hand the fathers of the church had such a vivid awareness of God's transcendence that they would never have dared to apply our human philosophical concepts to him. For them our concepts when applied to God, while expressing something that is true, always keep in some way the versatility and distance of metaphor. That is why the writings of the fathers breathed a sense of the sacred and of mystery, and suggested an interpenetration of the human and divine, one that finds a plastic correspondence in Roman and Byzantine art.[13]

Moreover, Louf thought, the fathers never teach on the basis of conjectures or deductions; they teach about a country they are going to. That such a theological statement could be near one's own experience imparted enthusiasm to those monk-students who at around this time met Dom Jean Leclercq, the great Benedictine savant who was giving the course at the Université Saint-Anselme that would soon become the book *L'amour des lettres et le désir de Dieu.*[14] In this masterpiece Leclercq revealed the beautiful harmony existing in the me-

13. Deseille, *Étapes d'un pélerinage*, 8.

14. Jean Leclercq, *L'amour des lettres et le désir de Dieu: Initiation aux auteurs monastiques du moyen âge* (Paris: Cerf, 1957); Jean Leclercq, *The Love of Learning and the Desire for God,* trans. Catherine Misrahi (New York: Fordham University Press, 1961). In one of his first articles Louf expressed his debt to this book, which had inspired the method for his work: "Marie dans la parole de Dieu selon Saint Amédée de Lausanne," *Collectanea Cisterciensia* 21 (1950): 31.

dieval monastic culture between Scripture and the search for God, witnessed by the works of these men who had "renounced everything but the art of writing well," as Étienne Gilson, the first to have taken seriously this theology born in the monasteries, expressed it.[15]

But Dom Leclercq went further. Besides the speculative theology rooted in Thomistic philosophy, he had discovered the existence of another theology, founded on biblical authority and the fathers, and supported by experience. With that theology, he argued, there was no longer any question of reasoning from what one conceives intellectually, but rather of "beginning with the mystical life itself, and of trying to take it into account, even when rational concepts show themselves as too strict and rigid to express mystical experience adequately."[16] Knowledge becomes an expression of experience. Louf belongs to that stream of tradition, which, although marginalized by the supremacy of scholasticism, has never stopped sprouting in Western contemplative milieux.[17] That stream requires theologians not to deliver a handsome discourse, logical and coherent, but rather with it to open up the ways of the heart.

The "Second Profession"

In this climate of a return to the sources, the idea of giving new life to what had hardened over the centuries found an

15. Étienne Gilson, *La théologie mystique de Saint Bernard* (Paris: Vrin, 1934); Étienne Gilson, *The Mystical Theology of Saint Bernard,* Cistercian Studies series 120 (Kalamazoo, MI: Cistercian Publications, 1990).

16. André Louf, "Cîteaux et Bernard de Clairvaux," unpublished conference given at Saint Petersburg, ADMC, June 1998.

17. On the division between theology and mysticism see Dominique Salin, *L'expérience spirituelle et son langage: leçons sur la tradition mystique chrétienne* (Paris: Éditions jésuites Facultés de Paris, 2015), 120–22.

echo in some leading religious figures. Such was the case with the abbot general of the Trappists, Dom Gabriel Sortais. With a clear-sightedness that anticipated the Council by fifteen years, Dom Gabriel initiated a renewal. His decisions were marked by a wish to alleviate the austerity of observances and to reduce a kind of excessive ascetical rigor. These moves were rather bold: making the horarium more flexible, reducing the fasts, shortening the liturgy, uniting the choir religious with the lay brothers, and so on.[18] But this initial *aggiornamento* was not enough for the students who surrounded Dom Gabriel. Louf was ready to contest the point. With his ability to lead, he provoked theological discussions on the priesthood of monks in the Generalate, defending the lay character of the monastic state.[19] He also sowed dissension by demanding more flexibility in observances. This argument was too much for the abbot general. He wanted to avoid the spread of new ideas, so just as Louf was preparing to defend his doctoral thesis under the direction of Père Lyonnet, Dom Gabriel and a portion of the Curia decided to terminate his time in Rome and to send him back to Mont-des-Cats, without appeal.[20]

The news soon reached Dom Achille, who no longer knew which way to turn. Should he once again let Louf go? Through Père Lyonnet Dom Achille let Louf, who was still at Rome, know that it would be well for him to look for another abbey and that, after all these vicissitudes, his return at such a time

18. Dom Emmanuel Coutant, "La Généralat de Dom Gabriel Sortais (1951–1963)," in Marie-Gérard Dubois, ed., *L'Ordre de la stricte observance au xx*[e] *siècle*, vol. 1 (Rome: OCSO, 2008), 247, 253; André Louf, "Bernard de Clairvaux et les Cisterciens," *Études* 373, nos. 1–2 (1990): 91–92.

19. André Louf, *À la grâce de Dieu: Entretiens avec Stéphane Delberghe* (Namur: Fidélité, 2002), 65.

20. André Louf, "Autrement la grâce n'est plus la grâce," in André Louf, Denis Huerre, and Marie-David Girard, *Dieu intime: Paroles des moines* (Paris: Bayard, 2003), 15.

might be unacceptable. Louf took this news hard, since he had followed an interior path that had confirmed his desire to return to Mont-des-Cats. A few weeks later he informed Dom Achille that he was leaving Rome. The abbot, however, stood by his position and insisted that Louf look for another community. "I repeated my desire to return to the monastery of my profession," Louf recalled. "He did not oppose it, but on one negative condition: any possibility of teaching should be resolutely excluded." Dom Achille asked, did Louf accept this condition, that was also a kind of punishment? "My answer was given," continues Louf, "but it came from somewhere else, from some other person: 'Yes, my Reverend Father, by the help of God and the assistance of your prayers.' " We can recognize there the ritual answer of the ceremony of solemn profession. They are the words that came spontaneously to Louf's lips at this highly important moment, words that he would later qualify, when re-reading his own history, as a "second profession."[21] It was as if on this June day of 1958 he had re-formulated with greater freedom and depth the commitment he had made on February 2, 1954.

21. André Louf, *Journal Spirituel*, 1 Nov. 1961.

CHAPTER 4

Discovering the Internal Man

The return from Rome began the decisive years of Louf's life—those from 1958 to 1962. Having returned behind the walls of the enclosure without alternative and without possibility of flight, the thirty-year-old had no choice but to confront the great equations of his existence: the search for a difficult equilibrium between his intellectual and spiritual life, the tug of war between his desires for self-forgetfulness in prayer and for the influence he could exert by pastoral action, the search for the right amount of common and of solitary life, and the apprenticeship of humble love in patience and in peril. By dealing with these tensions during four years of trials and temptations, Louf discovered, little by little through his daily falls and risings, both the mercy of God and the "interior man"; these are the principal threads with which he came to weave his teaching.

A Year of Repentance

But first, here he was in June 1958, back at Mont-des-Cats, where Dom Achille was inflicting upon the rebellious student a time of punishment and separation. Louf had to return not only to the ranks, but to the last place in the order of seniority. Pictures of the epoch portray the young monk, though unable to use his hands for anything except Scripture or piano, still awkwardly bestirring himself at the dairy. Although he felt that humility was unattainable without humiliations, as he would often repeat as time went on, yet he was suffering a martyrdom. On July 28 he wrote in his journal, "Returned from Rome. Isolation, repentance, tedium. To agree to be like Abraham: poor, alone, despoiled, and naked, without children or friends."[1] The 27th: "Feeling dull. Lack of activity, of movement, of new impressions." The next day: "Since this morning an irresistible need to weep at the thought of my abandoned friends, and of the doctoral thesis, probably lost." The perspective of an "eclipsed life, without initiative and without formation, depersonalized,"[2] gave him panic and fright. It was not easy for this singular person to be like the others, without anything to distinguish him anymore.

In September, however, he met with Père Lyonnet, who helped him to live through this time of discouragement. "Frère André," he told him, "I have the pope's confidence, of him who asks me to compose his encyclicals, and I have the confidence of my superiors. I am adored by my students. You have nothing, and I envy you."[3] Lyonnet also invited Louf to profit from his trial. Was it not the occasion for him to be configured to the poor Christ, alone and abandoned? "O Lord," wrote Louf, "I thank you for having deprived me of the confidence of my superiors and for having barred the way to 'careers' for me. Pardon me if I weep at times, and grant me your light, so that I may live in this grace: the supernatural beauty of a life forgotten and hidden in you."[4] Dom Achille was right again; the giving of a penance to his monk had been

1. André Louf, *Journal Spirituel* [hereafter JS], 24 July 1958.

2. Louf, JS, 22 Feb. 1959.

3. André Louf, "Compagnons de route," *La Vie*, "Les essentiels," 26 Feb. 2009: 44.

4. Louf, JS, 19 July 1958.

of very great benefit to him, enabling him finally to abandon himself and to open himself to grace. "My second conversion has begun."[5]

The Paradise of the Cloister?

When communities are founded on pardon and the climate they breathe is one of peaceful acceptance of each one's wretchedness, fraternal living can provide a real healing power.[6] Every abbey has meek and humble brothers who support the physical and psychological infirmities of others without judging them. Such are the hidden treasures of communities. Contact with these icons of the serving Christ brings about the experience of being accepted as one is, along with both fragilities that people are no longer afraid to expose and their personal gifts, which the love of the community brings to light.[7]

People need time to discover this balm of community life. If graceful illusions can let a young monk believe at the start of a journey in the existence of a *paradisus claustralis*, to use a Medieval Latin expression for an entirely rose-colored paradise, it does not take long for him to shed that illusion. The real world, with its portion of unjust or offensive situations, of opposing superiors and false brothers, quickly opens his eyes, especially to the ambiguity of his own initial euphoria. "If he identified himself so easily with a community, it was also because that community corresponded to the flattering image he had of himself without his realizing it," Louf later theorized. "That is the source of the irritation that envelops him every

5. André Louf, *À la grâce de Dieu: Entretiens avec Stéphane Delberghe* (Namur: Fidélité, 2002), 67.

6. Jean Vanier, *La communauté: lieu de pardon et de la fête* (Paris: Fleurus/Bellarmin, 1979).

7. André Louf, "Vivre en communauté fraternelle," *Vie Consacrée* 56 (1984): 152.

time the real world starts to threaten his expectations."[8] The young monk also discovers by contact with others how much the community reveals his own limitations and weaknesses to him, Louf writes: "The brothers manifest our poverty. The storms of aggression, rivalry, and jealousy that they unleash in us are the test. It is our own scars that begin to bleed again and our own weaknesses that we feel are threatened."[9]

During 1959–1961 Louf painfully experienced this ascesis of the common life. It was like a mirror being ceaselessly held in front of his misery. He stumbled in a special way against his persistent inability to forget himself and to avoid looking at himself. It was as though he were in prison. He could not help trying to win over his interlocutor in a personal relationship, to capture his attention, or to obtain his agreement. "Illuminating grace," he writes in his journal, "for my lack of internal simplicity. Very detailed self-examination; folding back on myself through which I admire myself and want to admire myself; difficult to describe; I take myself too seriously. I sense myself present in all that I do, especially when I speak or write. Emerging from this impasse will be the fruit of a long, courageous ascesis. Begin by humbly accepting the humiliation of this fault in front of other people who surely will be aware of it."[10]

In January 1959 Dom Achille put Louf in charge of a course in Holy Scripture, though taking it from him a few weeks later because Louf continued to be drawn by the progressive ideas that continued to weigh upon him. He wrote at this time, "At the moment of beginning to teach, O Lord, I beg of you to take away from me every desire to 'succeed,'

8. André Louf, "L'acédie des cénobites et des ermites," in *Tristesse, acédie, et médicine des âmes: Anthologie de textes rares et inédits (XIIIe– XXe siècles)*, ed. Nathalie Nabert (Paris: Beauchesne, 2005), 167.

9. Louf, "L'acédie des cénobites et des ermites," 168.

10. Louf, JS, 1 Dec. 1960.

to form a school, to have important and decisive influence, to form disciples or spiritual or intellectual sons. Let my only desire be that of being entirely spontaneous in your hands for your task."[11] He gave the impression of being afraid of his own power of attraction, as if he were aware that there was danger that this attraction, this charisma, could serve his own glory instead of God's. He who so aspired to simplicity felt himself engulfed by a social personality: "I am terribly artificial, and I play the part of a comedian in front of other people. I always think I am important. O Lord, give me your humility, that mystery I have still not understood."[12] But this narcissistic frailty kept him from loving as Jesus loved, without reward for himself or sentimental reflection. These were trying months, when the heart overflowing with tenderness buried itself in the desert of affectivity and experienced all its dryness and aridity, devoting the apprenticeship of humble love to each work, the love that he called "the summit of friendship."[13] It was a disinterested love, chaste and purified from all selfishness, whose only occupation was "service, self-effacement, and promotion of other people."[14]

Experiencing the True Face of God

The experience of a life hidden inside a large community of monks, incognito, unknown, in the last place, confronted by his own old demons, caused Louf to grow at full speed. In December 1958 he recorded these thoughts: "Today I am 29. Lord, I have the impression of finding myself mature and adult, ready to face life for the first time. Thank you for

11. Louf, JS, 28 Dec. 1958.
12. Louf, JS, 1 Nov. 1958.
13. Louf, JS, 11 May 1961.
14. Louf, JS, 25 Sept. 1960.

having hastened this process during these last few months."[15] The complete absence of expectation taught him to abandon himself to his circumstances: "To accept humbly and confidently the fact that the future is an absolutely closed book, and to accept that I have no future."[16] The wounds inflicted by community life sharpened his naked faith in the presence of God, who was invisible in the trial:

> It is necessary never to stiffen against suffering, but humbly to accept being crushed by it, without a disguise and without a mask, without playing the martyr or the hero, but to descend all the way to the bottom of pain, all the way to the touch of discouragement. And in that moment not to be discouraged. To call upon the name of the Lord in the darkness, despite our tears. To give infinite thanks, to believe against all evidence to the contrary that he is on the way to make us grow. That is indeed the liberation of Easter. It is after this Passover that another calm and another certainty will grow in an unexpected way in our heart. It will be the real Easter morning. That peace and joy will not belong to us, but it will come from the Lord.[17]

Engulfed by suffering, Louf thought he was sinking, in an impasse, the prisoner of his own frailty. But it was just at this moment of discouragement that he had a decisive spiritual experience, as if, at the point of exhaustion, tired of fighting, he finally consented to lay down his weapons and let grace work. It was July 21, 1960. A violent conflict arose between him and the prior of the monastery. There was a loud argument. Louf scrutinized the contempt he felt, wanting to fight it. That evening, the strain having subsided, he knelt down by

15. Louf, JS, 28 Dec. 1958.
16. Louf, JS, 23 March 1959.
17. Louf, JS, 18 March 1960.

the stalls in church, trying to excuse the unfading affront, but of himself he could not do so. Then in prayer all at once it was given him to discover with complete clarity the true face of God, his pure infinite mercy. "This staggering experience," he wrote long afterwards, "transformed my life of faith."[18] God's mercy immediately softened Louf's hardened heart, and the next morning he awoke overflowing with tenderness for his prior. "So much so," he continued, "that I seemed to love him more than any of my friends, and that I begged the Lord to give me as much tenderness for them. These moments are the only ones in life that are worth the trouble."[19]

"The Ceaseless Murmur of My Life"

Louf was not spontaneously inclined to that trusting abandonment to grace; his education in the family, at high school, in the youth movement had developed according to the principles of effort and will power that then colored all Christian education, and that considered prayer carried out in common to be an exercise one had to perform. "During the time of my adolescence," he wrote in a testimonial,

> a certain number of "ways" of prayer were in vogue, recommended by respectable traditions. We chose to try them out, thereby surrounding them with a large amount of generosity. Very soon we had to recognize that prayer was not the infallible fruit of such generosity or of any method, however experienced. My tactical error, let us say, was the desire to attain prayer or even to construct it outside myself as the object of my own efforts. Such was the case until the day it was given to me to understand that prayer was not to be searched out externally,

18. Louf, "Compagnons de route."
19. Louf, JS, 25 July 1960.

> but that it was given to me internally in the deepest part of my heart. Prayer had already been given me internally, even before any effort or any application of method on my part.[20]

When it comes to interior life, the wrist is useless except in finding that the door one faces is closed. Instead we have to let ourselves be taken by grace, to follow grace humbly, to be on call by the interior person, that "hidden man of the heart" (1 Pet 3:4).[21] During 1960 and 1961, a decisive period for Louf, that interior person coincided with his own awareness, as he wrote during that time:

> A great desire for interior life with Jesus. There is only one reality that counts, and it is more irresistible every day: the person of Jesus, his presence in the heart, at the root of my being. This reality would come like an internal breathing, like the unceasing murmur of my life. Perhaps the only gesture to learn is to relax, to let oneself go, to loosen one's attachments to sensible and passing things. Once that center of interior life is released, everything becomes simple and easy. The life of God is always there at the very source of our being.[22]

At the beginning of 1961 Louf entered still more deeply into contemplative experience. With the consent of his spiritual father, Frère Marie, he emphasized asceticism along with longer times of solitude of the desert: "One Sunday a month in complete intellectual abandonment with only the Bible and prayer, in silence with the Lord."[23] He also rediscovered those

20. André Louf, Témoignage inédit sur la prière, ADMC, 2005.

21. André Louf, "L'Homme intérieur ou la liturgie du coeur," *Collectanea Cisterciensia* 72 (2010): 334.

22. Louf, JS, 17 Sept. 1960.

23. Louf, JS, 22 Jan. 1961.

two traditional monastic observances: fasting and nightly vigils. "Fasting," he wrote, "awakes a thirst that is much more essential, that torments us at the roots of our being."[24] It assails us, he understood, in the mysterious universe of our desires, and it seems to resonate with prayer all the way to the deepest region of the flesh. Recalled during the nocturnal vigil, the image of Christ praying alone in the night always greatly moved Louf.[25] He felt himself drawn by this practice, which answers the invitation addressed by Christ to his privileged apostles: "Could you not watch one hour with me?" (Matt 26:40).

As the months passed, Louf understood that this practice would be a privileged moment of his intimacy with God.[26] "I watched with you," he wrote in his diary. "Thank you for having taught me this *hesychia*. I continued to be aware, always more profoundly and more vitally, that you are the root and the source of my being. What a marvelous story that we live together for always!"[27] This term *hesychia* can be translated "peace," "quiet," or "tranquility"; a hesychastic monk is given to solitude, contemplation, search for repose in God, and unceasing prayer,[28] the orientation that emerges. Louf was thus a hesychast, as at this period he discovered the prayer of the heart, this prayer that consists in calling upon Jesus in one's heart by the slow, unceasingly repeated invocation of the phrase by the publican in the Gospel: "Lord Jesus, Son of God, have mercy on me, a sinner." Supported by the

24. André Louf, "Faire pénitence?" *Sources Vives*, no. 108 (March 2003): 84.

25. Louf, "Marchons vers notre Pàques intérieur," *Panorama* (April 2002): 26.

26. Louf, JS, 21 April 1962.

27. Louf, JS, 12 August 1962.

28. André Louf, "Quelques constantes spirituelles dans les traditions *hésychastes* en Orient et en Occident," *Irenikon* 74 (2001): 496.

breath, this rumination produces a great internal sense of peace, as if Jesus surrounded one's whole being and became one's breath and inhaling of life. Clearly Louf was now descending toward his interior cell, the oratory of his heart, with the prayer of the Spirit that is never interrupted. "Very strong attraction, irresistible and pacifying at the same time, for prayer," he wrote in January 1961:

> To be sweetly "present" to the Lord, "to walk with him" unceasingly. For the life of prayer the most important thing is first to find the organ. It is placed in the deepest darkness of our interior, and most people are unaware of it. All the great spiritual writers tried to give it a name: *the heart, the noûs, the mens*, "the refined center of the soul." It is the deepest source of our being, the profundity that our awareness does not reach except at moments of rare spiritual fullness. It is a universe that only the saint has explored and where he pitches his tent, but every monk should at least suspect its existence.
>
> It is the place where our being is in permanent dialogue with God, the point of contact where God's love unceasingly reaches us and re-creates us, the most ardent hearth of our being. It is the only place of our eternal baptism, where, whether we know it or not, our soul can be in an uninterrupted state of prayer, under pain of falling instantly into nothingness. The poets and the philosophers had a certain natural intuition of this core of humanity. But only the spiritual senses, enlightened by faith, can "work the earth of their heart" to find there the hidden treasure and to snatch up the slender thread of prayer that almost in spite of our efforts wells up there forever, that slight breath that on the morning of our creation God the Father blew into our soul."[29]

29. Louf, JS, 8 Jan. 1961.

CHAPTER 5

The Grace of Collectanea

April 1959. The Procurator General of the Trappists came from Rome and climbed the hill of Mont-des-Cats to ask Dom Achille if it was possible to establish there the secretariat of *Collectanea Cisterciensia*, the important official review of the Order. This review of monastic history and spirituality had been begun in 1933 "with the desire of helping souls in their ascent to the love of God."[1] These intentions are summarized in the journal's device: *caritas cum scientia*, "Love with knowledge, or through knowledge."[2]

Dom Achille agreed and thought instantly of entrusting the publication to Louf. The leaders of Cîteaux who had discerned the uncommon skills of the monk during his sojourn at Rome also promoted this move, considering that this highly gifted man had completed his year of repentance and could now humbly take his place in community life. It was time for him to move out of the ranks. Louf accepted the challenge, secretly glad to find a place at last to express what he had at heart.

1. Armand Veilleux, "Rayonnement culturel," in Marie Gérard Dubois, ed., *L'Ordre de la stricte observance au xxe siècle*, vol. 1 (Rome: OCSO, 2008), 395.

2. Lorraine Caza, "Mon passionate 'Chantier cistercien,' " *Collectanea Cisterciensia* 50 (1988): 6.

The Bursting Forth of the Word

At the time of his acceptance of this new responsibility, Louf was facing an intellectual and spiritual crisis. Because of his exegetical training and a personal preference for scientific work, the Bible had become for him a book chock-full of linguistic riddles ready to be deciphered. *Lectio* had become impossible. He was bogged down in a dry, critical approach that did not allow the spirit to enter in.[3] In one of his homilies he shared his experience: "One could be a brilliant exegete, could collect information, historical, philological, and theological data in the Bible, study it frequently and assiduously, and attain competence in it without ever having really heard the Word."[4]

Three years passed from 1959 to 1962 as Louf served as head of the review, important ones for his experience. Thanks to *Collectanea* his curiosity turned away from recent fashionable publications to profit from sources on monastic life. He avidly read all the current publications he could find on Greek and Latin patrology. He examined ancient texts in the Syriac language. Through this exegesis by the fathers, studied also by Henri de Lubac, he came across a book by Lubac that had just come out, one that greatly surprised Louf.[5] From it he understood and experienced that "the Spirit is enclosed in the words of Scripture,"[6] and that it is for that reason that the lectionary is incensed and kissed. Little by little the patristic approach let him reach a kind of synthesis between the

3. Benoît Standaert, "In Memoriam Dom André Louf, O.C.S.O. (1929–2010)," unedited document, 2010.

4. André Louf, Homily for the twenty-third Sunday of Ordinary Time, ADMC, 1997.

5. Henri de Lubac, *Exégèse médiévale: Les quatre sens de l'Écriture* (Paris: Aubier, 1959).

6. Louf, "Une expérience de *lectio divina*," *La Vie Spirituelle* 81 (2001): 477.

two dimensions of science and spirituality, one that he would find fruitful from then on. He saw that it was important to keep in mind both extremes: neither to bury oneself in pure criticism nor to be engrossed in a heedless spiritual exegesis. Rather, one should reconcile the two points of view and be persuaded that such reconciliation will someday cause the light to shine. In fact for Louf the word itself shone.

This position, so profitable for Louf personally, was popularized by him in an article he published in 1960, a kind of *manifesto* of the rediscovery of *lectio*.[7] In it he expressed enthusiasm for the results of scientific exegesis, and while insisting that the reading of the Bible depended on those results, he put his readers on guard against what he called "a theological manual."[8] All the attainments of science will get us nowhere, he said, unless they lead us to an authentic spiritual experience of the word of God. Here is another instance of his former desire to promote a monastic theology: "We understand by that a theology that is the likeness of the theology of the great patristic age, a theology that is born of spiritual experience and aims in turn toward promoting spiritual experience."[9] Such a theology is knowledge linked to the spiritual life, flowing from it and acquiring its taste for intimate connection with the reality of God.

The Soul of the Tradition

The church of that period, as has already been mentioned, was seized by the irresistible need to plunge into the tradition as if into a bath of youthfulness. Especially in France in the

7. André Louf, "Exégèse scientifique ou *lectio* monastique? Autour d'un livre récent," *Collectanea Cisterciensia* 27 (1960): 225–47.

8. Louf, "Exégèse scientifique?" 230.

9. Louf, *À la grâce de Dieu: Entretiens avec Stéphane Delberghe* (Namur: Fidélité, 2002), 26.

middle of the twentieth century, a network of patristic studies was rising with its collections, its chairs, and its confreres, attaining a stunning density.[10] After Sources Chrétiennes began publication in 1942, Bibliothèque Augustinienne followed in 1947. At the same time as this flowering of texts was taking place, in the universities a whole new generation of academics emerged who gave academic visibility to the fathers of the church. In 1943 Jean Daniélou guaranteed the teaching of patristic studies at the Institut Catholique in Paris. In 1945 Père Henri Marrou instituted the discipline at the Sorbonne. In step with the crowd, the publication of texts and studies multiplied.

Louf himself began to translate passages of the *Philocalia*, the Bible of Oriental mysticism, into French.[11] Wanting to lead *Collectanea* into that stream of publications, he entreated the authors of *Collectanea* to do studies of some ancient authors and translations of others. The celebrated American Trappist Thomas Merton wrote articles for the review at Louf's request and did not resist the invitation to take part, writing to Louf, "I am glad to see you have discovered Saint John Climacus, Saint Peter Damian, and Blessed Giustiniani. We need to see more English and French translations of their works. If you can teach some of your young monks to do this work, it is one of the most urgent tasks needed in today's monastic movement."[12]

10. Dominique Bertrand, "L'Envol de la patristique en France au milieu du xxe siècle (1949–1958)," *Bulletin de l'Association Internationale Cardinal Henri de Lubac* 7 (2005): 42.

11. André Louf, À la grâce de Dieu, 152.

12. André Louf, Letter to Thomas Merton, 30 March 1961, Centre Thomas Merton, Université de Bellarmine (Kentucky), Section A - Correspondence (hereafter CTM). [In fact the French volume refers to no response from Louf and provides no source for Merton's letter. BK]

But digging up ancient texts is not enough; they must be lived. Under Louf's leadership *Collectanea* endeavored to return readers' minds to this idea: tradition "is not a well-wrapped package passed on from one generation to another. It is rather an act of transmission, always both gift and creative reception at the same time. Beginning with what we have received, we must discover what is useful today."[13] Louf continues by saying that learned works, translations, and historical studies are only the first step. After that it is still more important to make these texts pass into experience in "the creative discoveries of life," so that they become a "living link of the chain of tradition." The latter, he continues, "is a life in action, a life being lived still at that very moment. To judge it, it is necessary to be in touch with the stream that carries it."[14] He goes on: "And so, listening to the tradition means listening to one's own heart. It does not at all mean turning away from the present to bend towards the past, but rather to make the best of the past coincide with the most urgent appeals of the present in our hearts when they are entirely transformed by the Spirit."[15]

At the Outposts of *Aggiornamento*

As the months passed, Louf involved himself more and more in the review, which gave him the sense of weighing the changes that were taking place.[16] He discovered little by little the role it could play in the renewal that was taking form and that he was seeking to follow by defining the contemplative

13. Louf, *À la grâce de Dieu*, 28.

14. André Louf, "Écouter la tradition," *Collectanea Cisterciensia* 25 (1963): 5.

15. Louf, "Écouter la tradition," 7.

16. André Louf, Letter to Dom Gabriel Sortais, Abbot General of the Trappist Order, ADMC, 5 June 1960.

aspect that he shared with Thomas Merton: insistence upon solitude, interiority, and reform of souls more than structures. Sealed by this agreement, a friendship grew up between these two monks who, hand in hand, from one side of the Atlantic to the other, would warm the monastic life with the fire of interior prayer. "I sense that I am entirely in accord with your point of view, and that proves that the Holy Spirit is at work in the same way in our different young generations of monks," wrote Louf to Merton, who had not long before published the *La nuit privée d'étoiles*.[17] "Yes, it is certainly this contemplative inwardness that we must rediscover at any price. It is worth all the ritual, all the chant, and all the externals of the monastic life."[18]

A few months later Louf wrote again to Merton: "How I find myself in communion with all that you have written on today's monastic movement! Yes, something is stirring among our youth. But it is not institutions that we must first take hold of, it is souls. True poverty, real solitude, great interior life is still possible for individuals in the majority of our communities."[19]

Louf put *Collectanea* noticeably at an outpost of *aggiornamento*. From 1959 until 1962 the review counterbalanced insistence upon the classical elements of monastic life "with an openness to modern thought and an effort to make a synthesis between given elements of tradition and modern mentality."[20] It is no surprise then to find some years later in 1965 that the Council caused the breathing of a new spirit that led to the rethinking of the orientation of the review. Two monks inspired this "second wind."[21] Merton and Louf each wrote an article programming this new era by way of

17. *La Nuit Privée d'étoiles* (Paris: Albin Michel, 1956).
18. André Louf, Letter to Thomas Merton, CTM, 30 March 1961.
19. André Louf, Letter to Thomas Merton, CTM, 16 Sept. 1961.
20. André Louf, Letter to Dom André Fracheboud, ADMC, 3 Feb. 1962.
21. Lorraine Caza, "Mon passionnant 'Chantier Cistercien,' " 35.

prelude.[22] If there had not in fact been collaboration between the two friends, it is still true that their articles both show an important convergence of viewpoints.[23] They expressed the same intention of having the review confront the great contemporary problems, the same desire to contact the fathers, the same concern to propose knowledge capable of making the spiritual life bear fruit. In the vision Louf traced in his article, he dreamed of *Collectanea*'s becoming a center of dialogue between the monastic life and the contemporary church:

> By opening its pages copiously to the spiritual uplift that rises, sometimes chaotically but very fervently, with a promise of the future, a bit all over the monastic order, the review can hope to be more efficaciously present to a church in dialogue and in becoming . . . . It will be a common effort of long duration, and it should be undertaken on every level from the novitiate and the course of theology all the way to the General Chapter. The review will have the task of reflecting these diverse efforts, of inspiring them, and of orienting them. God willing, they may end up one day in a monasticism that while remaining solidly in the soil of tradition will still have acquired full rights of citizenship in the church of its time, speaking its language and taking up its preoccupations internally. It should respond, interiorly but confidently, to its best aspirations. So the review will necessarily have from then on as its primary objective the interior life of contemporary monasticism with its problems and its hopes. It will hear the requests of the

22. Thomas Merton, "The Function of a Monastic Review," *Collectanea Cisterciensia* 27 (1965): 9–13; André Louf, "Pour une revue monastique," *Collectanea Cisterciensia* 27 (1965): 3–8.

23. André Louf, "La fonction d'une revue monastique selon Thomas Merton," *Collectanea Cisterciensia* 56 (1994): 23.

> spirit, receive them, and try to formulate them and make them heard. It will seem tedious and dull to us if we do not read in it what is deepest in our hearts, if it does not convey to us the living word for the sake of which the monk has left all things.[24]

An Intellectual Style

Under Louf's direction *Collectanea* traced new paths, plowing the ground toward new horizons. At first Louf guided it toward rigorous scientific methods. His ambition was to raise its level, to make it an intermediary with the whole world that could not be distorted. In this spirit, in April 1959 he created the Bulletin de Spiritualité Monastique, a section in *Collectanea* of about twenty pages that mentioned and reviewed, in a problematized synthesis, most of the books that had recently appeared in the realm of spirituality and monastic history. In his editorial for the first number, Louf described his intention: to place the results of the most recent research at the disposal of contemplatives and to arouse interest in universities, that is, to create a place of dialogue between academic research and the religious world.

The Bulletin quickly established the general prestige of *Collectanea*; even today it "remains one of the joys of *Collectanea*,"[25] "a gold mine for researchers."[26] The second contribution of the Bulletin was its expansion of *Collectanea* beyond the Cistercian world, as Louf intended that the articles he published would increase "the horizon of the review

24. Louf, "La function," 3–8. The ellipsis is that of the author.

25. Armand Veilleux, "Rayonnement culturel," in *Le bonheur en Dieu: Souvenirs et reflexions du père abbe de La Trappe,* ed. Marie-Gérard Dubois (Paris: Robert Laffont, 1995), 395.

26. Caza, "Mon passionant 'chantier cistercien,'" 37.

to Christian monasticism in general (and not only Cistercian) and to ecumenism."[27]

Finally, Louf felt it necessary to reinforce the dimension of lived experience. "Our readers require something more than simple erudition," he wrote to Thomas Merton. "They want testimony."[28] In fact the review touches two extremes: serious science, but unceasingly confronted by and at the service of interior experience. "Too many reviews of this kind are tempted by a sort of vain academic science, but monastic life has no use for such pretense," he declared. "It has to remain unceasingly at the call of experience, that of the past as well as that of the present, and therefore open to wisdom that is living and life-giving for the future."[29]

It was not long before this dynamism bore fruit. Under Louf's direction the review acquired an authoritative standing. With regard to its success Louf himself had mixed feelings: he was proud on the one hand to have his work praised, but at the same time anxiety about potential vainglory because of this recognition made him uneasy. His journal reflects this ambivalence: "The message of *Collectanea* includes and reflects praise. It is really an exciting business. But it is necessary at all cost that it be and remain entirely the Lord's work, not mine. It is necessary not to let myself get befuddled by it. I have a strong sense of the danger of showing off. Making the work of the kingdom 'one's life's work' always means a risk of spoiling the whole enterprise. Humbly seek occasions of withdrawal."[30]

Louf gave *Collectanea* his complete attention for three years. He rushed headlong into its affairs, and he devoted whole hours of his time devouring new periodical arrivals to

27. Veilleux, "Rayonnement culturel," 395.

28. André Louf, Letter to Thomas Merton, CTM, 23 May 1956.

29. Louf, "La fonction d'une revue monastique," 23.

30. Louf, JS, 27 Nov. 1960.

enrich the Bulletin. The time required was excessive, and he ended up endangering his internal balance, which was already precarious. "Arranging a personal office and a typewriter required by many needs, encouraged by the recognition received on account of the review, I quite simply ran the risk of no longer living for anything but the review,"[31] he recalled. His life in fact took on a clear intellectual aspect. One part of him was glad and expansive; this attraction for studies was important for him. On the other hand, he had a foreboding of spiritual danger, especially that of losing himself in curiosity and of turning away from prayer.

Beginning in October 1961 Louf's workload was such that he asked the abbot's permission to pay regular visits to the neighboring abbey of Belval. Every three or four months he went to spend several weeks as chaplain for the nuns. But these arrangements in his schedule cost him something. "The work of editing that has been done up to now," he wrote to a member of the abbot general's Council, "can no longer be guaranteed by one man alone in the context of a regular life. It is not the work, however intellectual, that I wish to avoid. But what I find too heavy and cannot continue in the same way is the fact that the work robs me practically speaking of the least strength for contemplative living, when I wish to return to the regular life of the community."[32] That was basically the problem. He felt a "desire" rising in him "for a hidden life entirely given over to prayer."[33] He judged the intellectual quality that his life held prejudicial to that vocation.

31. Louf, *À la grâce de Dieu*, 76.
32. André Louf, Letter to Dom André Fracheboud, ADMC, 3 Feb. 1962.
33. Louf, Letter to Dom André Fracheboud.

CHAPTER 6

A Solitary Soul

While struggling with *Collectanea* and living an intellectual life, active, productive, and marked by external influence, Louf was tormented by a desire for solitude, for escape, for "freedom" to be with God, that desire that had stung him in the heart since his youth. Like a sleeping volcano this propensity awoke at the end of his studies in Rome, but especially at the time of his isolation at Mont-des-Cats when his abbot imposed a hidden life upon him. During his first years as a monk, 1947–1954, he had longed to be a diocesan priest and exercise a pastoral ministry. Now he was haunted by a diametrically opposite vocation: that of embracing the life of a hermit, of isolating himself still more, to be exclusively present to God in prayer.

"The Problem of a Vocation"

At the Trappist monastery of Mont-des-Cats everything was done in common: work, prayer, meals, even *lectio* (which took place in a huge hall or study called a *scriptorium*). In this common life where every minute was regulated, the only solitude offered a monk was that of a little cell a few feet long in the dormitory, where he could only go during the six hours prescribed for sleep. Louf needed more than that.

Doubts again tortured him. Was the cenobitic life really made for him? Was not a Carthusian monastery or an outside hermitage the place for him instead?

This desire for a deeper experience of solitude was blended with another desire: to resign from *Collectanea*. The review did not quench Louf's "thirst for life."[1] Already in October 1958 Louf had written to Dom Achille that he felt "pulled in two directions": the attraction for study on one side, and that for "a more humble, poor, and hidden life" on the other. "During my Roman sojourn," he explained, "I had a quasi-assurance that the mystery of my own life of intimacy with the Lord would one day be fulfilled in a very poor and very hidden life with no human comfort."[2] So this tendency gave him no rest. "Very much attracted by a very simple, peaceful, and quiet life," he wrote in his journal. "A '*hesychastic*' life where nothing would happen to impede or trouble the remembrance of your name."[3] "Wept this morning at the thought of my situation," he complained. "Tied to *Collectanea*, tied to the Bulletin, tied to so many obligations; along with that a great hunger for prayer, for meditation, for silence, for the one thing necessary."[4] In his mind intellectual work was now an obstacle to contemplation.

In June 1960 Louf submitted to Dom Sortais, the Cistercian abbot general, what he called a "vocational problem," because Dom Sortais had just prolonged Louf's service at *Collectanea* by a year. Louf was afraid that this prolonging would fix his life in an intellectual direction for good and that such a development would be an "infidelity" to his life of solitude and abandonment. He wanted to be disencum-

1. André Louf, *Journal Spirituel* [hereafter JS], 7 July 1960.

2. André Louf, Letter to Dom Achille Nivesse, abbot of Mont-des-Cats, ADMC, 29 Oct. 1958.

3. Louf, JS, 8 May 1960,

4. Louf, JS, 7 Oct. 1961.

bered from all activity, perceiving a solitary life to be what he was called to. "My dear Most Reverend Father," he writes, "I am thirty-one years old, and I still find myself only at the threshold of monastic experience, but it seems to me that in forty years I will be very much disappointed at being no more than a specialist in monastic spirituality, and at being forced to admit as well that I had often failed to tell my superiors that there were occasions when I seemed to hear the Lord's call to a deepening of my monastic vocation."[5]

Solitary Variations

Solitary, humble, poor, hidden, effaced, contemplative, silent, buried, disencumbered, unrelieved, inactive, without human scope. These words, with which Louf described his vocation during this period, shows the extent to which his vocation was indistinct and imprecise. For a year and a half it was also incarnated in a succession of projects whose pace was staggering.

Not without a certain romanticism, Louf first thought of forgetting himself in "some miserable Christianity in the near East."[6] At the time there was a plan for a Trappist foundation in Egypt. Placide Deseille was even dispatched to the land of the Pharaohs to study the possibility of a Melkite rite foundation.[7] Louf followed his friend's adventures with interest, but he would have preferred to take root among the Copts. "Contrary to Melkite Egypt," he wrote to Dom Sortais, "The Coptic Church is very humble, and its Catholic branch is, from a humanistic viewpoint, insignificant. That is the reason that I am drawn to try it. Such a foundation

5. André Louf, Letter to Gabriel Sortais, ADMC, 5 June 1960.

6. Louf, Letter to Gabriel Sortais.

7. Placide Deseille, *Étapes d'un pélerinage: Autobiographie spirituelle* (Saint-Laurent-en-Royans: Monastère Saint-Antoine-le-Grand, 2015), 20.

would have no hope of brilliant development or of any future progress. It would have no other success than that of being there and remaining there for the love of the Lord."[8]

At other times Louf thought of being enclosed in a hermitage, even though he knew that if freed for the life of solitude in that way, he would run the risk of being victimized by illusions. Monastic tradition teaches, briefly, that it is dangerous to become a hermit before having been tried for a long time in the common life. "I have better understood," he wrote lucidly, "what could be the dangers of the eremitical life. There is a risk of self-absorption under many forms. Instead of contact with God one finds oneself. That can only be avoided if the postulant hermit has reached a high degree of self-forgetfulness, of constant charity for others, and a certain habit of continuous prayer."[9]

What if the common life of a Trappist monastery was the best way to find the poor and humble Christ? After having idealized an Orient like a postcard, Louf became aware of the possibilities of the Cistercian way of life for holiness. "I understood better the extent to which I should desire a life that was truly humble," he wrote. "Certainly not with the humility that is fictional or romantic, like that of a foundation or a desert, but with the true, real, concrete humility of the common life."[10] "I have understood better that my Athos is certainly here," he wrote of the fraternal life at Mont-des-Cats. "What an immense possibility for interior life, for humility, for obedience, and for humble service! I really have no more to wish for, unless it be a little less publicity and a little more hiddenness!"[11]

8. Louf, Letter to Gabriel Sortais.
9. Louf, Letter to Gabriel Sortais.
10. Louf, JS, 18 Sept. 1960.
11. Louf, JS, 12 Feb. 1961.

But the eremitic seed did not take long to sprout anew. After the Oriental foundation and the hiddenness at La Trappe, he was struck again by a new idea: joining the *Fraternité de la Vierge des Pauvres*. The latter was a foundation made in 1956 to promote a simple and poor monastic life in the way traced by Charles de Foucauld.[12] A few weeks later it was instead the Carmelite hermitages of Roque-brunes in southern France that he thought of visiting.[13] Then at the end of December 1961, his desire fixed on the Camaldolese at Frascati, near Rome, a community where he had made retreats when he was a student in the eternal city. Founded in Italy in the eleventh century by Saint Romuald, the Camaldolese lead a life similar to the Carthusian, with individual hermitages grouped around a church and central buildings of general use. Louf rediscovered them at a time when he was deeply interested in a Western hesychastic tradition. He was considering Saint Peter Damian as a theologian of the eremitical life,[14] and in the process he came across the writings of Saint Romuald and his disciple, Blessed Justinian. "Their ideal," he wrote to Merton, "seems to me to be a peak in Western monastic spirituality. Alas! What is left of it today is a continuous sentence. Cost what it will, I must save this magnificent ideal."[15] His journal betrays the same enthusiasm: "I feel that I am now more than ever a Camaldolese postulant in the strict sense of the word. I have now discovered Blessed Paul Giustiniani, and I weep at the thought that the Lord might use me to rekindle the fire that he brought into the monastic world."[16]

12. Louf, JS, 7 Oct. 1961.
13. Louf, JS, 12 Dec. 1961.
14. André Louf, "Un grand docteur monastique: saint Pierre Damien," *Collectanea Cisterciensia* 23 (1961): 261.
15. André Louf, Letter to Thomas Merton, CTM, 30 March 1961.
16. Louf, JS, 29 Oct.1961.

The Obsession of Influence

It appeared to Louf that the Camaldolese incorporated all that he was searching for: a balance of solitary and communal life, flexibility of rhythms adapted to the needs of each member, ample possibilities of fasting and of nocturnal vigils. But the order was not really in good health, and Louf knew that behind his desire to join it was an idea of contributing to its recovery. As we have already seen, however, he always avoided anything that could put him in the limelight, in front, first in rank. Instead, he sought a way of being "without human succor," "without fame"; he wanted to avoid exposure "to any personal triumph," to use his own words.

From that point of view the responsibility for *Collectanea* and the courses in Holy Scripture, which Dom Achille had entrusted to him in April 1961, were a trial for him. He was exposed; his reputation grew along with the personal influence that radiated from him. He was more and more in demand in the Belgian and Dutch abbeys. His intellectual gifts and his joviality attracted attention. He knew it, and it made him suffer, because success and public esteem nourished the narcissism he so wanted to rid himself of. "As long as I still give in to the desire to be known or to be renowned (by teaching, articles, conferences, etc.)," he wrote, "the Lord cannot undertake anything through me for the sake of the kingdom."[17]

Louf's persistent desire, then, to have no further objective in the world can be seen as ambivalent. On one side it corresponded to a positive call to solitude, to an unencumbered life, one more strictly confined to the essentials, to prayer and love. On the other side it appears in a more ambiguous guise as sacrificing pastoral activity, whose influence he had to resolutely escape. But this fear of success, of attracting attention, of the limelight: what is its name? Should he violently, as his sacrificial

17. Louf, JS, 16 Oct. 1961.

voluntarism led him to think, stop teaching and writing if he wanted to travel the path of humility? Wasn't the upshot instead that he should learn to humbly practice the skills that were part and parcel of his personality, without self-reflection?

Louf was solitary and pastoral at the same time. If he willingly accepted his solitary dimension, the apostolic area would be the place of his combat. While he experienced the need to write and teach for his personal equilibrium, he felt that success in these domains intoxicated him, centered him in himself, and distracted him from God. Being the captive of a spirituality of suffering, he solved the problem in a radical way: the only way to shake off what the desert fathers called *vainglory*, Saint Augustine called *self-love*, and the spiritual writers of the seventeenth century called *love of one's own* consisted, he thought, in renouncing his gifts without cutting off an important part of himself. But in so doing he committed an error of evaluation, not seeing that behind his self-reflection was not pride, but his ancient bleeding wound, an extreme image whose only cure consisted in its being noticed by others. The solution to the problem would be the continuation of his apostolate, enlivening him by getting him to accept his weakness humbly and tenderly.

For the moment he thrashed about in the middle of his own contradictions, with a mind divided between a desire of quitting *Collectanea* in order to go into solitude, and another desire to have some pastoral influence, especially at the head of a community of monks. "Lately I have sometimes had occasion to wish for, or rather to experience a little bit, the desire to be a superior. I have understood better how the abbot, even today, especially if he is more than an administrator, truly represents the summit of the monastic ideal. A work of extreme ascesis and of extreme love."[18] Unable to decide

18. Louf, JS, 16 Sept. 1960.

between these two attractions, he chose to let the Lord make him his own work, to be "like a little baby in his hands."[19] So he encamped on a range of availability to God's will: "I belong to him, my life is his. It is he who will deploy it as he wills. Hermitage or *cenobium*. Humble service of the community or scientific influence, or even pastoral activity: nothing will be mine; I will receive all from his hands."[20]

"You lead me, and I will follow you"

Christmas 1961. Upon re-reading the year's entries, Louf understood that the months that had passed had definitively "confirmed him in his contemplative vocation." There was no longer any doubt about his attraction for the eremitical life. He had only one aspiration: "To leave absolutely everything, to burn all my boats, to destroy every bridge, and to live by faith alone in the veiled presence of Jesus."[21]

At the beginning of the month, with Dom Achille's permission, Louf had gone to meet Pierre Doyère, prior of the Benedictine Abbey of Wisques.[22] People came from all over France to consult him to discern their vocations to solitude. Dom Doyère approved Louf's vocation. It seemed to him that there was no question in Louf's case of a passing fancy, or of a slightly romantic dream. Louf had rightly understood the

19. Louf, JS, 16 Sept. 1960.

20. Louf, JS, 8 Dec. 1961.

21. Louf, JS, 25 Dec. 1961.

22. Doyère, who wrote the entry "Érémetisme" in the *Dictionnaire de Spiritualité,* admired the witness given by hermits for "the stress on the absolute with which they proclaim the primacy of the supernatural." According to him, "the hermit is a humble person called to witness by his hidden repentance that the true relationship of humans with God is that of a naked wretch before the majesty of the unique presence" (Bernard Hingrez, Préface to Pierre Doyère, *Benoît Labre: Ermite Pélerin* [Paris: Cerf, 1983], 5).

point of this life as a trial of faith and of privation, writing in his journal, "Such a life obliges us to look upon our own face and to accept our nothingness and insignificance. By depriving us in this way of all our supports—especially our secret pride, which ambushes every solitary, but of which solitude itself, when it is embraced with generosity, cannot fail to heal us—solitude reveals to us little by little the presence of Jesus, imperceptible before, in our hearts and in our entire existence."[23]

The first few months of 1962 passed in expectation and abandonment. Louf lay in wait for God's time with confidence, listening for the movements of the spirit. In his journal he wrote, "Refuse nothing, nothing to the spirit. Do not extinguish it, but let yourself be led by it. Only desire humbly to be as closely united to Jesus the Savior as possible, humble, misunderstood, hidden, praying, fighting, suffering, all that is in the lowest degree of the religious and ecclesial hierarchy, hermit or recluse, buried and forgotten. But this again never as a personal project, but always as a grace awaited."[24]

In this climate of self-reduction Louf was overtaken in March 1962 by his old pastoral hunger, that irrepressible desire to teach and to preach. After all the interior distance he had covered, that desire profoundly humbled him. "The Lord knows the wherefore of these contradictions," he wrote, perplexed.[25] A week, later as doubt continued to darken his mind, he confessed,

> I am still a child. I no longer know what I want. I desire to have everything at once, but there is pride in every one of these desires; there is vanity, greed, and attachment. My desire to experience solitude is sincere, but I

23. Louf, JS, 21 Nov. 1961.
24. Louf, JS, 29 Jan. 1962.
25. Louf, JS, 4 Feb. 1962.

> feel too much attachment to the influence I get from *Collectanea* to seriously strive to obtain it. Then I desire painfully to gain still more influence: preaching retreats, giving conferences, seeking a chair for monastic spirituality at Rome. Perhaps that will be the eternal drama of my monastic vocation. There is only one answer: let circumstances, superiors, obedience, that is to say, you, O Lord, make the choice for me.[26]

This interior division closed up during the months that followed. Louf was at peace. His wish to join the Camaldolese appeared to him so striking that he took the initiative in May 1962 to express it fully to the Cistercian abbot general, writing,

> Before my conscience I cannot doubt the authenticity of my attraction to the eremitical life with which the Lord has inspired me. You can easily guess that this departure for the family of Saint Romuald will by no means call into question my deepest attachment to the Cistercian ideal, to my superiors, and to my brothers. Quite to the contrary, I owe my whole monastic grace to Cîteaux and to those who have introduced me to her. But it seems to me that it is by the grace of God that I have felt this attraction, and I believe it to be a call in the earth of my heart.[27]

In June three weeks spent at Belval strengthened his decision by letting him taste the sweetness of solitude. "Every hermitage," he wrote under the influence of the grace of his retreat, "is a sanctuary of the Trinity; the Trinity is its refuge and its guesthouse."[28] "I feel a peaceful certitude," he wrote

26. Louf, JS, 11 Feb. 1962.
27. André Louf, Letter to Dom Gabriel Sortais, ADMC, 10 May 1962.
28. Louf, JS, 10 June 1962.

later, "and a rapture of being deeply united with a love that my whole life will not be long enough to assimilate."[29] He continued, "The presence of Jesus scatters problems, purifies fears, empties out feelings of anguish, chases away uncertainties. But it is not any human certitude that replaces them. It is much more like a fringe of the absolute, but within the faith. It is a love that finishes all. It is finding the truth of one's being in Jesus and in a relation with him. Solitude robs us of all that is fake, so that our truth may appear in Jesus' presence: the truth that we are sinners who have been pardoned."[30]

But a month later, in July, at a time when he was peacefully settled in his choice, rumor spread that he was a possible future prior at Mont-des-Cats. This hypothesis baffled him anew: "Let me be crucified by this impossible choice. Not to choose. To prefer whatever happens."[31]

Impossible Eremitism

When a choice is slow in being made, Ignatius Loyola, founder of the Jesuit Order, recommended an exercise: write down in black and white the advantages and disadvantages of such a way of life and weigh the respective merits. When it is hard to choose, he recommended the use of reason: "Consider and reflect how many advantages and how much profit flows for me from the responsibility of the benefice in question, in view strictly of the praise of God, Our Lord, and the salvation of my soul, and in the opposite sense consider as well the disadvantages and the dangers that accrue from it."[32]

29. Louf, JS, 12 June 1962.

30. Louf, JS, 17 June 1962.

31. Louf, JS, 6 July 1962.

32. Ignatius of Loyola, *Exercices spirituels* (Paris: Desclée de Brouwer/ Bellarmin, 2008), 111; Ignatius of Loyola, *The Spiritual Exercises* (Chicago: Loyola Press, 1992).

That is what Louf set out to do in August 1962—to judge between his rival desires. In the document he wrote, he made clear his "love and respect for the Cistercian tradition," and he asked himself whether his duty was not to stay at La Trappe in order to "balance by means of a life of prayer the tendencies toward activism and intellectualism that threaten me."

Despite this loyalty, his heart leaned toward the solitary life in the Camaldolese form. The primary merit of this way of life, he noted, was that it accumulated the advantages of the desert (interior deprivation) along with those of community life (renunciation of self). Its second attraction came from its flexibility that allowed life to bloom more easily. Louf had had this experience: "The design of a strict communal life has a tendency to put to sleep spontaneity and enthusiasm in me. The risk is that everything becomes routine and habit. Personal engagement seems more intense to me and truer in a solitary life removed from a social framework, to which I yield too easily."[33]

The choice of the Camaldolese, seen from the point of view of renouncing a spiritual/intellectual influence in the Trappist Order, also seemed to him linked to his refusal of any kind of "human success," which he had tried to maintain since the beginning, though not without being captured by a kind of sacrificial heroism: "Inclined to make again today in a more concrete way, truer and clearer, the sacrifice of any worldly career, which I made at the age of seventeen and at the moment of my solemn profession."[34] More deeply, the solitary

33. André Louf, Élection entre la vie cistercienne et la vie camaldule, ADMC, 15 August 1962. Louf was impressed by the argument of flexibility. He often regretted the hardening of religious formulations, writing for example in his journal, "Monastic families rise up against one another as if they were foreign to one another. The creation of different formulations, structures, and organizations is certainly a strength in Western monasticism, but it is a weakness when they harden, as is the case today."

34. Louf, Élection entre la vie cistercienne.

life seemed to him to be the true foundation of his vocation, the course that had guided him from the beginning. "The question of the eremitical life has always been posed to me," he wrote. "My fifteen years of cenobitic life were like a providential preparation for a more rigorous desert. My feeling is that it was for the sake of this desert, this hermitage, that I vaguely opted when between my fifteenth and seventeenth years I chose La Trappe. From this point of view, Cistercian life never gave me complete peace of soul. I was always looking for something else."[35]

Comforted by this choice, Louf left for Rome in September 1962. There he met the procurator general of the Carthusians, Dom Jean-Baptiste Porion, whose contemplative intensity had so fascinated him when he was still a student. As Nathalie Nabert writes, "Thirsty for the interior life, the young student betook himself often to watch the procession of the pontifical retinue, that endless parade of abbots, bishops, and archbishops leading the pope, only to look at the stunningly recollected face of Porion, who was for him the very countenance of that contemplation for which he longed with all his being."[36] But now Porion explained to Louf that it was nonsense to leave La Trappe at once. Since he had already reached a certain spiritual maturity, the lifestyle had little importance. The important thing was "to abandon oneself to providence and to let oneself be fashioned by it like a wisp of straw floating on the water."[37] This conversation shook Louf, but he nevertheless clung to his idea, writing, "What I feel myself drawn towards is the life of a hesychast, the spirituality of solitary prayer. I have never understood it so clearly or so unhesitatingly."[38]

35. Louf, Élection entre la vie cistercienne.

36. Nathalie Nabert, Introduction to Dom Jean-Baptiste Porion, *Lettres et écrits spirituels* (Paris: Beauchesne, 2011), 19.

37. Louf, JS, 6 Sept. 1962.

38. Louf, JS, 8 Sept. 1962.

But hardly had he made this affirmation than he sensed something uncertain. Significantly, two days later, after having sounded the bugle of his certitude, he copied out in his journal this passage of a letter that for him praised the attraction of communal life: "Except that everything follows the slow, soft rhythm of cenobitic life in the tranquil peace of the Benedictine lifestyle, which is organized self-forgetfulness and by that very fact lets us meet God without realizing it! It is a fruit that ripens without being shaken from its branch: accepting sun and rain, wind and heat as instruments of the Lord."[39]

In mid-September Louf learned that the Cistercian authorities had agreed to release him from the responsibility for *Collectanea* and that the way was open for him henceforth to have an experience of "western hesychasm."[40] He then spent a week with the Camaldolese at Frascati. He had several conversations with the brothers and superiors, and a seed of doubt was sown in his spirit. "The Camaldolese form of life really seems ideal to me, but," he writes, "is all that worth the trouble of leaving an order that I love passionately, where the Lord can lead me to high holiness?"[41] A meeting with Dom Étienne Chenevière was the finishing stroke. Chenevière was a Trappist monk who had between 1955 and 1957 made a trial of life among the Camaldolese at Frascati and had written a book there, *L'Hermitage*, a veritable breviary of solitary life. Jean-François Holthof has said of Dom Étienne's experience, "At first the experience seemed decisive, since he took the novice's habit in July 1958, but he ended up six months later deciding to return to the Trappist way . . . . The book, *L'Hermitage*, is nothing more than the publication without any editing of the spiritual notes taken by Dom

39. Louf, JS, 11 Sept. 1962.
40. Louf, JS, 15 Sept. 1962.
41. Louf, JS, 21 Sept. 1962.

Étienne during his sojourn with the Camaldolese."[42] These notes pin down the small congregation: lack of recruits, low intellectual level, a community with its own spirituality. "Coming from La Trappe, Dom Étienne determines, one has the vivid impression that what one loses is not compensated for by what one finds."[43]

Before leaving Frascati, Louf buried a miraculous medal and a medal of Saint Benedict, the father of monks, in a corner of the cemetery near the hermitage, and he supplicated the Virgin, Benedict, and the hermits who lay buried there to bring him back there to stay always, if such was God's will. But in his heart something had snapped: "I no longer feel attracted to this congregation."[44] On the return road to Mont-des-Cats he realized that it was time to break off, to stop the procrastination in which his irresolute character had engulfed him: "It behoves me no longer to prolong this time of reflection and hesitation. Above all, not to get settled in it. Once definitively determined upon an irrevocable commitment, I will lose all my hesitation. Temperamentally I am inclined toward anguish and perpetual hesitation about a choice to be made between two possible ways. I will mistrust this weakness."[45]

"To be thankful for mercy"

On his return to Mont-des-Cats Louf scrutinized the arguments for the Carthusians: "Above all one finds the solitude there that one brings to it. The Trappist who has not found solitude in himself will not find it among either the Carthusians

42. Jean-François Holthof, Préface to Un Moine, *L'Hermitage* (1968) (Paris: Ad Solem, 2005), 7.

43. Louf, JS, 21 Sept. 1962.

44. Louf, JS, 22 Sept. 1962.

45. Louf, JS, 21 Sept. 1962.

or the Camaldolese."[46] He finally realized that the place is secondary. The important thing is fidelity to the Word and to unceasing prayer with fasting and vigils; those are the practices that are at the heart of hesychasm. "All the graces of the past years have their meaning here," he insisted. "Whether at La Trappe or at Camaldoli or anywhere else that the Lord wills, my role will be to realize as well as I can this vocation to *hesychia*. Even at La Trappe there is a place for 'spiritual anchorites.' Whatever happens to me, it is at the side of anchorites that I should always sit down in one way or another, as if on my own center of gravity."[47]

The haze and irresolution that darkened his future anchored him nonetheless in an abandonment that kept deepening. Louf renounced himself, returned his life to God, and let Christ choose for him: "This morning I wept for joy, because I felt that my whole life from now on is in Jesus' hands and that I have no other choice than what he wants. I no longer fear anything. I believe blindly that all is grace; he will see to it that everything brings me close to him and involves me at my place deep inside the church, my place that he has chosen himself."[48]

In this state of mind at the beginning of December, Louf left for the abbey of Belval to bring the abbey's records up to date. It was there on December fourth that he learned of the sudden death of the abbot of Mont-des-Cats. "Now the community is plunged in mourning and suffering, and the anxiety of choosing a new father is already here."[49] On the ninth he was informed that his name was going around on the list of possible successors. At first sight nothing could have been more contrary to his hesychastic desire than the abbatial existence. But at the same time, he said to himself, "with a certain

46. Louf, JS, 11 Oct. 1962
47. Louf, JS, 21 Oct. 1962.
48. Louf, JS, 8 Nov. 1962.
49. Louf, JS, 4 Dec. 1962.

depth of privation and of death to oneself, being a hermit or being an abbot amounts to the same thing."[50] In fact he no longer knew what to think. He was lost, divided between irreconcilable attractions: "Sometimes I feel as though aspiring after the poverty of the desert and the humble, hidden joy of 'unceasing conversation with Jesus,' and sometimes on the other hand I feel the tenderness of a father and the desire to bury myself in humility and unceasing service of others."[51]

Can one imagine the suffering to Louf caused by his permanent search of vocation, his inability to fix himself finally in any position? Ever since he had entered the abbey in 1947 he had been looking for his place. Every time he thought he had found it, it disappeared; he had to leave again, to go on the road. Each stage required a new giving up of his certitudes, his choices, his desires. What with privation upon privation, hardly anything was left for him, now a thirty-three-year-old monk, except to have understood what was most important: the necessity of abandoning oneself in Jesus' arms and of confiding in him. On December 30, 1962, a few days before the abbatial election, he wrote,

> Reclusion, a life of poverty on a skete, spiritual fatherhood, bearing witness for the humble love of Jesus: none of that seems contradictory except to human reason. Every intervention of Jesus in our lives is a new discovery, a veritable new creation out of nothing; for him all these attractions become one and are in harmony with the concrete vocation that he has chosen for me, although I still do not know how they shape up. But everything prepares me for that vocation, through his hands, and always has. I want to settle in deeply and to abandon myself to this certitude of faith. All the seeds

50. Louf, JS, 9 Dec. 1962.
51. Louf, JS, 16 Dec. 1962.

that Jesus himself has planted in my heart will bear their fruit in their own good time, and no desire of mine that really comes from him will fail to be satisfied beyond all measure. *Tecum paupere:*[52] these two Latin words softly repeated in Jesus' presence have given me much peace in all the anguish about the future. I want to be pure and empty of all desires, of all self-will, and of all self-love, just as the human Jesus was in his sacred humanity concerning the divine activity in himself.[53]

52. "With you, the poor man."
53. Louf, JS, 30 Dec. 1962.

CHAPTER 7

Habemus Abbatem

The end of December 1962. After having spent two weeks as chaplain of the Trappistines at Belval, Louf returned to Mont-des-Cats. The abbey was still in mourning, but the abbatial election had been set to take place in a few days, on January 10. What was his state of mind? He secretly hoped that the successor of Dom Achille would have the same kindly disposition toward his eremetical leanings as the deceased abbot had had. Louf prayed and prepared himself internally for this election, which was a delicate turning point in the life of the community. On January 2, 1963, the anniversary of his baptism, he wrote, "I feel a strong attraction for solitude and for the way of life in a skete," and he again asked for "the grace to fall into the way of a recluse."[1] On the ninth, the day before the election, he had a sense of more inspired discernment: "It seems very likely that I will not be elected."[2] On the following day the votes of his brothers placed him at the head of the community. At the age of thirty-three there he was, abbot of Mont-des-Cats.

1. Louf, *Journal Spirituel* [hereafter JS], Jan. 2, 1963.
2. JS, January 9, 1963.

"A Little Pentecost"

This choice was a "complete surprise."[3] André was short of the canonical age of thirty-five, and he had never had any important responsibilities in the monastery. Instead his repeated absences had placed him at the fringe of the community. The vicissitudes of his early years as a monk were not forgotten. They were not ideal characteristics for a monk. Jokingly he would say that it was his sojourn at Belval, far from members of the council, that was the determining factor; absent brothers have a better chance to be elected because their good qualities will be taken into account, without their faults being seen.

The election began during the morning of January 10. Voting came around by turns. At each scrutiny Louf kept winning more and more votes for his name. "My heart began to beat, to beat, to beat with extraordinary speed," he testified.[4] The monk hesitates. If a quorum of votes is attained, should he accept? Can he escape it? He accosted his spiritual father in the cloister between two rounds. The latter counseled him to accept, even making him consider it a duty. In the course of the morning, and of the winning votes, a kind of clarity was felt by each participant. Louf compared it to an epiclesis, a descent of the Holy Spirit. The Spirit took hold of each one of the voters and, while respecting the freedom of each one, peacefully imposed a choice that became a consensus.[5]

In reporting the event to the sisters at Belval, Louf would confirm his election: "As the voting proceeded, one listened to the other, then God's will became sweetly more certain,

3. André Louf, "Autrement la grâce n'est plus la grâce," in André Louf, Denis Huerre, and Marie-David Giraud, *Dieu intime: Paroles de moines* (Paris: Bayard, 2003), 59–60.

4. André Louf, First meeting with the community of Belval, ADMC, Feb. 6, 1963.

5. Louf, "Autrement la grâce n'est plus la grâce," 13.

more precise, and more clear, and we bowed to that will. That one was chosen who was obviously chosen by the Lord. It was a little Pentecost for Mont-des-Cats."[6] For him there was no doubt about it. The election was a visitation by God, who intervened as he habitually does, in an unforeseen way. "It was really a work of the Lord among us," he said. "After the election a brother used this expression: 'It was like a liturgy. All we had to do was pray!' Yes, humanly speaking this election was hardly foreseeable. There were many candidates, which would have made it difficult; yet the Lord intervened in a way extremely perceptible, palpable even."[7]

Meanwhile in Louf's mind a chaos of contradictory impressions dashed against one another. Perplexity was dominant above all else, as he was confronted by the disconcerting mystery of God's plan. "Just when I was ready to go away to a hermitage, thinking I was faithful to an interior call, I was propelled to lead a community as its pastor," he recalled.[8] Yet strangely enough, he also sensed that it was precisely there in that place that he was expected to be for the moment, and that the isolation of a superior who faced alone a responsibility so daunting was perhaps the form of solitude and deprivation that God had chosen for him. That is the sense in which he wrote to Thomas Merton, "An abbot's life is far from being a hermit's life, but it does seem to me at times that the two graces are not so far apart from each other."[9]

So Louf accepted the responsibility, but he said to himself that it was a question of a provisional service, that in ten years he could offer his resignation in order finally to respond to his vocation as a hesychast. Leaving the voting chamber,

6. Louf, First meeting.

7. Louf, First meeting.

8. André Louf, *À la grâce de Dieu: Entretiens avec Stéphane Delberghe* (Namur: Fidélité, 2002), 90.

9. André Louf, Letter to Thomas Merton, CTM, Feb. 25, 1963.

he noticed an old laybrother, very old, who congratulated him before flinging this warning: "You will have the best portions, but also the worst, but you will never have cause for complaint. It is what you wanted!" Implied in these words was this: "Profit from present joy, since it will be of short duration. You cannot yet suspect into what abysmal distress this abbatial service will lead you!"

A Pardoned Sinner

To express the spirit with which Louf wished that his ministry should be exercised, he chose a device and a cry. His abbatial device was an expression inspired by the primitive texts of Cîteaux: "With the poor Christ" [*cum Christo paupere*]. It was a question not of material poverty, but of a wish to be an abbot who did not confide in his own strength but expected everything to come from grace, like a man poor at heart and poor in spirit.

The cry was the one uttered by Christ at the moment of his agony, when he was thrust down into the lowest depths of human desolation: *in manus tuas*: "Into your hands." These words express the almost childlike confidence with which Louf dived into his new life. On January 18, after having left aside his journal under the pressure of events, he wrote: "Chosen abbot of Mont-des-Cats after a good week in an election where the Holy Spirit was visibly at work. I was chosen by the Lord, in the Lord, and for the Lord. Nothing more belongs to me. All is his, all is his work. Without any doubt it is a very great grace for me, but one for which I cannot account or know what it means today. I desire only complete transparency as regards this grace and this task without any self-reflection and without any complacency."[10]

10. Louf, JS, 18 Jan. 1963.

A few days after the election a meeting was arranged between Louf and the abbot general, who had to confirm the election. Louf was anxious. For over a year he had deluged the abbot general with requests to withdraw into solitude. Dom Sortais remembered that it was not long since Louf had had one foot in Cîteaux and the other in Camaldoli; he wanted to sound out Louf's intentions and assure himself that the election had really banished his eremitical temptations. "He would tell me later," wrote Louf, "that he was afraid I might transform the monastery into a laura[11] for hermits or a charterhouse."[12] The meeting of the two men was a moment of intense brotherhood that André remembered with immense gratitude.

Dom Gabriel could identify with this young freshly styled abbot, since he had also been placed at the head of the community of Bellefontaine at the age of thirty-three. He opened his heart to Louf, and for hours at a time he shared his successes, his failures, and his regrets. He initiated Louf into his future profession by confiding to him the key to everything, as Louf later recalled: "I should base myself on my experiences of the weakest performances in my past life, of which he was not unaware, in order to derive from them an increase of comprehension and of mercy for the weaknesses that I might find in other monks. By mentioning himself as well as an example, he specified, 'God sometimes allows some weaknesses in a person with responsibilities, so that he can understand and help his brothers to bear their own.'"[13] Louf also received from the brethren words of encouragement like those of the abbot general. One said, "We have a prelate who will be able

11. *Laura* is a technical term, derived from Eastern monasticism, for a system of individual hermitages surrounding a central house or church. "Charterhouse" is the English for a Carthusian monastery.

12. Louf, *À la grâce de Dieu*, 90.

13. "Autrement la grâce," 16.

to have compassion on our weaknesses, because he has experienced them all himself." Inspired by Georges Bernanos, another went further: "He has enough sins to know how dark we are."[14]

Soon afterward Louf received a postcard signed by his teacher, the Benedictine monk Dom Jean Leclercq. On the back of it were scrawled these few words: "I do not congratulate you: you are not there for nothing. Neither do I pity you: God is all powerful."[15] To consent to be a vehicle of grace, to believe that the Lord would work through his poverty: that was the note to be sounded of his abbatial tenure.

A few days before his abbatial blessing Louf spent an entire night in prayer: "Lord Jesus, in this vigil in the darkness of this night, give me the heart of an abbot. I need you terribly. No function seems to require as many contradictory qualities as this one: a life of intense activity and of unceasing union with God, firmness and sweetness, a taste for reflection and the thought and qualification for action. a clear vision of principles and tireless adaptation to each one's potency. From the human point of view this synthesis is impossible."[16] A few days later, again: "Here I am, with you, on your mountain, in prayer and waiting for your Spirit. The adventure has begun. I am your abbot. I belong to you as I have never belonged to you. Create your sacred history in me. Make over your whole life in me."[17]

"I would like so much to be a holy abbot"

Just before Dom Achille's death, while Louf was still at Belval, he composed a "prayer for the election of an abbot." This text would serve him as a schema, as a standard, when

14. Louf, First meeting.
15. Louf, "Autrement la grâce," 22.
16. Louf, JS, 12 March 1963.
17. Louf, JS, 19 March 1963.

he wanted to examine his conscience and "keep a straight course against wind and sea."[18] It traces a kind of abbatial archetype. Forgetful of himself, directly depending on the Spirit, perfectly identified with God's will, the abbot, as Louf imagined him, has entirely renounced the seduction of the world. His only horizon is love. He radiates humility, sweetness, and Christ's mercy. An unprofitable servant, he is among his brothers as the one who washes their feet and occupies the last place. While carrying the cross of material cares, he is never distracted from the one thing necessary, from prayer, which is his essential task, rumbling unceasingly from his heart.[19] This portrait of an abbot, which is not without an evocation of a saint, suggests an ideal as elevated as it is inaccessible. Significantly, during the first months of his actual abbatial experience, Louf sadly found how great was the distance that separated this dreamy icon from reality.

How can the presence of Christ be kept alive in a frenetic life shaken by concerns, voyages, and all kinds of claims? The discovery of the innumerable constraints of his abbatial charge profoundly disoriented Louf during the first few years of that charge. He wanted to be "a man of prayer," but so many things turned him aside from that goal: "Turmoil, business, so many problems to solve and questions to answer, letters to write, so many conversations, telephones ringing, all the time, all the time."[20] Even when on a trip, he was not at peace. Hardly had he arrived at the Swiss abbey of Fille-Dieu, for example, when he found that a whole pile of work had preceded him: "The mail was already waiting on my desk. Reports upon reports always came from all the corners of the Order on the subject of *aggiornamento*, inclusion of

18. Louf, "Autrement la grâce," 17.

19. André Louf, Prayer for an abbatial election, ADMC, Dec. 1962.

20. André Louf, First meeting.

the brothers, etc. I would need a night train and a day train to get through all that."[21]

In that context he had a presentment that his fidelity to prayer would be both a vital need and a harsh combat at the same time. If he did not want his contemplative life to sink in the swamp of everyday life, it was necessary for him to make the time dedicated to prayer a sanctuary, to arrange spaces of solitude in the concrete organization of his life. Once a week he confined himself as well or as poorly as possible to a quiet day in a small hermitage near Mont-des-Cats; every five or six months he made a longer retreat. But the principal stake was the transformation into prayer of everything that cluttered his day; he longed after all to be "a permanent spiritual presence."[22] For a great many months he asked for this double grace: "the grace of evangelical life, that is to say: to be like Jesus in everything—and the grace of continual prayer—to be with Jesus in everything."[23] The regular framework of his existence moved by sudden bursts. His life became a journey. He had to learn to be in motion, in a strong wind, to find his stability in Christ, to have nothing more than "an unforeseeable track where God is found in every day, which is forever new and forever disconcerting."[24] It is the present moment. "Jesus," he writes in this spirit of abandonment to circumstances, "you will be the only reality of every moment, of every encounter, of every interview, of every Chapter, of every letter, of every trip. In every event you allow to happen I will feel that you are enclosing me like a recluse in his hermitage."[25]

21. André Louf, Letter to the community, ADMC, 26 Nov. 1964.
22. Louf, JS, 15 April 1963.
23. Louf, JS, 3 June 1965.
24. Louf, JS, 28 Feb. 1964.
25. Louf, JS, 22–23 Feb. 1964.

After several months as abbot, it is necessary to note that these generous resolutions and this good will led to an impasse. From morning until night Louf knocked against his fragility and his limitations, butted against his powerlessness to pray, to become the humble servant of his brothers, to get out of the prison of himself, to forget himself, to die to himself. "I do not know how to love," he writes, "because I stick to myself. Disconnect me, Jesus, from myself."[26] And again: "Thank you, O Lord, for beginning the destruction of the citadel of my vain complacency. So continue to force me to unlearn how to be witty in front of others and to show off concerning your grace."[27] In January 1965, two years after his election, he wrote, "I arrived at the hermitage with great interior poverty, deeply aware of my spiritual frailty. I am attached to my work. I find it very natural to be an abbot. Do I still listen enough to my brothers? I am lax in making an effort to pray, even while willingly assuring myself of long intervals spent in church where I can be seen. I find trips tempting, especially on business of the Order. I love to be entrusted with certain responsibilities."[28] A few months later: "All kinds of temptations, attachments, gluttony, vanity, dryness concerning the Word, weariness about my work. And I would like so much to be a holy father abbot."[29]

Briefly, in the space of two years, Louf's ideal image of the abbot had shattered into a thousand pieces. Blessed was the crisis that helped him recognize all that the ideal covered up concerning the search for his real self. Engulfed by his failings, Louf understood no longer intellectually, but according to the flesh, that he must be an abbot not according to his personal ideas, but by following the traces of God's will: "What

26. Louf, JS, 6 Dec. 1963.
27. Louf, JS, 21 Dec. 1963.
28. Louf, JS, 29 Jan. 1965.
29. Louf, JS, 18 March 1965.

I have to accept," he writes in a profound conversion, "is to drop unceasingly 'my' ideal of an abbot, in order that you, O Lord, may yourself realize your ideal in me: that is the witness you expect from me. It is for you to invent me and for me to let it happen."[30]

The experience of Louf's misery had another merit, which he expresses in a neat formula: "It throws me into the arms of his mercy; literally; it subdues me to his mercy. And I am full of joy, because I sense that God's love needs my sins. Our misery is the chasm of his grace." Sin was no longer an obstacle for him. It was now a path. "There is no real prayer possible without a certain realization of our radical poverty, and of our sin," Louf assures us. "Prayer is always *de profundis*, from the deepest part of our distress. It is from there that a cry rises from us. Blessed are you, Lord Jesus, because you reduce my pretension of justice to nothing, and you wish me to be counted among the sinners."[31]

A glimpse of nothing had brought about a salutary reversal. There was no longer any question of success by way of his virtues, but rather of letting grace work through failure. The power of God is deployed through human weaknesses. For Louf this discovery was a source of happiness and of a deep liberation. He knew that his consent to his poverty let God derive great glory, and that God was working miracles through Louf's insignificance: his mediocrity was God's instrument, which he used to make the kingdom advance. It was useless then, he saw, to stiffen himself against this whole bundle of insufficiency. It made more sense to accept it and to expose himself to God's love. "Let my brothers discover what I lack," he writes in a prayer, "in order that they may not be surprised by your action in me. It is by not hiding my misery, but by accepting it as it is in front of everybody that

30. Louf, JS, 25 Sept. 1965.
31. Louf, JS, 28 July 1976.

I will leave a place open inside me for Jesus' glory and for his action. Not to hide it, nor excuse it, nor defend it, but before everyone to confide it to the mercy of the Lord."[32]

In 2005, invited to cast a glance back at his journey, Louf compared his abbatial tenure to a "second novitiate": "With its joys and trials it constituted a new formation that threw me down into a depth hitherto unsuspected; there one ended up noticing that the brothers held their own and made progress, but not because of any qualities I thought I had. Despite my qualities, but instead because of my lacks and failures, which became for them a purifying fire, they progressed. But what a consolation it was to know that even from faults and failings God can derive some good."[33]

Apprentice to a Trade

A good friend of Louf's wrote just after the election saying that Louf was a "mushroom abbot," who had sprouted all of a sudden without warning.[34] In fact he had become head of the abbey without any preparation, free of any experience of responsibility in a monastery, without ever having touched its machine oil with his hands or put his hands on its functioning or its government. The community of Mont-des-Cats was like a small beehive, with eighty brothers and an economy based on a farm and a cheese production; it operated with a full regime, real estate, a complex administration, an organized novitiate, and daughter houses that had to be visited, all things whose management was not subject to improvisation. No one is a born abbot, but one becomes an abbot in the course of patient apprenticeship. Thanks be to God,

32. Louf, JS, 25 Oct. 1963.

33. André Louf, Homily on the occasion of his sacerdotal Jubilee at Mont-des-Cats," ADMC, 25 June 2005.

34. Louf, First meeting.

André was fortunate in having a team to depend on, one that had already assisted his predecessor to shoulder the burden of responsibility. During the first few months the apprentice abbot gained the soul of a disciple, listened to these men's advice, and refined his formation among them. "I am surrounded," he told the sisters of Belval, "by a troop of instructors; I have teachers of canon law, of liturgy, and of finance who show me the regular things that I should do, because I know absolutely nothing about them, nothing at all."[35]

To help him in his government André was assisted by a pastoral council. Although Dom Achille had rarely consulted this group, Louf decided to call their meetings regularly and to associate the members with his projects and decisions. "It was a novelty," he remembered, "which did not go without saying. The members of the council, whose opinions obviously did not always agree, had never been confronted with such a situation, nor had their young abbot. It was only after some time that I noticed how these 'sharing sessions' were reduced most of the time to a long abbatial monologue, during which I made known my own point of view."[36] The atmosphere at the time was one of consultation and deliberation. Led by that inspiration, Louf encouraged the formation of all kinds of structures, which emerged according to the immediate needs of the community: a finance committee, a work committee, a liturgy committee, all created to put into practice the *aggiornamento* that had been determined by Vatican II. "There was even room," he said, "for a committee whose purpose would be the beautification of the regular places"; he ended up calling it, for want of a better name, "the good taste committee."

In spite of his openness to democratic structures, and in spite of his ability to accept criticism, André would always

35. Louf, First meeting.

36. Louf, "Autrement la grâce n'est plus la grâce," 25.

keep something of the abbot of the *ancien regime*. Not at all because of a taste for pomp—of this he was absolutely devoid. No, it was his tendency to decide for himself, of which for example his decision to appoint Père Jean-Marie Couvreur master of novices is an instance: he acted against the advice of his council in virtue of an intuition—which was proven correct—that the latter would reveal all his talents for the service of the community in that post.[37] A former abbot bore him witness: "It should never be forgotten that he came from the pre-conciliar world, in which the abbot was elected for life and considered an absolute monarch, and when anyone met him, he was supposed to kneel and kiss his hand. Dom Louf grew up in that culture and passed through it into the contemporary world."[38]

In another domain Louf also had to feel his way in the beginning: fraternal relationships. "The manner of making remarks, in community or one on one, belongs to an art that has to be learned, and perhaps no one has ever perfectly mastered it. It was undoubtedly," he regrets, "the aspect of my ministry that left most to be desired."[39] In fact he wavered between excessively strong interventions that hurt some of the monks and other decisions that were too weak or slow, aimed at others; he endeavored for a long time to find his own style of authority. One evening after he had very strictly scolded one of the brothers, he found in his mailbox a short note darkened by this citation from Saint-Exupéry: "A friend is first of all the one who does not judge!"[40] Louf kept this note with him always as an invitation to prefer mercy to justice.

37. Jean-Marie Couvreur, conversation with the author.

38. Dom Guillaume Jedrzejczak, Louf's successor as abbot of Mont-des-Cats, conversation with the author.

39. Louf, "Autrement la grâce n'est plus la grâce," 32.

40. Louf, *À la grâce de Dieu,* 56.

CHAPTER 8

A Flemish Staretz

In Orthodox monasteries a distinction is often made between the *hégumenos*, the hierarchical superior of the community, and the *staretz*, who is its soul. This distinction is almost comparable to that between the cenobitic abbot, voucher for the community and for fraternal unity in the monastic tradition emanating from Saint Pachomius, and the abbot in the eremitical sense, whose role is to start his sons off on the way of interior prayer, following a tradition that itself goes back to the Desert Fathers. Louf's solitary tendency colored his abbatial style, so he takes his place in that second tradition. His idea of the abbot was above all that of the *staretz,* who communicates the life of the spirit to his sons.[1]

"The abbot is first of all the spiritual father of his monastery," Louf proclaimed in an unpublished document defining his approach to Cistercian identity.[2] For him the abbot's

1. Armand Veilleux, abbot of Scourmont, and Jean-Marc Thévenet, abbot of Acey, conversations with the author.

2. André Louf, "Questionnaire en vue du chapitre général de 1967," ADMC, 1966. "The preparatory commission for the 1967 Chapter, in its meeting of October 1966, sent out a preliminary questionnaire intended to invite the members of the Order to make known what they thought and desired. The results of the questionnaire were examined after the beginning of 1967" (Marie-Gérard Dubois, "Les débuts difficiles de la rénovation

ministry is entirely confined to the service of spiritual fatherhood, and the one responsible for the community bears the title "abbot"—"father"—precisely because his essential role is that of transmitting spiritual experience to his brothers in a particular way, and to the community in general.[3] If each abbey has its own style, it owes that style to a particular *abba,* who imprints his own deep mark and breathes a certain spiritual climate. How did Louf exercise this ministry? What was his spiritual pedagogy? "To feed the flock by prayer, to tend them by example, and to care for them by means of the words" of their abbot: that is the famous trilogy with which Saint Bernard sketched out the image of the shepherd he wanted to be in the midst of his brothers.[4] If Louf could in his turn take up the three elements of this triptych, that would characterize his paternity.

A Performative Word

A brother of Mont-des-Cats later remembered, "We read very few of his writings. For us Dom Louf was before all else a word that most of us received with a disciple's heart."[5] That word was the principal vehicle of Louf's teaching. He issued it especially on two occasions: in the chapter talks that he held every morning after the office of Prime, and in his homilies at Sunday Mass. He gave great importance to these

---

post-conciliaire de l'ordre: 1965–1970," in *L'Ordre cistercien de la stricte observance au XX*[e] *siècle, Vol. 2, Du concile Vatican II à la fin du siècle,* ed. Marie-Gérard Dubois [Rome: OCSO, 2008], 28).

3. André Louf, *À la grâce de Dieu: Entretiens avec Stéphane Delberghe* (Namur: Fidélité, 2002), 59–60.

4. Cited by André Louf, "Bernard, abbé," in *Bernard de Clairvaux: Histoire, mentalités, spiritualité: Introduction aux œuvres completes (Colloque de Lyon-Cîteaux-Dijon),* Sources Chrétiennes 380 (Paris: Cerf, 1992), 357.

5. Daniel Curely, monk of Mont-des-Cats, conversation with the author.

chapters, which are the privileged place of the transmission of the monastic grace. He prepared his talks in great detail.[6] Although he ended up commenting on the Rule of Saint Benedict in the last years of his abbacy, he did so little early on, preferring instead to focus on certain general themes of spirituality, which during several days or weeks at a stretch he approached from every angle. Or he commented on some ancient or recent spiritual writer through whom he might examine the elements of spirituality. Homilies also played an important role. It was undoubtedly in these Sunday sermons that he most magnificently expressed his own spirituality.

Louf wrote his homilies on small slips of paper that he took from his desk before going to the pulpit to preach to his brothers. Later his secretary recast them and distributed them to the community. "We received a printed sheet," recalled a brother, "and read it over, because it was really quite good. There was great appropriateness of style, originality in the approach to the Gospel, and always a closeness to the text; no external elucubrations at all, but the meditations were strongly evangelical."[7] This word was complemented by his exceptional oratorical gifts. Louf possessed the art of winning over his listeners by the clarity of his thought, the beauty of his expression, and his graceful gestures, especially when he moved his long, slender hands. "In front of an assembly," remembers Dom Marco-André Di Péa, "he used to say he felt like a tribune, and he was transported, transcended."[8]

"Every morning at chapter," Louf loved to repeat, "I create my community."[9] For thirty-five years he distilled his teaching

6. Jean-Marie Thévenet, conversation with the author.

7. Guillaume Jedrzejczak, conversation with the author.

8. Père Marco-André Di Péa, abbot of Mont-des-Cats at the time of the writing of this book, in conversation with the author. His abbacy ended in 2021.

9. André Louf, *Journal Spirituel* (hereafter JS), 7 Nov. 1963.

in his homilies, chapter talks, and spiritual conferences, and it planted seeds in the hearts of his brothers. The community was formed by this teaching, and even today it forms "the hidden tapestry"[10] of that community.

The Spirituality of Temporalities

Louf also exercised his spiritual fatherhood through his decisions, even those that seemed material and concerned with the temporal administration of the abbey. He was endowed with an intellectual temperament that inclined him to the realm of ideas. He was not well known for a knack for material things, nor for a practical sensitivity, of which he was almost completely destitute.[11] In a letter that breathes no flattery, an elderly brother reproached him with an incredible liberty of expression:

> Since you invited me to give you some subjects for reflection, I am sending you this verse from an unknown romantic poet about an albatross that fell on the bridge of a ship: "Its giant wings keep it from walking."[12] I ask myself if that is not the case with you. You solve the big problems and seem to be disarmed by the little ones; you undertake experiments for the good of the order without asking yourself whether you set the young against the old in your own monastery. You are an oracle for the whole order, and you fail to make Brother Pierre obey you. Obviously the first impression we have of you is a sail's length . . . and the second impression that of an absence from concrete problems (I am slightly exaggerating—we know you make an effort).

10. The words of Guillaume Jedrzejczak in his "Homelie pour le jubilé de Dom André" for June 2005.

11. Jean-Marc Thévenet, conversation with the author.

12. *L'albatros* by Charles Baudelaire.

> Maybe the solution would be to try to strengthen the awareness of the important immediate problems that confront the people near you in the domain of sensation, in their flesh, and in their psychology. Concretely, you should avoid undertaking too much. The monastery is a construction site from top to bottom and on all levels. If we do not want to go on to a drama that would not be a revolution, but a general discouragement, it is necessary to stop undertaking and occupy ourselves first with finishing: finish the WC, finish the henhouse, finish the church, finish . . . finish . . . finish . . . but gently. Excuse me, my Reverend Father, but the phrase has often come to my mind concerning you: "but now remain at rest!"[13]

Dom Louf always kept this letter with him, so full of good sense and so sharp, inviting him to keep his feet on the ground.

Louf was careful to focus his efforts on the spiritual accompaniment of his brothers and on spiritual teaching. He willingly delegated all that concerned the material and concrete management of the community whose upkeep tired him. During his abbatial tenure he depended very much on his cellarers, who succeeded one another and whom he chose with much discernment. "He had the artistry and genius," recalled one brother, "of naming good people for key positions. And he did this especially for the brother and for the community's sake to such a point that he was capable of placing in strategic posts people who did not seek them, or with whom he had stormy relationships, but those whom he judged competent and open to the service of the common good."[14]

Although he was of his own volition hardly inclined toward practical affairs, like his model, Saint Bernard, Louf was not

13. Un frère du Mont-des-Cats, Letter to Dom André Louf, ADMC, 16 July 1964.

14. Guillaume Jedrzejczak, conversation with the author.

for all that unconcerned. "Never complain," he wrote at a time when he became aware of it, "of 'being material.' God is there too, up to the neck. If God is even concerned about the lily in the field, why should I not be preoccupied with a kitchen garden, or a wheat field, or a cow? . . . but always along with him."[15] In a conference he gave for some nuns on the relation between prayer and work, he talked about "a new budget concept," about the importance of foreseeing a liquidation," and about using "a certain rigorous management," all ideas that show that he was not an ethereal being flying in the sky of ideas.[16] He was not unaware of reality, nor did he renounce the taking of responsibility; he did not fail to mark the material management of his monastery with his own style, especially when the latter revealed important spiritual objectives.

From that point of view certain decisions Louf made were authentic words of life. Such was the case with the remodeling of the church, which owes much to his good taste and sensitivity. Under his influence the neo-Gothic architecture was refined. A gentle configuration with new windows to diffuse the light peacefully creates a silent quality for a contemplative ambiance that surrounds this house of prayer today. He also considerably simplified the economy of the abbey. Before his time the economy was characterized by a multiplicity of little jobs that absorbed the brothers in every sense. Louf unified all activity around the production of cheese. The same concern for simplicity inspired him to undertake a kind of pruning of the inherited property of the monastery to the profit of an environment conducive to contemplation.[17] These few measures did not exhaust his accomplishments in the sphere of

15. Louf, JS, 15 March 1963.

16. André Louf, "Prière et travail II," *Le lien des contemplatives*, no. 80 (Jan. 1987): 16.

17. Jean-Marc Thévenet, conversation with the author.

temporal administration, but they show that his fatherhood extended to decisions leading the community in a direction that was very definitely spiritual.

Teaching by Example

Adding to the abbot's oral teaching and to the environment created by his decisions was the paternity he exercised by example, whose value was expressed first of all in a certain lifestyle characterized by simplicity and sobriety. Louf was not a worldly abbot in love with pomp and ceremony. His form of life was modest, without glitter, his clothing light, his regime ascetic—only a piece of fruit and a hot drink in the morning to feed his large body—1.91 meters.[18] However, he was careful never to boast of this practice of poverty. He showed great self-mastery when he was with others. "When we traveled with him," testifies a brother of the abbey, "he would always take us to a restaurant to please us. Since I am Italian, like my mother, it was often a *trattoria*. But when he was all alone, he traveled like the poor and contented himself with a sandwich gulped down in great haste and a Coke, a drink he was fond of."[19] Dom Jean-Marc Thévenet, who was abbot of Tamié and father immediate of Mont-des-Cats at the time, recalled their first meeting in 1980: "He insisted on having me visit his native city, Bruges, with a detour to Gand to see the triptych of the *Agneau Mystique* by Van Eyck. With him commentaries were thrilling. The chief attraction of our trip was our stop at the Duc de Bourgogne, one of the largest restaurants in Bruges, at the edge of the canal. I see him still at the moment of paying the bill for our excellent repast, when he noticed that he had forgotten his blue card and that he had no pocket money. We thought we would have to wash

18. Jean-Marc Thévenet, conversation with the author.

19. Daniel Curely, conversation with the author.

the dishes! His everyday manner of life was extremely sober, but when he wanted to entertain a friend, he could put himself out and create a festive atmosphere."[20]

To his brothers Louf primarily exemplified a person of rare contemplative insight. "His teaching," affirms one of the brothers of the abbey, "also arose from his prayer life. I have never known him to miss an Office. When he returned late from a trip, there he was in the morning present at Vigils. This faithfulness to prayer really impressed us."[21] "In all that he said," observed another brother of the abbey, "and in all that he wrote, there was a breath of life, a soul."[22] Especially during the Divine Office, which he celebrated in a very recollected way, he gave the impression of falling into prayer, as if some interior weight pushed him there. "Most of the monks," recounts a monk of the Abbey of Saint-Lioba, where Louf ended his life, "'make' their prayer and end up loving it. For André it was different: we sensed a deep attraction. During the Office I had the stall next to him. I sensed the intensity with which he lived the period of silence after the psalms had been sung, as if the liturgy of the word was prolonged in his heart. It was very palpable and most impressive."[23]

20. Jean-Marc Thévenet, conversation with the author.
21. Marc-André Di Péa, conversation with the author.
22. Daniel Curely, conversation with the author.
23. Frère Muban, monk of Saint-Lioba, conversation with the author.

CHAPTER 9

The Exegete of Aggiornamento

In 1963, when Louf became abbot of Mont-des-Cats, the bell of the Second Vatican Council was sounding loudly. The Church was carried forward by a powerful wind of return to the sources, an updating to meet the new expectations of the contemporary world. The teaching that the new abbot dispensed to his brothers in chapter every morning reflected that climate. He found support in a return to the sources that had enriched the ancient monastic teaching. These sources had been inaccessible before, so his catechesis became an exegesis for the time of confusion that was coming. He tried to propound a spiritual meaning for the *aggiornamento* that was confusing so many of the brethren in their habitual thoughts. He wanted to confront the problems that it raised and to integrate its practical consequences into their daily lives. He endeavored to let the fresh air of the council blow into the monks' observances and minds.

A Time of Crisis

Looking back over the passage of time, it seems that the evolution introduced by the Council happened by itself, that all was done in a kind of infantile clarity, as if the sense of history were transparent. But at the time there was confusion.

Aggiornamento opened up a time of deep crisis when communities were provoked and torn apart, and when those in charge of initiating change needed time for coordination. Louf's spiritual journal, which was for all that impassioned by the possibilities that were opened up for his generation, also bears witness to those difficulties: "Taking up this extremely particular cross of the pastors of our generation, which is that of standing fast at the heart of the restlessness of our time and of facing it with the peaceful certitude of the monastic grace,"[1] he wrote in 1965. It was difficult to see one's way clearly in the changes on the move, to discern the signs of the times, and to measure the relevant or precipitate character of such and such a reform:

> We do not see *aggiornamento*. We are in front of a wall; we are in darkness; we have the certainty, however, that it is the Lord who guides us and guides the Order. He knows what direction to follow. It will be clear for our successors and for the historians who follow. The whole witness of abbots consists in the obligation of announcing this direction without knowing it, by trusting only in the Lord. Thanks to this lack of light God traces the curve of his sacred history through the small successive options that we have to take in the total absence of human certitude, in the renunciation of any will of our own and fidelity to every divine glimmer of light, there where it seems to flicker.[2]

It is necessary to remember that it was in this climate of uncertainty and tentativeness that Louf spoke the word in chapter every morning to try to set free the sense of renewal while producing it. His only sense of direction was a kind of blind availability to the Holy Spirit. Besides, he was convinced

1. André Louf, *Journal Spirituel* (hereafter JS), 25 Dec. 1965.
2. Louf, JS, 10 July 1964.

that the best way for *aggiornamento* to succeed and to judge its evolution as well was this personal fidelity to prayer.

The effort of resourcefulness asked of monks by the Council may be summed up in a formula: "Less quantity to assure better quality." At another period the life of abbeys had been overloaded with Offices, litanies, and processions that gave monks' days a hellish rhythm, detrimental to recollection. To free prayer from such a straitjacket, the Council wished to alleviate these practices, imprinting on the monastic day a more peaceful rhythm. For Louf the reforms introduced in the wake of Vatican II were all ordered toward this search for contemplative interiority. If none of the great pillars of monastic life escaped these arrangements, neither, beyond doubt, did the liturgy; its *aggiornamento* has most profoundly affected Cistercian life since the Council.

The Liturgy, a Way of Prayer

In the space of ten years a widespread reform had renewed the liturgy of the monasteries: simplification of its structure, reduction in the number of Offices in choir, reorganization and curtailing of texts, composition of new music, abandonment of Latin, the ancient sacred language, in favor of the vernacular (French at Mont-des-Cats), and introduction of concelebration with the community gathered around the altar, and the Eucharist, which became the high point of the day.[3] At the close of this movement of deepening and of simplification, monastic liturgy rediscovered the role that it had had throughout history: allowing "the internalization of the words and rituals in the service of contemplative prayer."[4]

3. André Louf, "Vue d'ensemble sur la situation présente," in *L'Ordre cistercien de la stricte observance au XXe siècle,* Vol. 2: *Du concile Vatican II à la fin du siècle*, ed. Marie-Gérard Dubois (Rome: OCSO, 2008), 205.

4. André Louf, "Quelques leçons d'un centenaire," *Collectanea Cisterciensia* 60 (1998): 223.

Obviously none of this was done without a hitch or without a shock. Some monasteries were divided into two camps, with the partisans of reform on one side and the champions of the *status quo* on the other. The transition at Mont-des-Cats was much more peaceful, even if inevitable tensions did appear. The *opus Dei* is at the heart of monastic life; reform is impossible without some hurts or wounds. How can anyone not understand the reserve of those brothers who saw at one stroke rituals disappear to which they had fervently dedicated themselves for years, texts and melodies that had sustained their devotion and prayer? Nor should we forget the legitimate questions induced by the movement of renewal. Did not the passage to vernacular language risk depriving the Office of part of its beauty and of its dimension of prayer? And then the older brothers had been formed with a "Trappist" mentality in which they had to acquit themselves of a certain number of efforts to be "in order" with the Lord, so the alleviation of the Office brought up another fear: "of no longer doing all that was asked of them, and so no longer being prompt in their service of God."[5]

Louf was anxious to relieve the tension and to convey the meaning of the reforms in progress, so he often repeated to his brothers that the external rituals of liturgical actions were important, but secondary. From Lumbwa, an African abbey where he celebrated the feast of All Saints, he wrote to his community:

> I still notice to what degree our liturgical experience is linked to certain external rituals, a language, and a melody. Change brings in a certain bewilderment. The force of any religious experience bestows the ability to be so attached to its expressions that are impregnated with the life that comes from the Holy Spirit. But this

5. André Louf, *À la grâce de Dieu: Entretiens avec Stéphane Delberghe* (Namur: Fidélité, 2002), 29.

> is also its weakness, because external rituals run the risk of limiting and impoverishing the experience. And the life of the Spirit always remains beyond all forms of expression. It is necessary always to continue learning to discern this life behind the multiplicity and variety of its expression.[6]

Louf insisted on two extremes to be kept in tension: the external rituals, and the internal thrust of the spirit. "Prayer can never be pure externalization or a simple obligation that we have to fulfill, whatever it is worth. Nor should it ever be pure interiority, a prayer—freely rolling like a wheel—definitively unconnected to any sign that can be sensed. In the first case we would have a hardening of a ritualistic, pharisaic prayer; in the second we would have the illusion of false mysticism."[7]

Surrounded by the turmoil that unsettled so many habits and set on fire the abbeys of the Order, Louf reflected extensively on the meaning of liturgy and on its place in the life of a monk today. There again his thought moved around interiority, the indwelling of the Holy Spirit, and the rumination of the word of God, leading the monk "through the liturgical celebration to contemplative intimacy with the Lord."[8] While visiting Taizé with a group of Orthodox monks, he wrote to his community,

> The liturgical experiences that have been entrusted to us for some months now . . . have been much more exacting than a mere change of language or a simplification of ritual and of structure. It is a whole spiritual climate, and an ambience of mystery and of reality at

6. André Louf, Letter to the community, ADMC, 31 Oct. 1967.

7. André Louf, *L'Oeuvre de Dieu, un chemin de prière* (Paris: Lethielleux, 2005), 152–53.

8. André Louf, "Bernard de Clairvaux et les cisterciens," *Études* 373 (1990): 92.

> the same time, where God speaks to the heart, and one's being becomes a complete and absolute response, which we have to rediscover. The contemplative authenticity of this liturgical experience is the guarantee of this search. It is necessary for us to question ourselves often on this subject with all loyalty: Is our renewed liturgy for us all from now on really the place where the word of God resounds with all its power, where we meet God, and where he is sensed by our hearts? And finally, does this touching by God really free a whole wave of contemplative prayer inside us?[9]

A beautiful liturgy, then, is judged by its ability to put the monk into a state of prayer that is sensitive to the contemplative dimension of the Office. Louf loved that ancient practice of the Desert Fathers who stood still for a brief space after each psalm in silence to taste its meaning. The Council reintroduced this practice, letting the readings be followed by what it called *sacrum silentium*, a holy silence intended to let better profit be made from "the sensitive energy of the word."[10] It is then that the word reveals itself, thanks to a secret touch of the Holy Spirit, takes fire, shatters, and becomes material for prayer, often in the form of an invocation or what is called an ejaculation, thrown like a *jaculum*, a fiery arrow aimed at God. According to Louf the quality of these silent pauses was of the highest importance. He even went so far as to write that their reintroduction into liturgical celebration had constituted "the most important spiritual measure" of all those proclaimed by the Council, which built "a bridge between the liturgy of text and ritual, and the liturgy celebrated in our hearts."[11]

9. André Louf, Letter to the community, ADMC, 17 August 1968.

10. André Louf, "À l'école des psaumes," *Christus* 96 (1977): 419–31, repr. in André Louf, *À l'école de la contemplation* (Paris: Lethielleux, 2004), 183.

11. André Louf, *L'Oeuvre de Dieu*, 156.

So all of Louf's teaching had the purpose of emphasizing the link between liturgy and interior prayer. He often reminded his monks that the celebration was not over when it was concluded in church: "When the celebration is done, it is then that it begins."[12] Lived internally and deeply, in simplicity and sobriety, in restfulness and a certain silence, communal celebrations are an impulse "from points of departure, from springboards, from which we thrust ourselves forward towards interior prayer."[13] There is, then, a tendency in the liturgy "to spread all around, to prolong itself over the length of the day, to invade all the available places in time, in space, and especially in praying hearts. It always bears fruit beyond itself, fixed on life, tending to transform life completely into an unending liturgy."[14] Inspired by the *Livre des degrés*, a fourth-century text of Syrian monasticism, Louf repeated that this liturgical prayer, celebrated in stone-built oratories, is called to emerge as the prayer that all believers celebrate in their heart of hearts, in their spiritual oratory. "It is necessary," he said in a homily, "for us to get all the way through to that interior sanctuary, every time we cross the threshold of our church. No matter how splendid they are, they are still only a portal, a vestibule through which we can reach God's dwelling place in our most interior part."[15]

An Inspired and Inspiring Word

As a parallel to liturgy, *lectio divina* of Scripture also profited from *aggiornamento*. Led by the renewal of biblical studies, the Council wanted to restore the value of that slow, meditative reading, done in God's presence with confidence

12. André Louf, "Gouvernement et accompagnement dans les communautés contemplatives," *Vie Consacrée* 58 (1986): 352.

13. Louf, *À la grâce de Dieu*, 134.

14. André Louf, *L'Oeuvre de Dieu*, 157.

15. André Louf, Homily for the dedication of Latran, ADMC, 1997.

in God's powerful word, which reveals itself to those who approach it with faith. In a monk's or nun's day *lectio* occupies a more and more important place, a sanctuary in the arrangement of time. In his catechesis Louf unceasingly praised such reading, which he described as "the veritable lung of monastic experience."[16] The word of God is the key that opens the road to interiority. Scripture was not only inspired at the time of its redaction; it remains inspired forever. God's spirit continues to live in it and to touch the souls who hear it in the liturgy or in private. "Scripture vivifies," Louf explained,

> that is to say that it awakens the sleeping heart that has become deaf to hearing other sounds. There is a blinding flash that every word of God is able to release in a man's heart, and this is of the highest importance in a spiritual path. As long as this man has not had the experience of a simple word from the Bible, which has most often been already heard many times and heard again without any apparent result, but which all of a sudden explodes with rays of brightness and meaning, he will only with difficulty perceive interior space or the things of God taking place in him. It is only, then, at that moment, that he will "sense" his heart, and from that moment on he will be able, by a simple comparison of his different memories, to discern that which comes more directly from God.[17]

In another place Louf pursues these thoughts: "Undoubtedly it is the vocation of contemplatives in the heart of the church to remain so absorbed in the Word, to inhabit it with a burning heart, to have a presentiment of it in the name of all others, of all those who see without seeing, in order to

16. André Louf, *À la grâce de Dieu*, 140.

17. "Pour un coeur de chair. Interview with Dom André Louf," *Unité et charismes* no. 3 (2001): 29.

give God the joy of seeing his Word partly understood on earth, so that it can be born anew in human hearts."[18]

With the Council, *lectio* was also extended to include ancient spiritual writers. The patristic rediscovery in the preceding years constituted a precious help from that point of view by placing the texts of the first monastic fathers at the disposal of Christians. Louf added his mite to this return to sources. As a young monk he had already offered his knowledge of ancient languages to translate the first texts. After he became abbot, despite his heavy responsibility, he had the premonition that "a work of translation, slow of course but persevering, could be an element of equilibrium in a life that would see more and more movement."[19] In the mid-sixties he started translating the works of the Flemish mystic Jan van Ruusbroec, a task that he completed at the end of the nineties, beginning at that point the rendering into French of the unpublished works of Isaac of Nineveh, a Syriac mystic of the seventh century.

During the 1970s and 1980s Louf collaborated on the series Spiritualité Orientale, a collection founded by Placide Deseille to publish Oriental monastic texts, parallel to the Oriental monastic series of Sources Chrétiennes. For that series he translated the letters of Saint Antony[20] and those of Macarius the Egyptian.[21] He was also the workhorse of some great editorial companies. His contribution to the French edition of the *Philocalie des pères neptiques*, that celebrated collection of Byzantine texts, was as decisive as it is unknown. The roles of

18. André Louf, Homily for the fourth Sunday of Advent, ADMC, 1999.

19. André Louf, *À la grâce de Dieu*, 153.

20. André Louf, Introduction to Saint Antoine, *Lettres*, Spiritualité Orientale, no. 19 (Bégrolles-en-Mauges: Abbaye de Bellefontaine, 1976), 7–36.

21. André Louf, Présentation to *Lettres des Pères du désert: Ammonas, Macaire, Arsène, Sérapion de Thmuis*, Spiritualité Orientale, no. 4 (Bégrolles-en-Mauges: Abbaye de Bellefontaine, 1985).

Placide Deseille, Dom Coutant, Olivier Clément, Boris Bobrinskoy, and Jacques Touraille in creating the French edition of the *Philocalie* are often advanced,[22] but Louf's is much less well known, though central. The archives of Mont-des-Cats contains a dossier on the publication of these writings on Oriental mysticism, containing his correspondence with Clément, Regnault, Coutant, and Bobrinskoy. He emerges there as the director of the work, calling meetings, initiating the dynamism, and offering advice on such and such a contributor.

Louf was also the prime mover in the publication of Sources Chrétiennes' *Oeuvres Complètes* of Saint Bernard. In 1986 he had taken the initiative of writing to Dominique Bertrand, S.J., the director of Sources Chrétiennes, to have *Le Dernier des Pères* published: "along with a group of abbots and abbesses we would like to speed up the French translation of our Cistercian fathers of the twelfth century, especially Saint Bernard, whose centenary (1990) is near."[23] Then Louf met Bertrand and put the Cistercians in motion. The historian Laurence Mellerin has judged Louf's initiative decisive: "On February 7, 1986, Dom Louf sent to 'Sources Chrétiennes' the letter that would decide the entrance of Saint Bernard in the collection."[24]

The Spirit of the Observances

In dealing with ascetical observances the Council oriented the efforts of monks in two directions: 1. To soften their ex-

22. Monique Simon, "*L'Oecumenisme dans l'ordre au XX*[e] *siècle*," in Dubois, ed., *L'Ordre cistercien de la stricte observance*, 2:372–73.

23. André Louf, Letter to Dominique Bertrand, ADMC, 7 Feb. 1986.

24. Laurence Mellerin, "L'édition des oeuvres de Bernard de Clairvaux dans la collection, 'Sources Chrétiennes,'" in *Actes du colloque "Journée culture cistercienne," Conférences du Collège des Bernardines* (Paris: Cerf, 2009), 129–48.

cessive rigor, and 2. "to rediscover their profound significance for today's anthropology."[25] It was in this second direction that Louf focused his teaching. He considered it essential to maintain ascetic practices, especially those that had always been a part of the great tradition (such as vigils, fasting, abstinence, solitude, and simplicity of life) but thought it was urgent to rediscover their spirit. In the past monks had placed great importance on the more or less strict manner in which those observances were put into practice. The value of an ascesis was measured by the weight of inconvenience, the amount of sweat and tears to which it gave rise. In reversing this point of view Louf had to confront the resistance of brothers who had been nursed by this athletic culture of effort. It was necessary to argue that observances were not first of all a collection of gestures to be practiced externally; they were supposed to be practiced internally from the grace that moved them.[26] Instead of external movement and quantity, therefore, emphasis was to be placed on interiority and quality.[27]

With a large pedagogical commitment, Dom Louf set about disengaging the spiritual sense belonging to each observance, the interior fruit that it contained. Fasting, he explained to his brothers, not only affects the external sense organs, but it also reaches "certain deep levels of the soul that have not yet been surrounded by grace."[28] Having deferred a meal awakens in one a much deeper hunger. The refusal to satisfy a sensible need at once also reveals a certain confusion in their desires "that is not without a link with their confused desire for God."[29] Another ingredient of ascesis, solitude,

25. Louf, "Vue d'ensemble," 206.

26. Louf, "Autrement la grâce n'est plus la grâce," 51.

27. Louf, "Bernard de Clairvaux et les cisterciens," 93.

28. André Louf, "Faire pénitence?" *Sources Vives* no. 108 (March 2003): 83.

29. Louf, "Faire pénitence?" 83.

also responds to a precise spiritual need: before becoming the place of *hesychia*, of rest, solitude is at first an arena of combat in which the solitary is never a winner, but a loser, "reduced to his simplest state: radical poverty that the desert has at last taught him to learn."[30] The spiritual meaning of vigils is still easier to discern. Are they not a self-conscious presence to the world and to God at a time when the universe is plunged into the unconscious state of sleep, and a way of composing oneself for the sacrament of waiting for the dawn, which is itself a prefiguring of Christ's return, when he comes to inundate us with the light of the Parousia?"[31]

Monastic tradition distinguishes interior ascesis—watchfulness of the heart by control over the thoughts, abandonment of useless concerns, suppression of vain distractions—from bodily labor, which includes all the practices that exert a certain pressure on the body, such as fasting, vigils, tiring manual labor, and living in a confined space. For Louf these latter penances were important precisely because they affected the body, which has for too long been disdained by Christian spirituality. Ascesis is the way not to enslave the body, but to treat it fairly, to reveal its true greatness. "*Glorify God in your body*" (1 Cor 6:20), he told his brothers, "is perhaps the loveliest expression of Christian ascesis. Every ascetical effort means to place the body in a state of availability for the work of the Spirit to be accomplished in us. It means to belong to the Holy Spirit, who redeems us entirely stage by stage, depth following depth; it is a continuous investment in humankind by the power of the Spirit."[32]

30. Louf, "Autrement la grâce n'est plus la grâce," 58.

31. Louf, "Faire pénitence?" 85.

32. André Louf, "L'Ésprit en nous," Unedited chapter talk at Mont-des-Cats, ADMC, Feb. 1971.

Human Effort and Grace

Louf's desire to evangelize monastic observances sometimes led him to introduce a theme that would become one of the pivots of his catechesis: the relationship between human action and God's grace. Louf loved to tell a story about a monk whose heroism was touching, a brother who was so irreproachable that he was called a "walking rule." His regularity was like a metronome; it led him to be given the job of bellringer. "But it was enough," Louf continued, "to see his attitudes and his approach close up, how inflexible and compact they were, to guess that his 'exemplary behavior' had to be the fruit of an unresting interior constraint, hardly that of an interior freedom." One fine day under this unceasing pressure his nervous resistance gave way, and he let himself be overtaken by a love affair. This disaster compromised the lovely image of himself that he had entertained by so many efforts, and it caused him to come to grief in a serious fit of depression.

Louf remembered having met this brother at that time. He was aroused by black anger, and he wished evil upon the whole world, but especially upon God himself, not knowing why he had permitted this fall after thirty years of such generous loyalty. "Suddenly," Louf continued, "he straightened up and angrily stared at me, shouting, 'Fr. Abbot, I cannot accept those words of the Gospel. Jesus was much too strict with the Pharisees, when even people of good will were doing their best!' That phrase betrayed him. It is exactly what he tried to do himself: have a good will and do his best. But without realizing it he had chosen the Pharisees' party, that is, those who Jesus regretted 'had no need of mercy.' "[33] This brother's story, he said, was emblematic of a heroic display of religious life that still haunts the minds of many Christians: there are

33. Louf, "Autrement la grâce n'est plus la grâce," 68.

always more effort, more sweat, more courage, and more tears. To be satisfied with one's own generous offering of virtue: this mentality has so deeply penetrated Western Christianity that a person is declared a saint for his or her heroic virtue, an expression that shocked Louf: "our virtues embarrass God if they are not the pure result of grace."[34]

Louf owed much to Martin Luther, whose criticism permitted him to rid himself of the traces of paganism that blemish Christian asceticism. Following Luther, Louf put his brothers on guard against the temptation to give precedence to a spirituality that emphasizes human effort and to believe that God is won by the force of the arm, by heroic acts, or by an irreproachable life. Instead, he taught, evangelical ascesis promotes "a spirituality of imperfection."[35] It reaches its objective when it causes the monk to feel his powerlessness and when, engulfed by failure in this way, the monk is obliged to give himself back to God. "Certainly, far from being the occasion for prowess or generosity," said Louf, "Christian ascesis is meant to become the place of our defeat, where only God's grace triumphs. Its purpose is to make evident our radical weakness, in order that the power of grace can finally be deployed."[36]

A fourth-century letter signed by Macarius the Egyptian, a monk of the desert of Scetis, helped Louf find the correct position to take among the controversies issuing from the Pelagian heresy on the relation between human effort and the gift of God's grace. In this text, which Louf found, translated, and introduced, Macarius adopts an original intermediate position: there is no question of choosing between divine or human action, he says. Both of them take the initiative.

34. André Louf, "Donnons à Dieu l'occasion de se manifester," *La Croix* 25–26 Dec. 1999.

35. Jacques Dupont, *Seul devant l'unique: Entretiens avec un chartreux* (Paris: Parole et Silence, 2016), 152.

36. Louf, *À la grâce de Dieu*, 78.

"What belongs to mankind," explains Louf in his introduction to Macarius's writings, "is not fruitless either. Nevertheless it cannot succeed by itself. It is even condemned to fail."[37] According to Macarius, then, ascetical effort should lead the monk to failure and to exhaustion, and through them to a double perception:

> First there is his own irremediable weakness, then the all-powerful mercy of God, who at every turn saves him from danger and from the touch of defeat. Such an ascesis takes the form of an unequal battle at every point, and it leads the monk even to the edge of despair before God's intervention assures him of a victory that he no longer expected. Upon emerging from such an ordeal the believer finally knows from experience that "it is God himself who makes him strong." Such an ascesis is an ascesis of abasement, that is, of humility, poles away from any prowess of spiritual athleticism, sometimes attributed to ancient monasticism. This asceticism breathes the pure air of the gospel. It is an asceticism of poverty, that is, literally, a little path.[38]

The Flexibility of the Spirit

In the wake of the Council a flowering of original monastic foundations took place. Deseille started a small community at Aubazine in Corrèze in the first Egyptian monks' simple style of deprivation.[39] His initiative was preceded or followed by an outgrowth of new creations. Mère Marie founded the Sisters and Brothers of Bethlehem, Père Delfieux the monks in the heart of the city with the Monastic Fraternity of

37. Louf, Introduction to *Lettres des Pères du Désert*, 69.

38. Louf, Introduction to *Lettres des Pères du Désert*.

39. Placide Deseille, "Une vie monastique en quête de la vraie lumière: Entretiens," *Lumière et Vie* no. 298 (April-June 2013): 12.

Jerusalem, Père Ermin the Little Brothers of the Virgin of the Poor, a community inspired by the monastic phase of Charles de Foucauld, and Père Enzo Bianchi the Ecumenical Community of Bose. Additionally, a band of Cistercian brothers came from the abbey of Achel and established themselves on the Isle of Bornholm in Denmark, to experiment there with a foundation whose structures were less rigid than was common in Trappist communities and to emphasize poverty. Louf sympathized very much with these efforts at a simplified monastic life. Beyond the emphasis they put on solitude, poverty, and simplicity of life, the evangelical climate of freedom attracted him. "Learn to stop putting your confidence in laws and structures, but trust only in the interior experience of the Spirit," he wrote in his journal.[40]

Despite his nostalgia for rules, Louf thought that rules could become a straitjacket and could stifle spontaneity of the spirit. He said to his monks,

> Monastic life cannot be reduced to a program or a *horarium*, still less to an ideal or a regulation. It is a call in our heart, an irresistible attraction that launches us on the road to a meeting with God who has touched us. Structures often have a tendency to absorb what is essential. Purification is unceasingly necessary. It is necessary to admit that *aggiornamento* has often purified us from constraint. So much the better above all for monastic life, for which it is a gain to be reduced to the simplest expression. Is it not itself precisely the simplest expression of things, of God, and of all that binds us to him?[41]

We often forget, Louf recalled, that the Benedictine Rule is above all the written record of an experience, that of Saint

40. Louf, JS, 5 May 1967.
41. André Louf, Letter to the community, ADMC, 20 Nov. 1968.

Benedict. "The letter of the Rule," he said, contains a life that is always capable of being awakened through the heart of a disciple who listens attentively." He put his hearers on guard against the danger of formality.[42] As the apostle of the weightlessness of the institution, leaving to each one the flexibility to find his own rhythm and respond to the unforeseeable initiatives of the spirit, Louf considered that the rules were there for beginners, to help them grow and to become free, that is, to be capable of regulating themselves internally under the prompting of the Spirit.[43] According to him, it is through the succor of this pedagogy of interior freedom that monasteries would attract or not attract future vocations. This development would entail their capacity to form spiritual people who were themselves able to perceive the touches of the Spirit, who directed their unceasing prayer beyond regulations, beyond rubrics, and beyond fixed hours.[44]

42. André Louf, Preface to *La Règle de Saint-Benoît*, Édition du 15e centenaire (Paris: Desclée de Brouwer, 1980), vii–viii.

43. Louf, "Gouvernement et accompagnement," 362.

44. André Louf, "Essayer d'ouvrir ce monde à Dieu," *La Libre Belgique* 2 Feb. 1994.

CHAPTER 10

The Book of Experience

August 1968. Dom Louf improvised visits to French contemplative monasteries for a group of Orthodox monks passing through the country. They were spending a few days at the Carthusian house of Sélignac at Ain, where Louf had close relations with some brothers. He profited from stopping here to write to his community about his enthusiasm for the Carthusians and their existence entirely devoted to prayer: "I had the deep happiness to know that God grants to certain ones in his church the grace of living so entirely and so virginally for the search and for the love of him. It should not be necessary for us to have any envy of them. Cîteaux is just like the Carthusians in being deeply marked by this love of solitude and silence, even if unavoidable needs—and profitable ones—of the fraternal cenobitic life lead us to have more openness and welcome for brothers."

After leaving Sélignac the small ecumenical team stopped at the sanctuary of Ars, where Louf prayed at length before the sanctuary of Père Jean Vianney:

> I remembered that the first abbot of Mont-des-Cats once undertook a pilgrimage to Ars while the saintly Curé was still alive, to ask his counsel on his own vocation: Would it not be better for him to renounce his charge

> and become a Carthusian? I do not think I would have asked the same question, but I asked him with all my heart that the Trappist monastery of Mont-des-Cats might be slightly of the sort of those Trappist and those Carthusian houses that he thought of for himself when the weight of his ministry grew too heavy for him.[1]

A certain feeling was abroad at that time greatly emphasizing community life and brotherly relations, and it was prevailing in the Order of Cistercians of the Strict Observance. Louf's position was quite different. If as abbot he did not disdain the cenobitic dimension, he placed the emphasis above all on the personal experience of each monk who did not bury himself in the desert to find brothers there, but to search for a quiet contemplative life, that precious pearl for which he had left all things. To get his monks started on the interior adventure, to give them a taste for solitude and silence, and to act in such a way that they would become, as Saint Bernard wished, *amicae quies*, of the quiet life in God—that was the other side of the teaching Louf gave his community.[2]

When a friend asked Louf how he composed his Sunday homilies, he gave this beautiful reply: "I expose myself to the Word, and I share with my brothers where I am from a spiritual point of view."[3] A man of prayer who shared his own life of prayer with his brothers: that was the whole secret of his ministry. What Louf gave to others in his sermons, his chapter talks, his conferences, and even his books, the literary fallout of his teaching, he had first experienced himself. He

1. André Louf, Letter to the community, ADMC, 17 August 1968.

2. André Louf, "Le Cîteaux de saint-Bernard," *Collectanea Cisterciensia* 61, no. 1 (1999): 50.

3. Benoît Standaert, "In Memoriam André Louf, OCSO (1929–2010)," unedited essay, 2010.

spoke only from what Saint Bernard called "the book of experience."[4] Louf later explained the relationship between his life as an abbot and the books he published: "To envisage the writing of a book would require large blocks of free time that I no longer had at my command in my abbatial tenure, so it became impossible. The few books that have been published under my name are a refitted collection of conferences given beforehand."[5] It is not surprising then to find in his teaching themes that emerged in the course of his pilgrimage and about the great turning points of his life: his discovery of the interior man, the stages of the spiritual life, heartbreak, the finding of mercy, the road of humility and of humble love—.

"I is Another"[6]

There are two 'me's in us: the little egoistic self within whose limitations we choke, we gasp for air, we feel confined; the other one our real self, as deep as an abyss, as wide as a prairie. That is where we breathe the perfume of Christ infused into us at the time of our baptism. The whole aim of the spiritual life, Louf explained, consists in passing from our surface personality to that deep being that Saint Peter (1 Pet 3:4) calls "the hidden person of the heart," and Saint Paul (2 Cor 4:16) calls "the interior man," the one who is our truest reality, the most internal, and the most hidden.[7]

4. André Louf, "Bernard de Clairvaux et les cisterciens," *Études* 373 (1990): 94.

5. André Louf, *À la grâce de Dieu: Entretiens avec Stéphane Delberghe* (Namur: Fidélité, 2002), 153.

6. *Je est un autre.*

7. André Louf, "L'accompagnment spirituel aujourd'hui (1)," *Vie consacrée* no. 6 (1980): 333.

"I is another": it is impossible to say whether Louf knew this expression of Rimbaud, but he took up the idea that our interior space is inhabited by another person.[8] The human being, he said, is the "temple of the Spirit" (1 Cor 3:16), "Christ dwells in him" (Eph 3:17), "the Father and the Son come to make their home in him" (1 John 14:23). The whole Bible attests the existence of this interior space inhabited by God, to which Saint Augustine devoted the most beautiful pages of his *Confessions*: "Too late have I loved you, O beauty, so ancient and so new! Too late have I loved you. Behold, you were inside, and I was outside, and it was there that I searched for you, and by the grace of the things that you made, poor disgraced me, I was thrown away! You were with me, and I was not with you. They held me far from you, those things that, if they had not existed in you, would not have existed at all!"[9]

"In our heart we possess heaven," Louf often repeated to his brothers, to move them to plunge into their real spiritual selves and discover what the Greek fathers called the "place of God," the Latin tradition the "hidden temple," the summit of the soul, or even the peak of the Spirit—so many words to express that space inside that escapes our clear awareness, where the Trinity has put his dwelling, and where our being rests in God.[10]

It is there in that sanctuary that the divine host unceasingly celebrates his eternal life, that prayer is always given to us, given in advance and given first, without effort on our part.

8. Enrico Parolari, "Nel ricordo di André Louf," *Tredimensioni* 9 (2012): 63.

9. Augustine, *Les Confessions* (Paris: Folio-Gallimard, 1993), 371.

10. André Louf, "L'Homme intérieur ou la liturgie du coeur," *Collectanea Cisterciensia* 72 (2010): 334–53; and *Au gré de la grâce: Propos sur la prière* (Paris: Desclée de Brouwer, 1989), 180.

"However extraordinary it may be, this gift is not exceptional," Louf declares:

> But it is the common lot of every baptized person. On the reception of the gift of God within him, and upon becoming in this way a son of God by adoption, the one who has been baptized receives at the same time the gift of the Holy Spirit. Now this Spirit is a Spirit always at prayer, who cries out untiringly in our hearts: "Abba, Father!" That is a real treasure, unheard of really, that every Christian carries in his deepest being, unknown to himself most of the time. Even if he pays no attention to it, the Christian is always partly at prayer. Or rather the Holy Spirit celebrates prayer inside him.[11]

There are certain moments of grace as rare as they are memorable, Louf writes, when we experience ourselves abruptly inhabited by a kind of warmth or sweetness never felt before, or even as though moved by an invincible urging or a mysterious attraction to interior prayer. All methods and techniques of prayer, then, have no object in view other than this: to put believers in contact with that divine prayer already at work in them without their knowing it, to bring it about that it flows into their awareness and into their sensitivity and their faculties of love and knowledge. How is this done? Obviously it is better to avoid crowded places and saturation of words and distractions. Anything that favors recollection, an undisturbed and quiet place or a sober lifestyle, is profitable. However, he continues, that is not enough:

> Such preparations are still very external. Christian prayer shares them in common along with many other techniques of recollection, and they usually belong to some tradition. But what is proper to Christian prayer

11. Louf, "L'Homme intérieur," 336.

> is the nature of the link that such preparations have with techniques. Well, if such is the case, preparation has no direct hold on the event of prayer, and the latter could not by any means be the natural consequence of the former. God remains the only Master of prayer, and he could just as well do without our preparations and quietly stride over all our obstacles. It is he who will cause our prayer to spring up "when he wills, as he wills, wherever he wills," as Ruusbroec says.[12]

Louf speaks of the event of prayer sometimes as if it were a "see-saw,"[13] or a "moving car"[14] toward interiority; at other times he speaks of it as if one came to be aware of it as of "the formation of an exact fit, slow and patient, barely perceptible, a kind of impregnation beginning internally."[15] Other times he calls it a unsealing of a spring that lets fresh living water flow in us.[16] This event accordingly remains always unforeseeable and uncontrollable. God is absolute Master of his gifts and favors, so the prayer of all believers is necessarily "a poor man's prayer exposed to visits by grace that are always awaited and always unexpected."[17]

A Pilgrimage to the Heart

Learning to recollect oneself in the presence of this murmur of the Spirit is not the work of a single day, nor can it be done without pain, Louf says. At our baptism we all received the life of God and all that it includes: the presence of the three

12. Louf, "L'Homme intérieur," 337–38.
13. Louf, *À la grâce de Dieu*, 128.
14. Louf, *À la grâce de Dieu*, 128.
15. Louf, *À la grâce de Dieu*, 133.
16. André Louf, Unedited conference on prayer, Dunkirk, ADMC, 1980.
17. André Louf, "Les cisterciens et la prière, unedited conference at Grodno (Biélorussie)," ADMC, 2005.

persons of the Trinity, unceasing motions of the Spirit, and progressive transformation into Christ. But this life has been given us as a seed, destined to grow and to occupy still more room in our psychology. To say it differently, just like any other life, God's life is called to increase and evolve, but it can also stagnate, regress, and even waste away and die. Saint Paul puts us on our guard: *Do not quench the Spirit* (1 Thess 5:19). What Louf calls "taking possession of our humanity by the divine life"[18] takes place over a long stretch. The spiritualization of the human being begins as a small seed; then it continues to develop with the grace of God, like a tiny drop of water trying to trickle down through the ground broken by our wounds.

Louf compares the besieging of the human being by the Spirit to a road on which every believer starts walking, moves ahead and makes progress, stops or draws back, and grows on the way on the narrow corners that must be negotiated and the decisive crossings that must not be missed.[19] In the course of this pilgrimage marked by trials, many assurances and external consolations will be taken away. In fact the believer will live this journey toward God with an alternation of joys and difficulties, a kind of going and coming—the goings and comings of the Bridegroom, as Saint Bernard would say. Louf describes it as a "balancing act between the oppression of the heart and its expansion that creates a fruitful rhythm, a paschal movement that inserts it more and more into the passion and resurrection of the Lord."[20] From the first stammering of faith this road ends at the summit of

18. André Louf, "Être formé à l'accompagnement spirituel," *Séminarium* 39 (1999): 553–68.

19. André Louf, "'À la recherche du bonheur' dans la règle de saint-Benoît," *Vie consacrée* 80, no. 2 (2008): 118.

20. André Louf, Homily for two brothers' taking of the habit, ADMC, date unknown.

interior life, a "stupor," "ecstasy," or "ravishment," something that "resembles a departure to the beyond, a surrender of the soul that is overwhelmed by the action of the Spirit and yields to it one's own action and conduct."[21] This inner experience is not reserved to certain hand-picked mystics. No, it is the concern of all believers, into whose hearts baptism has infused the seed. As Louf says, "It is this experience for which the Christian is later irremediably destined. Through temptations, through weakness, falls, and recoveries, through marvels of grace especially, one sometimes perceives the first glimmers of this experience."[22]

The Breaking of the Heart

If the discovery of the interior space where the Holy Spirit celebrates his liturgy of love depends on the gratuitous intervention of God, certain practices may favor that discovery, Louf writes. Two such practices are assiduous and frequent presence at the Word, and spiritual accompaniment. But for the approach to this sanctuary one transition is particularly important. Louf presents this stage as the "decisive turning point on the spiritual road, the fundamental Christian experience, the preliminary step, and the entry gate for all authentic mysticism."[23] A moment arrives on the spiritual road, he explains, when the believer is faced with a barrier at the entry to a new road; the road is steep and precipitous, and the crossing is so rough that a person will hesitate for a long time, perhaps an entire lifetime, before committing oneself.

21. André Louf, "Quelques constantes du parcours spirituel d'un chrétien," Conférence au Centre Paul VI, Milan, ADMC, 25 Sept. 2002.

22. André Louf, *Initiation à la vie spirituelle* (Paris: Seuil, 2008), 85.

23. André Louf, "Le coeur brisé," *Buisson ardent*, March 1997, 52.

Nevertheless, he warns, there is no escape; there is no avoiding the declivity, no getting away from this abasement.[24]

Upon entering this rugged road, which is a passage in the strongest sense of the word—this Easter—Christians have no suspicion of the point at which they will fall to the ground, touch bottom, experience that humiliation from which they will someday be reborn in humility. Up until the moment of that trial, humility will be no more than a vague moral virtue, the synonym of a low opinion of oneself. But true humility, that of which Louf speaks, following tradition, is no virtue. It is a state that corresponds to a concrete abasement, a sinking that is almost physical, in which one finds oneself as low as the soil. *Humus*, after all, is derived from the Latin *humilitas*.[25]

This barrier before which one is tempted to turn back takes many forms: a malady that declares itself, the death of a relative, shocks or temptations of all kinds, a chronic psychological failure, a complex that humiliates us, a limitation, a character trait against which one keeps butting, a persistent weakness. Despite the diversity of its expression, at its core the trial consists in the experience of one's own powerlessness: no matter what one does to extricate oneself from the obstacle, there is no escape, and all one's efforts fail. Humanly speaking there is no way out. It is an impasse, a cul-de-sac. "One finds himself confronted by his own weakness on the deepest level, by his limitations, his insignificance, his creatureliness," Louf writes.[26] To describe this crisis, which can provoke distress near despair,

24. André Louf, "Chercher Dieu au temps de la déréliction," *Vie Consacrée* 77, no. 4 (2005): 223–24.

25. André Louf, "L'humilité dans la vie monastique," *Le lieu des moniales*, no. 142 (July 2000): 8; Notes from an unedited conference on obedience, ADMC, 1997.

26. Louf, "Le Coeur Brisé," 53.

ancient monastic literature speaks of a broken heart, crushed, literally "reduced to crumbs."[27]

Even if such brokenheartedness is the lot of all believers, monks are preeminent in choosing ascesis. In fact, the time comes when contemplatives can no longer be proud of their own efforts to maintain their monastic purpose. Their natural energy gets exhausted, and their powers are disarmed. Celibacy, solitude, fasting, vigils all become impossible. "God," writes Louf, "comes to break the mirror that the monk paraded down the cloister."[28] The ideal image the brother had of himself flies to pieces, not without provoking violent internal shocks. What's more, the crisis does not delay in reaching the very desire that is at the heart of his vocation: to see and know God.

In a text written at the request of Paul VI, who wanted contemplatives to make known their impressions for the postconciliar church, Louf spoke of monks as "experts in atheism."[29] Before being a source of rejoicing, prayer is often put to the test during a crisis that plunges the brother into a dark night, a dereliction. God seems to disappear, to hide himself, unless he is quite simply nonexistent, like a lure or an infinite projection of our own desires. This desert is "a cold antechamber,"[30] "an obligatory vestibule for any contemplation,"[31] Louf writes, continuing, "Every contemplative finds himself confronted

27. Louf, "L'Humilité dans la vie monastique," 12.

28. André Louf, "Gouvernement et accompagnement dans les communautés contemplatives," *Vie Consacrée* 58 (1986): 345.

29. André Louf and Jean-Baptiste Porion, "Message des moines contemplatifs au Synode des Évêques de 1967," *La Documentation Catholique*, 5 Nov. 1967, no. 1504, 1907–1911.

30. Louf, "Gouvernement et accompagnement," 346.

31. André Louf, "Saint Benoît, homme de Dieu pour tous les temps," in *Fraternités monastiques de Jérusalem: Saint Benoît aujourd'hui*, Collection Épiphanie (Paris: Cerf, 1980), 22.

someday with unbelief, atheism, and irreligion."[32] It is as though God lightly detached the spiritual person from all the idols vaguely imbued with Christian ideas, idols in which he or she still placed trust.

Louf goes on to say that "The true God, the God of Jesus Christ, is quite different, he discovers after this crossing of the desert. There is no longer any question of reaching him by our own efforts, but of waiting untiringly and of letting ourselves be taken by him at the time set by his good pleasure, as unforeseeable as was Easter morning."[33] It is on this low ground of humility that one reaches the knowledge that "all is grace, entirely gratuitous."[34]

Whether it touches monks in their prayer or other believers in their life, then, heartbreak happens when one is tormented and exhausted by trials, humiliated and discouraged by one's weakness. Hopeless for himself, having become poor and reduced to his simplest manner, the believer has no outlet other than to turn to the Lord, to call for God's help, and to trust in God's strength. Louf continues, "He ends up lowering the arms with which, unknown to himself, he fought off grace, and surrenders by delivering himself, such as he is, to the sweet mercy of the Savior. His resistance is finally broken, his pride crushed. His true self can come out to daylight under God's benevolent gaze."[35]

When this crisis shows itself, believers invent a thousand stratagems: they go off on tangents, distract themselves, hide it from themselves. Anything goes to avoid facing the unbearable.[36] Nevertheless, Louf insists, the spiritual art does not

32. Louf, "Gouvernement et accompagnement," 346–47.

33. Louf, *À la grâce de Dieu*, 99.

34. André Louf, "Veilleur, où en est la nuit?" *Christus* no. 200 (Oct. 2003): 426.

35. André Louf, "L'acédie des cénobites et des ermites," *Études* 399, no. 6 (2003): 169.

36. Louf, "L'acédie des moines," 662.

consist in running away from trials or in stiffening oneself against them, but in taking them up, "in settling down in them peacefully without ever losing hope."[37] One must have the patience of the poor who put their trust in grace. "The danger to beware," he says, "is panic and what panic threatens to lead us to: disordered activity. Our clumsiness consists in wanting to act by ourselves, in reassuring ourselves of a successful issue. As long as we act thus, we deprive ourselves of the only issue possible, that of God's action. He it is who acts. Any effort that hardens our resolve prevents God's action. We need to stop, to desist, to give ourselves entirely to him."[38]

When believers consent in this way to abandon themselves, to accept their own weakness, and to accept the bitterness that ensues, this miracle happens without delay. They then discover that at the heart of their distress God will deploy his power. "It is by being a prey to temptation," Louf explains, "that a person perceives the action of grace in himself, through the groans that the very brutality of the attack wrenches from him, and these nourish his prayer, which then becomes constant."[39] For the believer heartbreak is of course good news. Divine pedagogy lets believers be engulfed by temptation to lead them back to prayer and to confidence. Louf explains, "The purpose of this being put to the test is to transform a love that at first was interested in 'chaste' and 'gratuitous' love. If the being that was loved seems at times to draw back, it is only to drive the loving soul to turn toward him and to feel itself succored by him."[40]

37. Louf, "Le coeur brisé," 54.

38. André Louf, Homily for the thirty-third Sunday of Ordinary Time, ADMC, 1974.

39. Louf, "L'homme intérieur," 339.

40. André Louf, "Saint Bernard et Sainte Thérèse de Lisieux," *Carmel* 3 (1997): 17.

Happy Fault

"He who sees his sins is greater than the one who sees God," said Isaac the Syrian in a phrase often quoted by Louf, who was persuaded of its truth. Sin is a *felix culpa*, a happy fault, a chance for salvation. Through it and the repentance it allows, the merciful God reveals himself and becomes perceptible to the heart.

Few spiritual writers have insisted on this point of the place of repentance. But Louf goes so far as to suggest that there is no other way truly to meet the Lord here below. "No one," he teaches, "could really admit his sin without having at the same time met God. As long as this revelation has not taken place, sin is still for the person nothing more than the breaking of a rule, not yet the moment of this privileged and unique meeting" that provokes conversion, the turning around of the heart of a person who has noticed that "his spark of anger, one moment feared, was silenced by a furnace of infinite love."[41]

As long as this phenomenon has not taken place, one's efforts to make progress on the spiritual road are met by the same ambiguity: the fervent believer is threatened by scruples; his fidelity may end up in Pharisaism. This pharisaic mentality considers sin to be a breach of a rule, so it is enough to respect rules to be law-abiding in God's eyes. Such edifying legalism is a disaster for interior life. For those who do not succeed in respecting the norms, this legalism generates from the first moment a sense of guilt that gnaws at hearts and provokes remorse, feelings of shame and nothingness. These torments imprison believers in anguish and in an abasement that often, Louf says, is "nothing more than wounded pride"[42] or a

41. André Louf, "Autrement la grâce n'est plus la grâce," in André Louf, Denis Huerre, and Marie-David Giraud, *Dieu intime: Parole de moines* (Paris: Bayard, 2003), 71.

42. André Louf, Homily for the 4th Sunday of Lent, ADMC, 1995.

"subtle search for preeminence"[43] that has nothing to do with repentance. Repentance is never oppressive; it is living, peaceful, free, and joyful under the influence of the Holy Spirit. But this legalism is also a catastrophe for those who follow directions literally. It starts them on a course toward perfection that mirrors the virtues they suppose themselves to have when they contemplate it. This category of believers maintains the sufficiency of legalism; they reek of self-satisfaction, satisfied with a surface-deep holiness; the Gospel says of them that they have no need of mercy, because they believe themselves irreproachable.

However, pursues Louf, virtue embarrasses God, who seems to be at ease with sinners. Real sinners, Louf goes on, are those who do not hide their faults or try to excuse them but who are at length reconciled with them, accept them, and expose them to mercy. God cannot resist such an attitude, says Louf. He even seems to be on the lookout for the moment of their fall, not to punish them, but to avoid their collapsing under the weight of discouragement and to embrace them with his love and his pardon. "And at that very moment," he insists, "at the very heart of this pardon, the sinner understands something of God's living reality within him for the first time."[44]

In Louf's eyes, taking up an idea dear to Saint Bernard, sin becomes part of mystical experience[45] and of divine pedagogy. God makes use of sin to proclaim his love and to reveal the superabundance of his mercy. "We might even say," he

43. André Louf, "Le repentir, clé de la vie en Christ," *Buisson ardent* Sept. 2003, 35.

44. Louf, "L'homme intérieur," 35.

45. André Louf, "Bernard, Abbé," in *Bernard de Clairvaux: Histoire, mentalités, spiritualité*, Sources Chrétiennes 380 (Paris: Cerf, 1992), 371; and André Louf, "La faiblesse, un chemin pascal selon Saint Bernard," *Collectanea Cisterciensia* 65 (2003): 15–20.

says, boldly, "that he has a need for the sin that has a share in the economy of salvation, since it detaches us from our self-love, from our false sense of guilt, and from our pretending to build our own spiritual edifice with our own strength."[46] We think we can reach the Lord by the deployment of our own efforts, the display of our virtue, but it is our misery that activates his mercy. Sin is "the combustible fuel of love": from the very moment that it is revealed to us, it has already been pardoned.[47]

It is then useless to panic or be ashamed of our sins. For Louf there is nothing worse than choosing to be a sinner who is so ashamed that he not only hides his wounds from others but even conceals them from himself, and consequently from God. Christ did not come for the healthy, but for the sick (Matt 9:12), he writes. It is the wounded for whom he looks, and whom he wants to meet with his bloody wound, right where it is most painful but where it will also do the most good, "there where Jesus, simply by a touch, a look, or a word, receives us just as we are and prostrates us with his tenderness. That is the mercy he wants for us, and it is so much more important in his eyes than our sacrifices or good works."[48]

Finally, and characteristically, Louf's teaching makes the soft refrain of the Gospel resound: whatever it may be, sin is pardoned, and this pardon is available for all sinners, provided they accept abasement before the lowly narrow door of repentance. Like Saint Benedict, who pictures perfection as a ladder to humility, scaled by descending, whose summit is an abyss of repentance, Louf asks that his brothers be neither

46. André Louf, "La métanoïa, lieu de l'Esprit," unedited chapter talk at Mont-des-Cats, ADMC, Feb. 1971.

47. André Louf, Homily for the fifth Sunday of Ordinary Time, ADMC, 1989.

48. André Louf, Homily for the tenth Sunday of Ordinary Time, ADMC, 2002.

supermen nor even righteous, but only sitting in the front row of sinners. He presents the perfect monk as an icon of the publican in the Gospel, satisfied with displaying his sins in God's sight and with repeating unceasingly in his heart, fixing his eyes on the ground and not daring to lift them up to heaven, "My God, have mercy on me, a sinner" (Luke 18:13).

Toward Humble Love

Whether they are tied to an experience of sin or one of shock, all these falls open up in the believer's heart discrete wrinkles that end up by pushing him into his own interiority. Grace, which comes along later to relieve his efforts, draws him to something outside himself that is strangely found in his deepest self, in his interior cell, where he is at home in God's presence. Cabled in this way at the source of his being, plugged in to a "long wave of the spirit,"[49] everything becomes different. Christians feel themselves directed by an unknown force and sense a profound peace. Recollection, so hard up to now, henceforth flows as if from a spring. Prayer is given internally and becomes like a "musical background," interpreting their activity and covering all other sounds with its sweet melody.[50]

The feeling that finally predominates in one who has been tested by this trial is that of unshakable confidence in God's love. "From then on such a man knows himself to be weak and sinful," Louf writes, "but he ends up turning his eyes away from his misery in order to no longer contemplate anything but God's mercy":

> The break in his heart has been imperceptibly transformed into love and thanksgiving. From this ascesis of

49. Louf, *Au gré de sa grâce*, 197.
50. André Louf, Unedited conference on prayer.

> poverty there rises every day a new man. He is entirely peace, benevolence, and sweetness. He remains stamped with repentance forever, but it is a repentance full of joy and love, which spreads out everywhere and always, and remains the background of his search for God. This man has reached peace for good, and it is a profound peace, because he has been broken and rebuilt in his whole being by pure grace. He has finally learned to lay down his arms before God, to stop defending himself against him. He has renounced all personal righteousness, and he no longer has a project of sanctity. His hands are empty, or they hold nothing but his misery, but he dares to expose his misery to mercy. God has finally become a real God to him, and there is nothing but God. That means *salvator*: Savior from sin. He is happy in recognizing his fragility. He retains nothing but his wounds, nursed and healed by mercy, have blossomed into miracles.[51]

This meeting with mercy has melted his heart, which now radiates the humble love of Jesus. There is now in this man a sweetness and benevolence, an overflowing tenderness for the whole world.

51. André Louf, "L'humilité dans la vie monastique," *Le Lien des Moniales* no. 14 (July 2000): 19–20.

CHAPTER 11

Spiritual Accompaniment

Along with the pastoral ministry of guiding the community as a whole, Louf considered it important that the abbot also be a spiritual father in the traditionally understood sense, that is, in a more intimate way, having a more personal contact with individual brothers, a way of infusing his government "with the environment, the procedures, and the fruits of spiritual accompaniment."[1] A few weeks after his election he spoke to the sisters at Belval about the kind of superior he wanted to be. He had already said directly, "The abbot is there especially to discern the call of God's love in every soul that has been entrusted to him." Then he confessed, "The Lord has put in my heart an attraction for the role of spiritual father. In fact it is the only thing that really draws me in the abbot's office."[2]

To become a listener to the confused desires of his son lets one discern God's call; then it blesses him, that is, it engages him on the path that he has discerned along with the one he is counseling. This bond, so particular, unites a spiritual father

1. André Louf, "L'abbé et l'accompagnement spirituel," *Collectanea Cisterciensia* 62 (2000): 230.

2. André Louf, First encounter with the community of Belval, ADMC, 6 Feb. 1963.

to his son in a total openness of heart; it was for Louf "one of the highest forms of human relationship."[3]

Spiritual Midwifery

Every life is transmitted by processes of fertilization, of begetting, and then of maturing toward the event of birth. It is the same in the spiritual life, where the one who officiates at the lying-in is called the accompanier. The role of this obstetrician is to help the one accompanied to bring forth the life of the spirit, to make that person discover, accept, and accomplish what the ancients called "the will of God," "not the will that the person might previously have made regarding his subject, but his wish concerning it, all of whose powers he displays little by little, being drawn secretly with extreme sweetness to the most intimate place in his heart."[4] Through the words of the one who accompanies, then, believers are made aware of God's design on their behalf, a design that they find really corresponds to their own desires and deepest aspirations.[5] Such an experience is so important in the spiritual life that both the one who helps that life and the one who is helped are able to call themselves, in Louf's phrasing, father and son.

The art of listening for the movement of the spirit in a believer's heart is not the subject of a decree. It is not a trade, an improvisation, or an installation, something a coach or psychotherapist might undertake. No one could arrogate this

3. Louf, "L'accompagnement spirituel aujourd'hui (1)," *Vie consacré* no. 6 (1980): 325.

4. André Louf, "Le discernement dans la tradition orientale," *Itinéraire Augustinienne* 30 (2003): 45.

5. André Louf, "Les moines d'Occident et le mont Athos," in *Vivere il regno di Dio Servitio degli Altri: Miscellanea in Onore del P. Olivier Raquez, O.S.B.*, ed. Mihai Frățilă (Barcelona: Galaxia Gutenberg, 2008), 113–33.

ministry to oneself. In the first place it depends on the trust of the one who presents himself to the father, not to the qualities, even spiritual ones, that the latter might possess. By recognizing the father's discernment with full confidence, a discernment that goes beyond a simple human clairvoyance, the son creates the father.[6] What is more, this charism of discernment is a gift received from the Holy Spirit. "The accompanier," the abbot explains,

> might be naturally endowed with a certain psychological flair that might allow him, better than someone else, to "guess" something about the person who comes to him. As far as that goes, there is no assurance that he can discern correctly among all the material that the one to be accompanied comes to entrust to him: what is a neutral inconsequential desire, what is a desire wounded by sin, or what is a desire from the Holy Spirit in the deepest region of the heart? Only the Holy Spirit, you see, can give a person the ability to "perceive" him spiritually.[7]

When Louf became abbot this practice had fallen into disuse in many centers of the church's life, even among religious communities. The many reasons for this loss greatly preoccupied him. First of all, there was a certain natural looseness that was the effect of a regrettable evolution: the director of conscience came to be confused with the confessor, in such a way that the opening of the heart often coincided with the self-accusation of sins, giving the spiritual dialogue

6. Louf, "Être formé à l'accompagnement spirituel," *Seminarium* 39 (1999): 553–68.

7. André Louf, "La paternità spirituale nel monachesimo d'occidente oggi," in *Evlogij di Vladimir et al.: Optina Pustyne' e la paternità spirituale, Atti del X Convegno ecumenico internazionale di spiritualità ortodossa. Sezione russa. Bose, 19–21 settembre 2002*, edited by Adalberto Mainardi (Magnano: Qiqajon, 2003), 178.

an authoritarian, moralizing, and legalistic style, very far from the style that the great tradition understood it to have. The contentious mentality that grew up during the sixties also played an important role in this recession. Christians more and more abandoned this practice, which they suspected of carrying on what was left of paternalism. In a significant way filial terminology (*father*) or vertical (*director*) gave way little by little to terms making the relation of spiritual master and his disciple a more horizontal and egalitarian one (*counselor* or *accompanier*).[8]

However, the term *counselor*, which is favored today, runs the risk of leading people into error on the true nature of this practice. The latter does not consist in multiplying counsels or giving orders. The dimension of teaching or informing on the broad principles of spiritual experience is not the heart of accompaniment; if that were the case, a strong course in spirituality or ethics would fill the bill. Instead a relationship seeks to lead the disciple into deep water, to make him "descend progressively to the deepest part of himself, in order to liberate the vital forces that are hindered there."[9] To attain this end the father listens to all that stirs and rumbles in his son's heart. From this dialogue, Louf explains, a desire emerges little by little: "that will be the Holy Spirit in him, the Word of God in the strongest sense of the term, and therefore a word that is really creative, capable of opening up a way that the disciple would hardly have dared to suspect. Blessed is the person who will have recognized on the lips of his father what comes from God at the very depths of himself!"[10]

The objective of accompaniment, then, says Louf, is to give birth to life, to life in the most absolute sense of the word "that the Latin fathers called *vita vitalis* or *vita vivida*, 'the

8. Louf, "La paternità spirituale nel monachismo," 157.

9. Louf, *À la grâce de Dieu*, 55.

10. Louf, "La paternità spirituale nel monachismo," 170.

living life' par excellence, that is to say the life of God in each one of us."[11] That is why the rediscovery of this practice is one of the most important stakes for the future of the church. It is a question of the transfer of life and therefore of the spreading of Christian faith, of catechesis in a broad sense. He goes so far as to say, "When we no longer know how to accompany in truth, the handing on of the faith is itself compromised."[12]

The Art of Discernment

By returning to the practice of accompanying, Louf says, Christians will rediscover little by little the art of discernment, that faculty of finding in their hearts the movement of the Spirit: "Spiritual discernment is not limited to the relationship between two persons in spiritual accompaniment," he cautioned in a letter to his brothers, "but it should be the particular grace of every believer. All of us are guided by the Holy Spirit at every moment of our lives, and we should all be ready to 'feel' him and to give an account thereof. It is one of the prerogatives of every baptized person. But it is true that it is rarely spoken of in today's church."[13]

Louf explained that the true art of interior listening, discernment, presupposes a refined sensitivity and acute spiritual senses. It is the "ear of the heart"[14] that is above all called for, he said, an ear whose drum should learn to vibrate at the rustling of the Spirit and to hear the Spirit's voice beneath its most silent murmur. The Lord, he explained, works permanently inside the heart of believers and leads them in a certain direction. By learning to decipher this interior word, believers

11. Louf, "Être formé à l'accompagnement spirituel," 556.

12. Louf, "Être formé à l'accompagnement spirituel," 561.

13. André Louf, Letter to the community, ADMC, 9 Feb. 1987.

14. André Louf, Homily for Br. Guillaume's taking of the habit, ADMC, 1982.

will be able little by little, by training, to find instinctively what the Spirit urges them to in the concrete circumstances of their lives.[15]

Following Christ does not consist in respecting the provisions of morality or the precepts of a system; it is lived in docility to the Holy Spirit. That is why it is so important to be able to discern the Spirit's motions and calls, so that one may conform one's life to him. According to Louf, this ministry of discernment within the reach of every Christian is at the same time "a necessary gift for the spiritual health of the people of God"[16] and a charism adapted for the present needs of the church in the act of passing in the wake of the Council from the regime of the law and observances to that of interior freedom. "If it is practiced correctly," he goes on, "the art of spiritual discernment turns out to be infinitely more exacting than any law or observance. It aims to free and to listen for the interior requirements of every person, in fact those of the Holy Spirit, that are never bound or exhausted by any law or regulation . . . . We will have an unceasingly growing need for believers who are experts in the detection of the most subtle movements of grace."[17]

To be unendingly plugged in to God's current, to sense the hidden urge of God's Spirit within oneself, and to let oneself be guided to act through it—this art of spiritual accompaniment and discernment, which traces out a true pedagogy of liberty, is, Louf says, "the most precious" good that monks can offer to the contemporary church and one of the church's

15. Enrico Parolari, "Nel ricordo di André Louf," *Tredimensioni* 9 (2012): 63.

16. André Louf, *La grâce peut davantage: L'accompagnement spirituel* (Paris: Desclée de Brouwer, 1992), 40.

17. Louf, *La grâce peut davantage*, 18, 22. The ellipsis is that of the author.

most urgent tasks.[18] "A rediscovery of this practice," he says, "faithful to tradition but taking into account refined sensitivity and modern psychology, could be decisive for the future of the faith in the twenty-first century." He concludes, "The stakes are high, because it is a question of the transmission of life, of the very life of God."[19]

A Spiritual Therapy

At the beginning of the sixties Louf took part with those religious who were bold enough to have a dialogue on the experience of the faith and the first interpretations of it as being put at risk by the human sciences. He attempted this hybridization with the subject of spiritual fatherhood, building a bridge between the traditional teaching sprung from the worldly practice of accompaniment and the most recent discoveries of psychology, psychotherapy, and psychoanalysis.

Even although, having entered the monastic life at the age of seventeen, Louf had slight human experience, and although he had never studied psychology, he was always intrigued by this side of human experience.[20] A born psychologist, he was endowed with remarkable intuition and a refined perception of existence and of situations. This fact emerges in a conference he gave for novice masters, where he sketched out psychological profiles of young monks with the moral expertise of the seventeenth century and the keen-sightedness of a

18. André Louf, "La dimension apostolique et contemplative de la vie religieuse," *Vie Consacrée* 3 (1985): 147–64 (repr. from *À l'école de la contemplation* [Paris: Lethielleux, 2004], 108–10).

19. André Louf, *À la grâce de Dieu*, 49. André's vision on the question is synthesized in Alexandro Saraco, *Discernement et accompagnement spirituel dans les écrits d'André Louf* (Nouan-le-Fuzelier: Éditions des Béatitudes, 2016).

20. Parolari, "Nel ricordo di André Louf," 58.

therapist. First, he described a novice with the temperament of a stationmaster: "Once he is on the rails, he does not get off, and God knows there are enough rails in the monastic life. More turns, more branches, more choices to make. Who will pass through this barrier? He is a regular maniac, closing and barring doors."

Another frequent subject was the "fervid novice," engaged on a course for perfection, prisoner of a rigorism that unveils an "image of himself puffed up with a need, at any price, for the affection that he perhaps never received." Louf continued with a profile of this novice's "identity": "No one has ever helped him to know himself, to identify himself, because no one has ever loved him for what he is. He has been loved for his work, his scholarly success, certain qualities, but for himself he has never really been there. He will try to construct for himself more or less habitually an identity easy to embrace, a monastic identity. He becomes hooked on an external image, to details like a beard, a hood, a habit. Will he exist without these signs of social recognition?" And then he spoke of the novice victimized "by a split between monastic ideology and concrete life, between *ratio* and *affectus*. He knows what he should do, and especially how he should answer the father master: be correct and irreproachable: that's the orthodox monastic ideology. But it doesn't sound right. He talks only with his head. His inner parts are not in harmony and do not vibrate."[21] These few examples, taken from a much longer list, show Louf's skill in perceiving the unconscious states of young brothers, the masks under which they try to hide their failings. How had he sharpened his view? Where did his knowledge come from?

The writings of the ancient monks offered an initial answer. Louf was intrigued by the psychological finesse of the mo-

21. André Louf, Notes for an unedited conference on obedience, ADMC, 1997.

nastic tradition, especially the apophthegms of the Desert Fathers and the letters written by the Palestinian monks of the sixth century, John and Barsanuphius, a veritable treasure of spiritual discernment.[22] He reported to his brother monks on a conference he had just given in Paris on the link between monastic life and psychology: "Exchanges have above all been held on the psychological snares that are inherent in all spiritual efforts toward a certain perfection. It is surprising to see that the ancient monastic literature was perfectly aware of these snares, and that they did not have to wait for Freud before suspecting spiritual behavior or spiritual pretenses that run the risk of destroying those who accept them."[23] In another letter he goes further: "The psychological wisdom of the ancient monks is really extraordinary, and it stands out even more when there is reason to clarify a point with the help of certain findings of the human sciences."[24]

The second source of Louf's knowledge came directly from the writings of some pioneers who were trying at that time to introduce the findings of modern psychology into the spiritual life. In his book on accompaniment Louf quotes some of them: Louis Beirnaert, André Godin, Raymond Hostie, François Dolto, Denis Vasse, Maurice Bellet, and the doctor Fred Blum.[25] An Anglican priest and psychotherapist, Blum exerted a great influence on Louf, especially through his book *Depth Psychology and the Healing Ministry*.[26] Louf met Blum several times, notably at Oxford, where they organized

22. Guerric Aerdese, from correspondence with the author. Louf later devoted an article to the spiritual paternity practiced by John and Barsanuphius: "Un accompagnement spirituel concerté: Barsanuphe, Jean et Séridos," *Collectanea Cisterciensia* 66 (2004): 35–50.

23. André Louf, Letter to the community, ADMC, 20 Jan. 1981.

24. André Louf, Letter to the community, ADMC, 9 Feb. 1981.

25. André Louf, *La grâce peut davantage*, 8.

26. London: Hyperion Books, 1990.

"psycho-spiritual" sessions for those responsible for the formation of young monks and nuns.

But he also owed much to Antoine Vergote, Carl Jung, and even Carl Rogers. "Psychotherapy," recalled Louf, "that is, to follow the original Greek etymology, the 'healing of the soul,' could not help influencing, intriguing, sometimes irritating, or even revolting, but also little by little interesting those who were responsible for the spiritual formation and maturing of their brothers. There would often be hesitations, serious objections, and even rejections and refusals."[27] He himself had no fear of confronting or even doing research into the ancient findings of the tradition, of which he was both a connoisseur and practitioner, exploring the recent findings of that depth psychology that traced a therapeutic path that he concluded could "illuminate in a new and positive way the classical methods of spiritual pedagogy, of ascesis, as well as of prayer."[28]

Louf also profited a great deal from the reflections and knowledge of two professional men whose aid and expertise he had regularly solicited at the abbey. First of all, Dr. Pierre Bour (1917–2003) came to the monastery every two months to meet with brothers who wished to speak to him, not to discuss psychoanalysis, but to share their problems with him. Dr. Bour owed his renown to employing a technique of psychodrama in hospital contexts. But he was also well-known as a practitioner of works of reflection. He was convinced that humans have hidden energies within their psychological makeup, like molten lava hidden deep within the planet. Freud called these psychic reserves *libido*, but this term was too fluid for Bour and too strictly confined to the sexual sphere.

A critical heir of Freudian psychoanalysis, Bour developed an elaborate theory of emotions in *Les Racines de l'homme*.[29]

27. Louf, "La paternità spirituale nel monachismo," 161.
28. Louf, *À la grâce de Dieu*, 185.
29. Paris: Robert Laffont, 1973.

According to him, psychotherapy should stop envisaging the person as torn between different emotions and instead watch for the unique emotion of self-affirmation, of internal expansion, which would permit unification. He criticized the psychoanalysis that reduced a person to emotions, and he criticized the behavioral psychology that was reduced to reflexes. He untiringly searched for the deepest level in every person, one's permanent unity, in a word, one's soul. In 1985, in *L'inconscient et la grâce*[30] he unveiled his Christianity. This iconoclastic person, famous scientist, writer, and explorer of the psyche in all its forms, was in his element with Louf. He was a specialist in psychodrama and in group dynamics; as a therapist he intervened at Louf's request to resolve fraternal tensions and to pour oil on the hardening of community relationships.[31]

At the beginning of the eighties Louf turned to the psychiatrist Hubert Ronse de Craene, like him, Belgian. A friendship grew between them, as a letter from Ronse de Craene shows: "Then I read your biography with pleasure. It is a little reminder of my visits at Mont-des-Cats. They were the most captivating moments in my career. There was a brotherly listening, but also your presence, your life among them."[32] Along with the doctors Bour and Ronse de Craene, Louf sometimes invited the Colombian psychotherapist, Alvaro Escabor Molina, to Mont-des-Cats. Louf later admitted,

> I do not insist on the good influence both of them [Bour and Ronse de Craene] have had on the lives of many of my brother monks, who were completely free to present themselves to them during their regular visits. I wish only to recall here how much they have helped me in

30. Paris: Éditions du Levain, 1985.

31. Jean-Marc Thévenet, conversation with the author.

32. Hubert Ronse de Craene, Letter to Dom Louf, 20 May 2003, Archives of the Ronse de Craene family.

> my burden of responsibility. Without ever dictating to me the conduct I should follow or reproaching me for my obvious blunders, a witticism nicely dropped would quickly draw my attention to an unconscious slip-up on the point of catching up with me. They knew how to mention in passing "a superfluous word" in my discourse, as one of them called it, one that betrayed the unconscious scenario in which I still had the tendency to seek refuge when a situation of opposition appeared on the horizon. The fact of "surprising oneself in an obvious misdeed" at such a time counted for nothing in the supportive and forbearing eyes of a person who was fatherly and friendly at the same time. In a way that was perfectly secular they undoubtedly led me to a presentiment of what spiritual accompaniment might mean in the order of grace.[33]

But Louf held that the essential element in his knowledge of the human psyche came from his own practice of accompaniment. In fact, as he spoke with his brothers, listened to their difficulties, and tried to disentangle the skein of their problems, this experience led him to perceive that the divine life is indissolubly linked to our psychological state, even if not completely identified with it: "The surgeon makes an intervention, because he is completely prepared to distinguish one organ from another, or a nerve from a vein. But his lancet will never cut the soul of his patient. By the same token no surgery exists that would allow for the exact tracing of what would be purely psychological, or what would be exclusively supernatural . . . . If we cannot separate in any concrete person the spiritual life from psychology, it is because the spiritual life in that person is necessarily supported by psy-

33. André Louf, "Autrement la grâce n'est plus la grâce," in André Louf, Denis Huerre, and Marie-David Giraud, *Dieu intime: Parole de moines* (Paris: Bayard, 2003), 23–24.

chology, in other words quite concretely by the positive and negative aspects of psychology at the same time."[34] Louf's explanation discovers in its wake that psychology is able to bring substantial aid in the spiritual life. As a kind of *catharsis* or internal purification, psychotherapy, if correctly applied, is in a position to prepare the area where interior life is lived, to identify certain obstacles and illusions without ever suppressing them, and to reduce their hindering effects.[35]

For all that, psychotherapy cannot be a substitute for accompaniment. Certainly there are similarities between therapeutic listening and spiritual accompaniment; for instance, there is neutral or even benevolent reception on the part of the therapist, as well as abstaining from any judgment or any condemnation. On the part of the patient there is sharing of deep desires under the form of temptations or dreams, emergence from suffering or internal wounds long repressed, or a reconciliation as peaceful as possible within certain limits.[36] However, these resemblances should not obscure the essential differences between the two approaches. First of all there is the nature of the relationship. Whereas in the therapeutic context that relation should be neutralized because of the phenomena that accompany what is communicated, the case is different in the relationship of accompaniment. Life force and healing, Louf explains, are at work in the bond that unites the spiritual father's heart with that of the son in the movement of the spirit.[37] He distinguishes the objectives of the two procedures thus: "Therapy aims at the healing of one or another of our psychological problems, whereas the goal

34. Louf, *La grâce peut davantage*.

35. *Paroles d'ermite*. Father André Louf, documentary, CFRT/KTO Sunset Presse 52 minutes, produced by Laurence Chartier, 2009.

36. Louf, "La paternità spirituale nel monacismo," 182–83.

37. Louf, "La paternità spirituale nel monachismo," 183.

of accompaniment is to prepare the heart for God's visit,"[38] to let the deep desire for the Spirit come to one's awareness, as well as one's vocation and the secret of one's freedom.

The Adventure of Desires

A brother of Mont-des-Cats recounted this memory: "At the moment of my taking of the habit, when the abbot asks the novice the ritual question, 'What do you seek?' I recited a brief exposition that was very pious in the hope of edifying the congregation. Dom André quickly detected it, and, starting over, he gently retorted, 'Thank you. That is very nice, but it is not what I want to know. This is what interests me: You, personally: what do you really wish?' "[39]

Louf was much marked by the spirituality of the twelfth-century Cistercians, who gave great importance to desire, "The lever of the person's unification."[40] He maintained that there is no one who goes on living in ignorance of his deep affections, who kills all passions in himself, who becomes listless. "It is an enterprise doomed to failure." he said. "A 'repressed' desire has quickly made a reappearance, more or less knowingly disguised. This proves that passions and desires are parts of us; they cause us to move and urge us to live."[41] Louf frowned every time he heard a novice master confuse the invitation of spiritual writers "to hate one's own will" with the repression of desires. "How can I calmly renounce them without harming myself, mutilating myself, or endangering my equilibrium? What are the conditions under which renun-

38. Louf, *À la grâce de Dieu*, 50.

39. Marc-André Di Péa, conversation with the author.

40. Xavier Morales, *Dieu est amitié: La spiritualité d'Aelred de Rievaulx* (Paris: Salvator, 2016), 11.

41. Louf, *À la grâce de Dieu*, 148.

ciation becomes spiritually fruitful?"[42] was his reply to this sacrificial spirituality, of which he had rid himself.

Louf's accompaniment was deeply influenced by this vision of the human being as a creature of desire. Moreover, he taught the brothers whose spiritual father he was first of all to try to see clearly the way through these complex diseases that in every sense took hold of their hearts, as he invited them to open their hearts to him through what the Oriental tradition calls *exagoreusis*, that is, a humble opening up of the heart. When the disciple feels confidence at the invitation of his spiritual father, with true love he entrusts to him all that forms the course of his life. This opening up goes far beyond any simple recounting of sins. It concerns his states of soul, his thoughts, and his deep inclinations. It is at this level that the spiritual dialogue takes place.

As Louf explained it, "There is not so much a question of a discourse on God or on what the virtuous life of one conformed to moral teaching might amount to, but rather of being open to the desire that dwells at the root of our heart."[43] He insisted on this essential point: this sharing of desires, apparently good and bad, should never issue in a condemnation or a sanction. The disciple does not open his heart with the idea of learning from the mouth of his spiritual father where good and evil lie, "but to be accepted by him and to receive from him authorization to be what he is, with his dark and light places under the gaze of his love. At bottom," Louf explained, "it is in order that the disciple may be regarded and accepted by his spiritual father as God himself regards and accepts the disciple."[44] To have in this way the right to

42. André Louf, Notes of an unedited conference on spiritual accompaniment, given at the abbey of Pierre-qui-vire, ADMC, 1997.

43. André Louf, *À la grâce de Dieu,* 55.

44. André Louf, "La paternità spirituale," 170.

face another person with all the desires that swarm inside gains for one a fabulous sense of freedom.[45]

Louf regretted that the sphere of desires had been made such a subject of guilt by Christianity, stamped by the Jansenism in which his infancy had been spent. "We were encouraged," he wrote, "to reduce our desires and to conform to rules and regulations. Attractions that we perceived in ourselves, even spiritual ones, were only accepted if we were assured of some obligation. Because of this reticence toward our desires, we could not let the desire of the Spirit rise in our hearts, and yet this desire of the Spirit in us is our true freedom."[46] In this inhibiting atmosphere, he said, the desires that young people venture to express fall under the knife of blame, of judgment, of being pilloried, along with the feeling of shame that is part of it, and the difficulty of appropriating one's capacity of being a man or woman of desires, otherwise called adulthood.[47]

For Louf, shame was never a positive sentiment. To be convinced of that view, he said, one must first remember that shameful thoughts do not exist.[48] The idea that there were evil passions in the human being was itself, he thought, the leftover trace of a heresy condemned by the church: Manicheism. He insisted that

45. André Louf, *La Grâce peut davantage*, 97. In 1961 Louf for the first time tasted the benefits of this opening of the heart with his spiritual father, Frère Marie, with some echoes preserved in his journal: "First experience of *exagoreusis* today. Impression of freedom. Feeling that this 'attention to thoughts' really constitutes a very important monastic activity" (JS, 3 March 1961). Again, "There was immense benefit in this frank humiliation every week, and it made me meek and humble, truer in front of everybody else"(Louf, JS, 10 Sept. 1961).

46. André Louf, "L'Esprit en nous," unedited conference to the Mont-des-Cat chapter, ADMC, Feb. 1971.

47. Louf, *À la grâce de Dieu*, 55.

48. Louf, Notes of an unedited conference on spiritual accompaniment.

> In God's eyes there are no fundamentally evil desires; there are only "distorted" and sick desires, desires sick with love."[49] What the fathers of monastic life called combat against "passions" does not consist of joining battle against one's desires, in stifling them with blows from the will, or in imposing silence on them, cost what it may, but in setting them right, in healing them by accepting them such as they are and exposing them to God's love. The opening of the heart, then, and the manifestation of one's thoughts constitute a real spiritual therapy; within love and warmed by love, desires previously distorted are little by little set right and find their rightful place, as a deep healing has taken place.[50]

To help his brothers escape feelings of guilt and shame, Louf taught them his "theory" of the disguising of desires. "You have made us for yourself, O Lord," Saint Augustine had already cried, "and our heart is restless until it rests in you!" Louf reformulated the idea thus: God has put into the human heart a mysterious thirst that nothing worldly can quench, but only God. The desires with which our days are woven are nothing more than remote signs, symbols, and discreet reminders of that fundamental thirst. "Our thirsts here below," he explains,

> are all disguised thirsts, so well disguised, in fact, that we rarely look beyond their momentary satisfaction. We are most often content with brief earthly drinks, left to find ourselves again disturbed and tormented by some new thirst, when the first has been hardly quenched, because all the brief drinks we try, succeeding one

49. Louf, "La paternità spirituale nel monachismo," 171.

50. André Louf, "Repentir et expérience de Dieu," in *L'expérience de Dieu dans la vie monastique,* ed. Denis Huerre (Abbaye Sainte Marie de la Pierre-qui-Vire: Les Presses Monastiques, 1973), 38.

> another, are nothing more than decoys, loaded up to fool our true thirst. The clearest proof of that is that all these thirsts, when added one to another, are thirsts not only for drinks, but also for realities of an apparent higher order: thirsts for possessions, for enjoyment, for power, for knowledge. All these thirsts are nothing more than travesties—oh, how ingenious and subtle—of another thirst that they hide. It is by dint of always having a thirst for something and then for something else, or for something better, or for more of something, that we end up noticing that all this covetousness hides something else that is, properly speaking, unquenchable, unsatisfiable, and insatiable: our desire for God.[51]

That is what the Carthusian Dom Auguste Guillerand calls "the singular secret of true and lasting serenity."[52] The source of happiness is not located where we think it is, in the innumerable objects of our desires that never stop drawing us on where they leave us empty and deceived. "It is Jesus first of all," says Louf,

> and then, as soon as we receive Jesus and the water he brings, and his Spirit, the source stays in us forever. It never leaves us, and it never stops welling up and freeing us from drawing more water elsewhere and from always starting over. Not that our other desires are then quenched or repressed or pushed aside. Far from it. It is never even necessary to renounce them. But those desires are no more than ephemeral fragments of a much more profound desire, on which they are called to signify and to deepen in us every day without ever letting us be dis-

51. André Louf, Homily for the third Sunday of Lent, ADMC, 2002.

52. Auguste Guillerand, *Silence Cartusien* (Paris: Desclée de Brouwer, 1976), 19.

tracted from it: the desire to be fully and unconditionally accepted in love.[53]

At the Risk of Love

To illustrate the virtues of listening and the way he tried to practice it himself, Louf often used the example of a certain woman who was in the grip of scruples; she had knocked unsuccessfully on the doors of many spiritual fathers and psychotherapists to find deliverance from this state. War-weary, she acted on the suggestion of a friend and presented herself to Abbot Maurice Zundel, a priest and spiritual writer related to Pope Paul VI. Zundel healed her after only one meeting. When she was asked what the priest had told her that cured her so rapidly, she answered, "He did not say a single word. All he did was listen. He saw my tears, and he started to cry with me. We cried together for a long time." Revealing the quality of listening that Louf kept for his sons, he concludes, "To sympathize so deeply with a brother's distress is sometimes enough not only to calm him, but to heal the wound that is hidden behind the tears."[54]

Through this attentive listening without judgment, so charged with a loving presence that it becomes active and efficacious and is sometimes enough to resolve problems, Louf allowed something of a mother's tenderness to be transparent. The mother unceasingly receives, lifts up, and forgets herself in order the better to promote the other. But Louf could also make his accompaniment take on a father's firmness in delivering a judgment. It is the image of God's love, so rich in contrasts; only the complementarity of the masculine and the feminine can approach it. Louf was then both

53. André Louf, Homily for the third Sunday of Lent, ADMC, 1982.
54. André Louf, "La paternità spirituale nel monachismo," 173.

father and mother at the same time, rouser of life and educator, sweet and strong, tender and firm:

> The love of God can be described neither by the image of a man alone nor by the image of a woman alone. Both are needed for the image of God to be complete. The love of God is so great and so rich in aspects and contrasts that if anyone wanted to find here below a sign and sacrament of it, he would have to appeal to both sexes to unite in love for the birth and growth of a human being. In God are united "mercy" and "truth," tenderness and firmness. The spiritual guide is characterized by this sovereign quality, which is at the same time paternal and maternal, charged with tensions indeed and with unavoidable uncertainties, since we are limited creatures.[55]

Consuming the whole register of affectivity, Louf, this maternal father, caused the human and spiritual growth of an incalculable number of men and women. For many of the monks of Mont-des-Cats he first spoke the teaching, illuminating, and sometimes even creative word at one point or another on their journey, the word that creates and directs one's whole existence. Dom Guillaume Jedrzejczak, who succeeded him as abbot, confirmed that "Many are those who keep a memory of an exchange, a look, or a silence that has transformed their lives."[56] Dom Jacques De Lesalle, another of Louf's successors, agrees: "For many of us his word and his presence illuminated the way and indicated in an unforgettable way the point of light that does not go out, *the* light itself, the Lord Jesus. If I am here today (and many of us could

55. Louf, "L'accompagnement spirituel aujourd'hui (1)," 332.

56. Dom Guillaume Jedrzejczak, Homily for Dom André's Jubilee, ADMC, 25 June 2005.

say the same) it is because I had the grace of listening to this word of life."[57]

Louf was a veritable "educator of the humanity of mankind."[58] Against the sacrificial spirituality of his youth, according to which one had to corset one's being and put one's aspirations in a bucket, he passed on to his monks a humanism that cared for their blossoming and for the deploying of their gifts. As soon as he detected in a brother an intellectual or artistic orientation, for example, and he sensed that it was in the noblest sense part of his life, that is, his personal vocation, the life God gave him, he encouraged him to follow it.

This spiritual paternity radiated far beyond the confines of Mont-des-Cats. Many French monasteries sent their new recruits to Louf to have their vocational anxieties cleared up by the light of his discernment, as his reputation had quickly spread everywhere.[59] The founder of the community of Bose, Enzo Bianchi, also testified to this irradiation of influence: "Many of us addressed ourselves to him for spiritual counsel, a word of confirmation, or an exhortation of trust and hope, finding in him an always-available father or brother. He impressed us by his extraordinary capacity to listen, his powerful intercession, his untiring ministry of consolation, his propensity always to extend the cloak of pardon over sin, and the absolute primacy he always gave to mercy."[60] Even outside the monasteries many people were profoundly reached, either by reading his books or by personal encounters with him.

57. Dom Jacques De Lesalle, Homily for Dom Louf's funeral, ADMC, 14 July 2010.

58. The expression belongs to Br. Denis Cazes, in conversation with the author.

59. Jean-Marc Thévenet in conversation with the author.

60. Enzo Bianchi, "André Louf has left this world for the Father," 13 July 2010.

Louf himself did not remain unchanged by these encounters. Constrained to verify God's action in the lives of others, he said, the spiritual accompanier is profoundly transformed; father and son "evolve together, and the growth of one calls forth the growth of the other."[61] But if the encounter causes growth, it also includes danger. Spiritual accompaniment is an adventure, a perilous crossing to the search for the desire of the Holy Spirit, hidden in the deepest part of the heart of the one being accompanied. Dom André had the intrepid temperament of pioneers who have no fear of the uncharted zones of the psyche, or of taking the risk of having this heart-to-heart contact with the brothers.[62]

At the beginning of his abbatial tenure Louf insisted on evoking the figure of the spiritual father: if he wanted to understand the breath of the Spirit in his sons, it was imperative "that his heart be silent, that certain noises be stilled, and that the voices of the passions be smothered."[63] Later he would rather say that the spiritual father should be aware that desires were still sick, were still active, and could falsify his discernment. "At least," he continued, "he is a convalescent who still has scars from his wounds. And these scars, inside a relationship that is sometimes as charged with affection as spiritual accompaniment can be, could open up and make the patient seek healing."[64]

Louf knew that by exposing himself to spiritual friendship in this way, he could cause his old wounds to start to bleed again. But he ran the risk, persuaded that friendship was a rung on the ladder of love that leads to God. Following Aelred of Rievaulx, Louf thought that friendship, when authentic, is an opening to the Wholly Other: "It means that the two friends

61. André Louf, *La grâce peut davantage*, 77.

62. Dom Guillaume Jedrzejzcak, conversation with the author.

63. André Louf, First meeting with the sisters of Belval, ADMC, 1963.

64. André Louf, "La paternità spirituale nel monachismo," 177.

realize their mutual love and let it bear fruit by letting it converge upon a third whom they love together. The love centered upon two lovers who look closely into each other's eyes is still egotistic. Friendship with the clause of non-exclusivity breaks egotism and opens love up to the outside by keeping the lovers from being centered and focused on the self."[65] Louf made the condition that he should humbly learn to practice accompaniment in a disinterested fashion, primarily in the interest of the other. In the beginning of the spiritual course the ability to love, he said, is still held in the web of *proprietas*, attachment to one's own. To become fruitful, this egotistic love has little by little to free itself from every turning back to itself. He warns, "It is obvious that for a certain period of time an intense affection that is still insufficiently integrated will play a role in such a relationship. Without dramatizing eventual outbreaks, the brothers will unceasingly be encouraged not at all to love less, but instead to love more and to direct this love to the preferential love of Jesus, which is our true vocation. When it is favored in this way, the adventure of friendship can not only introduce a real comfort, but even become a test of the authenticity of our love for God."[66]

It is clear that Louf spent some time on integrating this role of affectivity that was so lavish in him. The "long and patient apprenticeship in the gratuity of love"[67] was not spent without pain or in a single day. He was very lucid about this fragility of affectivity, enlivened by his own need to love and be loved. From the beginning of his monastic life he had realized that there was in him an "overflowing tide of tenderness," and he had asked God for the grace "of learning to love no

65. Xavier Morales, *Dieu et amitié: La spiritualite d'Aelred de Rievaulx* (Paris: Salvator, 2015), 84.

66. André Louf, "Vie commune, École de charité: Document de travail pour le chapitre générale de 1996," in *À l'école de la contemplation*, 43.

67. Louf, "Vie commune, École de charité," 24.

one but you, which is what I have done so badly."[68] During the first ten years of his monastic life he tried to love according to God's heart, humbly and self-effacingly, in order to help the other person grow. Sometimes he succeeded with the help of grace; at other times his charity slipped into self-love. For example, he wrote, "I felt at a certain point that I did not love my brothers enough with that total charity that is God's. At one point of the road my friendship came to a halt. I look at myself again. I am incapable of 'sympathizing' all the way, of coming out of myself in an ever-new way."[69] Or, ten years earlier: "Lord, it is clear that I cannot love others with that transparent, lucid friendship, entirely gift, without any self-regard. Until now for me to love anyone has always been more or less to create a 'sentimental attachment' in which I am myself central. Thank you for this humble enlightenment. Let my friendship be always disinterested."[70]

After his abbatial election Louf continued to pose this question of gratuitous love, free of all self-seeking, of the righteousness of taking one's own affectivity into account, and of one's need for tenderness. In 1956, for example, he noted, "There is a danger of personal attachment in my affections as father and head. I should never think about those whom I love without at the same time thinking about you, Jesus, or without a form of invocation or blessing."[71] But is it not precisely there that his boldness resides? In the fact that he had dared to run the risk of this danger of attachment and of exposing himself to his former demons, when the growth, to say nothing of the survival of certain monks, was in question? In fact, in the course of his abbatial tenure, he had risked personal engagement in continuing relationships with certain

68. Letter detailing the list of renunciations, ADMC, 1 Feb. 1954.
69. Louf, JS, 9 July 1968.
70. Louf, JS, 8 Nov. 1959.
71. Louf, JS, 26 August 1966.

brothers hindered by psychological weaknesses or past familial sufferings. Where other people would have pulled back, he considered that someone's salvation required that everything be tried, even leaving the beaten track. He had the compassion of a father who would do all he could to rescue his sons from going adrift. He was moved by their distress and anxious to relieve them from it. He watched over his monks in difficulty with a particular attention. Externally this compassion could pass as affection. Some people in fact reproached him for getting too emotionally involved, while others supposed that these relationships generated an excessively affective dependence; some even went so far as to say that he unconsciously exercised a kind of control over those recruits who imitated their abbot even to the extent of holding his cowl.[72]

The love that streamed from Louf could be the object of many analyses. A psychoanalyst would perhaps discern underneath his abundant affectivity the traces of a kind of narcissistic wound. Because of a father who never really "acknowledged" his existence, Dom Louf doubted himself all his life and tried to find in the regard of other people a kind of recognition. That would explain his propensity to seduce, to conquer the esteem, the sympathy, or the admiration of the other person. But more spiritual lenses would see instead a resemblance to the figure of Mary Magdalene. The abbot's surpassing love and his overflowing tenderness also resemble the woman in the gospel whom God pardoned so much because she had loved so much (Luke 7:47).

Louf often said that he had to fight his interior divisions with "a kindly stubbornness." "I love that expression," he continued, "because it lets us understand that we must renew *ourselves* every day with that patient and secret confronta-

72. That is the thesis developed by Alvaro Escobar Molina in *L'enfermement, Espace, Temps, Cloture* (Paris: Klincksieck, 1989), 258–59.

tion. It is certainly not a voluntarist and supercilious process, but an abandonment to God's grace in the confident certitude that he will correct our faults as he pleases, in the measure that he pleases, and when he pleases."[73] All his life he had dragged along an affective fragility that centered his attention upon himself when he so desired to forget himself. But if God, he insisted, lets us fight against our interior failings in this way, it is in order to humble us: "The saints themselves often experience this fact. They had a 'thorn' in the flesh—a persistent weakness—that kept them from giving in to pride."[74] Louf's holiness consists in that, in persevering in fidelity to his vocation despite the healing wounds and the blows that made him feel on the spot. Forced to drag along his bundle of misery, to fall and get up again, he experienced a salutary action: by accepting confirmation in a situation of misery, by a joyful acceptance without bitterness of all that galled him, his weakness became a fissure through which the Spirit was able to enter. In this way, little by little, his weaknesses became fruitful, and his failings were transformed into sources of life, into good results for the sake of other people.

73. André Louf, "Le Bon Combat," *Prier*, March 2007.

74. Louf, "Le Bon Combat."

CHAPTER 12

A Carthusian Heart

In April 1979, Louf, forty-nine years old, had been abbot of Mont-des-Cats for thirteen years and was a leader in the Cistercian Order. Books containing his teaching and translated into a number of languages had made him a famous spiritual master for contemporary Christianity. To rest from his activity, he granted himself a few days of retreat at the Carthusian house of Portes in Ain, where he was acquainted with certain brothers. There, in the course of a walk in the mountains of Bugey, he was drenched by rainfall; his rough Cistercian habit was dripping wet and had to be hung up in the drying room. In the meantime the Carthusians lent him one of their robes, which he put on with a great deal of emotion. "Today by chance (and with the tender love of Providence)," he wrote," I am wearing the Carthusian habit for a few hours. I would be wearing this habit today if the Lord had directed the events of the past eight years otherwise. Many of my weaknesses would not have appeared . . . but it is idiotic to dream about what might have been. Everything is really in Jesus' hands: both past and future."[1]

In these words Louf alluded to events that were opening a tumultuous new chapter in his already troubled search to know

1. André Louf, *Journal Spirituel* [hereafter JS], 24 April 1979.

his vocation: he had decided in 1972 to leave his abbatial charge and to enter Carthusian life, so to lead a life entirely devoted to prayer, a dream he had for so long cherished.

A Recluse at Prayer

In 1963, only a month after becoming abbot, Louf wrote in his journal, "I felt that my choice of the life of a hermit was not to be given up, but that the Lord would take it seriously some day in a way entirely unforeseeable as yet."[2] In fact his election had hardly caused an eclipse of his desire to lead the life of a recluse in prayer. Even while performing his pastoral service, he never lost sight of this eremitical vocation, which unceasingly beckoned him. In March 1967, four years after the election, the desire returned more insistently: "In this third day of hermitage I again felt the attraction of that existence entirely devoted to love and to the word of love that is a hermit's life."[3] A few months later, on his return from long trying weeks on a journey, he observed, "Every time I stop and remain partially solitary, a call to prayer makes itself felt."[4] In November of the same year, he for the first time formulated a hypothesis of laying down his abbatial charge: "I understood better in what sense I should envisage, beginning now, the wish to retire from the office of abbot. I have a great desire to show by my life what I have preached in words."[5]

But it was in the course of a pilgrimage to Mount Athos in August 1969 that the call became specific, during a visit with a hermit, an Orthodox monk, who lived a half hour's walk away from the monastery of Stavronikita, on the east side of the holy mountain. While the monk was busy with

2. Louf, JS, 16 Feb. 1963
3. Louf, JS, 22 March 1967.
4. Louf, JS, 16 Oct. 1967.
5. Louf, JS, 21 Nov. 1967.

the meal, Louf prayed in the modest chapel of the hermitage, facing the iconostasis, the sea visible through the window. Then he was struck by an absolute certainty: "Someday," he said, "somewhere the Lord would grant me the grace that would have been the grace of my being: to be with Jesus in prayer, unceasingly calling upon his most sweet name!"[6] This disclosure provoked joyful tears. Years later, when his plan to resign had received clear confirmation, he said of this moment, "Undoubtedly I would come finally to the realization of what has been the heart of my personal vocation, the sweet will of God for me."[7]

A year later, in April 1970, the evidence shone out again: "Passage to the Carthusian monastery of Sélignac. A deep interior call, as though I was beginning to wake up. Not a doubt about it. My interior attraction is most essentially to *quies*, to *hesychia* for God. There has been a desire for clear discernment that calls me back to my own truth."[8] There he was again, bogged down in the enigma of his vocation: "I am nothing more than a common laborer, very unskilled, hardly understanding what the architect intends to do."[9]

On April 17 he at last confided to his spiritual father, the Orthodox monk André Scrima, his plan to resign his abbatial charge: "He approved of my desire to profit from the next Regular Visitation to submit my mandate to the judgment of the community. It was toward reclusion that he directed me without hesitation, and he suggested on his own part an establishment in the shadow of a Carthusian house, without however abandoning the works of the fathers. I was at peace and in joy at the termination of this conversation. The life of

6. André Louf, Unedited witness on prayer, ADMC, 2003.

7. André Louf, "Le Coeur brisé," *Buisson Ardent* 3 (1997): 49.

8. Louf, JS, 14 April 1970.

9. Louf, JS, 18 Sept. 1970.

a recluse for the Lord is a deep characteristic of my call."[10] From that time on he authorized solitary retreats for himself on a more regular basis, either at the Carthusian house at Portes or in a small hermitage near Mont-des-Cats, in order to "refresh" his heart,[11] as he said happily when prayer diminished under the weight of his pastoral charge.

The Grace of a Carthusian

In his own house Louf felt that he was on the Carthusian path, which he qualified as a "marvel of equilibrium and of peace." During a retreat at Portes, he wrote in his journal, "In the cell my tears accumulate unexpectedly and sweetly. My peace is very great. The sweetness of solitude fills the whole being of God. Thank you, Lord, for having kept the grace of Carthusians in the heart of the church."[12] When he visited the Carthusian house of Arlington, Vermont, he was astonished: "Thank you, Lord, for this grace of Carthusian poverty, for these vocations that are consumed in your presence by their unceasing depth before you. There is much of the absolute here but much also that is sweet, and a great delicacy of charity. Saint Bruno should be here as well."[13] The great specialist in Carthusian spirituality Nathalie Nabert said of Louf that he had a "Carthusian heart."[14]

In fact Louf felt that he was fully alive when he was in a Carthusian house, when the deepest threads of his being started to vibrate. Everything in the order founded by Saint Bruno attracted him: the spirituality of the divine indwelling, the insistence on presence to the heart that is called to be an altar from which unceasing prayer is lifted up, a life drawn

10. Louf, JS, 17 April 1970.
11. Louf, JS, 4 May 1971.
12. Louf, JS, 8 July 1971.
13. Louf, JS, 18 Oct. 1976.
14. Nathalie Nabert, conversation with the author.

closer to what is essential, the face-to-face encounter with God, the silence and the solitude where God speaks to the monk's heart. It is just as an ancient Carthusian said: "In the Old and especially in the New Testament, almost all the most sublime and deepest secrets were revealed to the servants of God, not at all in tumult or in crowds, but when they were found alone."[15] Nor should one forget the importance of the cell, about which the Cistercian William of Saint-Thierry wrote, "The cell is holy ground and a holy place in which the Lord and his servant often talk together as a man does with his friend."[16] Finally Louf appreciated the equilibrium of the formula, this "precious dosage"[17] of the common life and the eremitic life, since, he wrote, the "Carthusian is a solitary monk who risks an isolation that is moderated by a discreet dose of fraternal life."[18]

While sharing deeply in the Carthusian life, Louf also had good relations with the brothers. On his journeys to Rome he often stopped in at the villa where Dom Jean-Baptiste Porion stayed. He admired the human and spiritual greatness of the man and his feeling for the contemplative life. Conversations with him on Flemish mysticism flowed. Dom Porion had entered the Carthusian house at La Val Sainte in

15. Guigues Ier, *Coutumes de Chartreux* (Paris: Cerf, 1984), 289.

16. Guillaume de Saint-Thierry, *Lettre aux frères du Mont-Dieu* (Paris: Cerf, 1975), 173; William of Saint-Thierry, *The Golden Epistle*, Cistercian Fathers series 12 (Kalamazoo, MI: Cistercian Publications, 1971), 22. Dom Porion, then the procurator general of the Carthusian Order, spoke similarly about this friendly intimacy in the Carthusian life: "We will be with God as though we were with a very dear friend. We do not speak words continually, but we are nonetheless happy to know him and to find ourselves at his side, and it is enough" (Jean-Baptiste Porion, *Amour et silence et autres textes*, rev. ed. (Paris: Ad Solem, 2010), 66.

17. André Louf, "Les lignes de force de l'aggiornamento monastique," an unpublished manuscript, ADMC, 1967, 13.

18. André Louf, "Saint Bruno," in *Documents d'épiscopat*, no. 12–13, 2001, 9.

Switzerland in 1925 and was procurator general, residing at Rome, from 1946–1981. Porion, one of the witnesses of the reforms of the Second Vatican Council, was known for the transparency of his spiritual thought, expressed in *Amour et silence*, but he also translated the poems and letters of Hadewijch of Anvers.[19]

During the 1960s Louf also visited the Carthusian house of Sélignac, where he met a group of brothers who would soon form the nucleus of the community at Portes. Noteworthy among them were Dom Marie-Paul Chapeau, Dom Pierre Anquez, and Dom Marcellin Theeuwes, who later became prior general of the Order from 1997 to 2012. In 2000 Dom Theeuwes asked Dom André to become extraordinary confessor for the Carthusian Order.[20] Portes, of course, was the Carthusian house where Louf often stopped, since it was located on his way to Fille-Dieu, the Swiss abbey of which he was father immediate. Dom Étienne Descamps, a former prior of Portes, recalls, "He stopped off with us along the road ordinarily once a year. I was bound with him by friendship, and I was always glad to see him. Our conversations were about the situation of contemplative monasteries in France. When he was with us, he would visit one or another monk of the community. He was considered an 'extraordinary confessor,' and each one could approach him if he felt the need."[21]

Louf's spiritual journal shows that certain brothers of Portes were bound to him with particularly deep ties. Some of them even considered him a spiritual father, from whom they awaited a word of life. For example, Louf kept this letter from Dom Anquez in his journal:

19. Dom Jean-Baptiste Porion, *Lettres et écrits spirituels* (Paris: Beauchesne, 2011).

20. Dom Jacques Dupont, procurator general of the Carthusians, in correspondence with the author.

21. Dom Étienne Descamps in correspondence with the author.

> I had hoped to receive your words of discernment concerning the simple research project outside the Carthusian environment on something that concerns me as a word of the Lord. I found it in your letter, where you tell me that you would like to entreat me to pray to remain in my cell in the Order. And there to live as a hesychast who owes nobody anything. I receive this word very respectfully as your spiritual discernment in the present instance, and I will keep that word with all the seriousness that it requires. Thank you very much; I beg your prayers in this regard . . . . So thank you for the words you have sent. Once again through your prayers the word has been received in my heart through my wish to listen.[22]

When in 1971 Louf's project of retirement in order to lead the solitary life took shape, it was naturally to the Carthusian Order that he turned his eye. He spoke of the plan to the prior at Portes, who did not close the door but could foresee the plan's difficulty; he would especially have to deal with the resistance of Dom André Poisson, prior general at La Grande Chartreuse,[23] who did not look kindly on this tenor[24] of contemplative life joining an Order that preferred anonymity and discretion. Louf recorded Dom Poisson's views in his journal: "According to him an eventual entry into the Carthusian Order was absolutely problematic. The opposition to overcome on the part of the prior of La Grande Chartreuse would be very great, because I was a *persona non grata* for the Order, too well known already because of my commitments to

22. Letter to Dom Louf, ADMC, 26 August 1972.

23. Dom André Poisson was elected prior of La Grande Chartreuse in 1967. This office made him minister general of the Order, with the task of proceeding with the *aggiornamento* of Vatican II. He kept that charge until May 1997.

24. I.e., an operatic star.

monastic *aggiornamento*." But Louf still clung to his desire, encouraged by his spiritual father, who in July 1971 demanded a straight answer: "In a twenty-minute conversation that was slightly blunt, he launched me on the road to solitude. Without putting it off any longer I should start by acting in such a way as to get the community to espouse my project."[25]

In due course Louf communicated with the Cistercian abbot general, at the time Ignace Gillet, saying he wished to retire from his abbatial charge. Dom Gillet showed himself favorable to that decision. In September 1971 André made a retreat of postulation at the Carthusian house of Portes and completed it with new assurance. Heart-to-heart conversation with God was a center of gravity for him, his profound calling. As he wrote in his journal,

> Intimacy with Jesus, abiding in him, in his word, in his love. A free gift beyond all expectation, beyond all merit. The cell is still that Easter cenacle where the urgency and imminence of salvation invests everything. Nearly at the same time the face of La Chartreuse is revealed: a humble and simple life where everything is oriented towards prayer and quietness with God, a certain absolute without any other possible issue, but also with great equilibrium and sweetness, good feeling, good humor, and discretion. Doing everything with Jesus without counting, without too much foresight, without measuring the passing time, since it is Jesus' time that measures us.[26]

An important conversation with Dom Pierre Anquez, then prior of Portes, closed Louf's month's retreat. Louf wrote of his conversation with the prior,

25. Louf, JS, 15 July 1971.
26. Louf, JS, 21 Sept. 1971.

> It seemed to him that the experience I had during these weeks could lead me to envisage a retirement in order to devote myself more completely to prayer. He even invited me positively to take this path. As far as solitude is concerned (temporarily excluding La Chartreuse), it seemed to him that I could not only support it, but even make spiritual progress through it. "There are no major obstacles," he said. "You have all you need for it to bear fruit." That was for his part the *nihil obstat*. Solitude really seemed to him a good path for me, the white stone the Lord had prepared for me.[27]

Louf later said of this conversation, which had validated his vocation, "After this sojourn at Portes something irreversible had taken place. I felt that I was recognized as what I really am; my identity was final before God and before men."[28] The weeks and months that followed were difficult. His return to pastoral activity gave him the impression that he was estranged from his true being:

> Those weeks spent at La Chartreuse led me by the grace of God to live at a different level of my being. I received proof of it yesterday at the end of my conference on Mount Athos. I again felt myself completely externalized, outside of myself, with the physical impossibility of an immediate return. At Mont-des-Cats, without any doubt, I live continually on the surface of myself. Truly solitude, vigils, and fasting go deep inside the heart again, and God sweetly makes himself present in them. And I would do anything, put anything aside, sacrifice anything in order to preserve this secret life, this plant that is so fragile.[29]

27. Louf, JS, 30 Sept. 1971.
28. Louf, JS, 1 Jan. 1974.
29. Louf, JS, 27 Sept. 1971.

La Chartreuse had summed up all the sides of his person, which had seemed discordant up to that point: "A growing sense of the importance of the one thing necessary, toward which all my desires are now converging, and all my ambitions as well. This sense is now so clear that every other desire, even spiritual, outside of *hesychia*, has disappeared. All the rest seems burdensome to me."[30]

In March 1972, during the regular visitation at Mont-des-Cats, Louf rendered his gathered teaching into a perfume. A month later, thirsty for silence, he granted himself another retreat at Portes. "Silence," he wrote, "is God. There are silences that are so dense that babbling becomes infidelity, adultery, treason."[31] On his return to Mont-des-Cats he presided at a historical chapter on the morning of April 24. Since the abbey was rife with rumors about his retirement, he decided to put his cards on the table. "A rumor is spreading about me in the Order and even slightly inside this house already," he began at once. "This evening I would like to bring matters to a head and tell you exactly what is the case. What is this rumor? It is very simple. The father abbot of Mont-des-Cats is resigning and is going to be a hermit. Actually the rumor is not quite exact. However, as the saying goes, there is never smoke without a fire. So what is the case exactly?"[32] Then he entered into the heart of the matter: "Since I became abbot I have had to bear this attraction all alone. Since it has begun to occupy my attention excessively, it has become too heavy to carry alone." The moment seemed to have come for him to put aside his abbatial service, he announced to his brothers, explaining,

30. Louf, JS, 10 Dec. 1971.

31. Louf, JS, 23 April 1972.

32. The passages that follow here are taken from his report to the chapter at Mont-des-Cats, given on April 2, 1972. ADMC.

> From the first moments when I began to fulfill my charge, I always had the impression that it was a question of a temporary engagement, of a stage that someday or other would lead me toward a deeper solitude, which has always remained the object of my desire and my prayer. Every day I have requested it earnestly and humbly as a grace that is not at our disposal, but that one receives from the Lord when the Lord wills. Over about the past two years many signs seemed to indicate that the hour might be near. The hour to abandon the word, the activity, even the pen, quite simply to devote my time to the thing I esteem as most important, not only for every one of us and for the Order today, but especially for me personally: namely silent vigils and prayerful waiting for the Lord.

With that said, he continued, nothing had yet been done. "Because of the role I have been able to play inside and outside the Order," he says, "it will not be easy for me to find a situation that offers every guarantee of solitude." So before retiring in proper and legal form, he proposed to take a sabbatical year to allow the project to mature, for himself and for the community at the same time, since the community needed time to prepare itself for his departure. "It is necessary that we travel this end of the road together," he said, "until God makes his will absolutely clear. In order for me someday to arrange my departure peacefully, I need a concrete action on your part—let us say an agreement or a consent, or something else of that kind. If my project is to be successful, it cannot succeed without your aid."

A few days after holding this chapter, Dom André submitted his project to a vote of the community. He reaped a shower of yes votes. The abbot was exultant. "I sensed that I was fully in accord with my vocation, that it was for this purpose that I was born. My whole life as a solitary will have this very special coloration, since it is grafted on to my life as a pastor, since it is confirmed to it."[33] On June 15 he met with the abbot of Sept-Fons, Dominique du Ligondès, at the time the father immediate of Mont-des-Cats, to receive his support.

Identity Crisis

As often happened in Louf's career, though, just when all the signs were green, when the road was clear, uncertainty arose like a thick fog to impede his advance. When traveling to La Grande Chartreuse to request official entrance, when he was just a few meters away, he was suddenly overtaken by the shadow of doubt. Was he on the wrong road? "At the foot of La Grande Chartreuse," he wrote in June 1972, "for an hour or two I was in complete disarray, even physically; I had the impression of being mistaken and desired to run away and turn back."[34] The following day he had overcome this trial, but there was a cold setback, a clear refusal, "very gentle, but very firm by the reverend father of La Grande Chartreuse." With a sure sense of discernment, the abbot made André understand that if he did have a real vocation to solitary prayer, he also had an apostolic soul in him that would poorly accommodate the Carthusian charism, where the only valid apostolate was that of silence. Louf had just published his first book. "In the prior's eyes that was sufficient proof," he recalled. "A Carthusian must be careful to break with the world completely, to the point of agreeing to be altogether 'useless.' Well, writing a book was still a means of presence to the world and of hope to be useful to it."[35]

In fact Louf was not and would never be a hermit according to the traditional image that the word conveys. "He would have been a good Maurist of the seventeenth century, leading

33. Louf, JS, 9 June 1972.
34. Louf, JS, 17 June 1972.
35. André Louf, *À la grâce de Dieu*, 92.

a life of prayer joined to a life of erudition," reflected a brother who knew him well.[36] "Despite an undeniable calling to solitary prayer," corroborates Nathalie Nabert, "he also had an apostolic charisma through writing, which could not have been exercised at La Chartreuse. In a certain way we can be relieved, because it would have been a loss for the world to be deprived of his books, which have been infinitely serviceable to so many people and to the church."[37]

In the meantime Louf was completely out of sorts. He had banked everything on this departure. "What can I do now?" he asked himself. "My attraction for solitary life was certainly linked to the Carthusian formula and to the admirable equilibrium it proposes. Lord Jesus, there is so little light at the moment, and I am again the prey of all hesitations. Make your will shine out."[38]

On June 30 Louf left Mont-des-Cats to seek isolation among the Camaldolese of Frascati and to work on the French translation of his book. First having been published in Dutch in 1971, the book then came out in 1972 in French—as *Seigneur, apprends-nous à prier*.[39] The novices at Mont-des-Cats talk about the book among themselves as "the little red book," because of the reddish-orange color of the cover.[40] In his journal at the time Louf addressed the recent events: "There is no bitterness in my heart. There is relief, surprise, and anxiety at the same time. There is also a little identity crisis: Who am I? What do you want of me, O Lord?"[41] More and more seriously he thought of looking for a solitary place "where a very small colony could gather with a firm decision

36. Denis Cazes, in conversation with the author.
37. Nathalie Nabert, in conversation with the author.
38. Louf, JS, 18 June 1972.
39. Brussels, Foyer Notre-Dame, 1972.
40. Marc-André Di Péa, in conversation with the author.
41. Louf, JS, 30 June 1972.

to put down roots and remain in a quiet state with God."[42] He even went so far as to describe the project concretely as a laura:

> An annex-house of the semi-eremitic type, profiting at the same time from the Camaldolese and the Carthusian traditions; open only to cenobites who were already experienced; emphasis placed on the cell and on reclusion; no heavy work for those living in cells; as a general rule no guests; nor should there be temporary or passing hermits; the one admitted must intend a stable effort; conventual Mass rare, but normally no Mass said in the cell; once arrived at the isle, no one ever leaves it except in the case of a serious necessity; there are two communities: those living in cells, whether priests or brothers, and those around the church, even priests; the latter more for serving and for external contacts. The one responsible is one of those living in cells.[43]

Louf had the impression that his best gift was solitude. That is why he asked himself, should he after all envisage a prolonged abbatial tenure? Should he make a foundation of hermits and assume their leadership? Should he try his chances at La Chartreuse on some future occasion? He had no idea. "Perhaps at the moment there is no choice to be made between Cîteaux and La Chartreuse," he concludes, "and what I should do is keep on living with this ambiguous identity: I am now a Cistercian abbot who would have wanted to be a Carthusian and who does not find himself anymore except at La Chartreuse."[44]

42. Louf, JS, 10 Sept. 1972.
43. Louf, JS, 15 Sept. 1972.
44. Louf, JS, 9 August 1972.

"The Future is a Cloud"

The following weeks did not allay the disorder of Louf's mind; he was not reconciled with the trial. Its meaning escaped him, and he stumbled against a future that seemed opaque, without perspective. "Wherever I turn," he wrote, "the future is improbable. I stay there projectless and surrounded by forbidden meanings. I weep, O Lord, because I have become unfit for the doors of La Chartreuse."[45] "To know no longer, to pretend no longer"—he returns to the heart of his trial—"to let myself simply alone with events. I have a foolish need to be quiet, to stop, to place myself in deep silence in Jesus. At certain times I want to cry about my sufferings and about the contradiction in which I find myself."[46] A few weeks later the same bell resounds: "Lord Jesus, I unceasingly bump into this refusal, this confrontation with La Chartreuse, and I try again to pack up. And I am ashamed that I do not understand. I do not understand this annoyance I have with the Cistercian life, nor this persistent attraction for solitary life. The mere idea of La Chartreuse fills me with devotion and fervor."[47]

Soon a new source of perplexity was added to the sorrowful feeling of living outside of his own truth. Just as in 1962, when he had been mentally divided between the call to lead a solitary life and the desire to shine by his pastoral activity, he was feeling a new attachment for the abbatial charge. With his chronic indecisiveness, his inability to follow a clear direction also returned, an inability that had already appeared during his solemn profession in 1954, and when he wanted to leave the Order in 1962 to join the Camaldolese. He himself made the connection between the two periods: "I re-read some

45. Louf, JS, 25 Dec. 1972.
46. Louf, JS, 17 May 1972.
47. Louf, JS, 31 August 1973.

passages of this diary, written in 1960–1962. The similarity of that situation is upsetting: the same strong beating attraction for solitude, and yet the intense difficulty of detachment from the 'role' that I then played in editing *Collectanea.*"[48] "Which only goes to say: that is how I am built, and I must learn to live with my weaknesses," he confesses. "After having chosen white, I will be tempted to go back to black. My choice should have some place partly outside of this psychological pull, which is almost congenital. It should not be affected by these doubts and these anxieties, these desires and regrets."[49]

Later Louf would talk about "psychological knots," which instigate a kind of "ambivalence about any decision, a difficulty in choosing peacefully and without remorse."[50] The same scenario recurred in 1979, when there was a possibility of his being nominated archbishop of Malines-Brussels. In June 1979 the abbot general informed him that he was being discussed at Rome in that regard. On June 13 Louf noted, "The noises concerning me on the subject of the archbishop of Malines are now being freely heard in Belgium, Paris, and Rome." On the 14th he learned that the nunciature of Brussels was making inquiries about him among the Belgian Cistercian abbots. Then followed long weeks when talk kept going and coming, sometimes putting him in the key position and sometimes removing him. He observed with astonishment the repetition of the same patterns: "Curious parallel with my 'eremitical vocation' of seven years ago. I have the impression of being called elsewhere, and all the internal sacrifices have been made, but the Lord finally intervenes to tell me that there need be no change. It is so good to be doing his will, as good as being a hermit, or archbishop of Malines,

48. Louf, JS, 14 March 1973.
49. Louf, JS, 26 Sept. 1971.
50. Louf, JS, 26 Sept. 1971.

or simply abbot of Mont-des-Cats. These are always miracles of the Lord!"[51]

On November 22 an article in *Paris Match* announced his nomination, but in December it was learned that Msgr. Godfried Danneels had been appointed. Such episodes multiplied, forcing Louf to live in the present and abandon himself to God's will: "Fortunately you did not ask me to choose: abbot, bishop, or solitary. I would not have been able to choose. You have chosen for me, and I bless your hand and your choice.[52]

Despite his lack of clarity, Louf was sustained by naked faith. "The future is cloudy," he wrote. "I let it cover me, with only this certitude: God is within, and he is ready to bring about a sign, a marvel that exceeds anything I could have hoped for."[53] Confident that the Lord was at work but hidden, during this unsettled period Louf abdicated mastery over his own future and abandoned himself to the present moment. He comforted himself by saying that whatever happened, his vocation would be realized in heaven: "It seems to me that the Lord has really destined me for a heavenly life, so to speak, at La Chartreuse, in other words as a full recluse in this great look of love toward him. This thought calms me. I know what is going on in my deepest being. Its sole expectation is that I must be the abbot of a Cistercian community as long as the Lord wills it. But there is still all eternity to realize my Carthusian grace little by little."[54]

Louf's attraction to the figure of Benoît-Joseph Labre[55] became clear in the light of these episodes: "It seems to me," Louf writes in his diary, "that all the saints would be wrong if the Lord had asked them to sketch out for themselves the

51. Louf, JS, 9 Nov. 1979.

52. Louf, JS, 14 Dec. 1981.

53. Louf, JS, 13 April 1973.

54. Louf, JS, 1 Jan. 1974.

55. An eighteenth-century French Franciscan tertiary, beatified in 1860.

role they would play in the church. From deprivation to deprivation God led them by the most unforeseen ways to get them to do his own work. It is necessary for me to be treated the same way, as well for my monastic activity as for my eremitical vocation."[56] It is that poverty that touched him in the itinerary of Labre, the vagabond beggar. Writing of Labre in what sounds like a self-portrait, Louf observed that Labre is always depicted as a marcher on a road that seems to have no beginning and no end. But Labre did not himself choose the road. At the start of the trajectory he was searching for a monastery where he could find shelter for his desired penitential and prayerful life, to make his search for God concrete. "At first he did not know," Louf continued, "that this road was taking him nowhere, and that even if every day conveyed him from place to place and from sanctuary to sanctuary, the road was on the point of turning into a dead end. His true vocation would not be to end up at any place, but to stay on the road, or what amounts to the same thing—to stay at rest at the dead end. It is the dead end of a road that cannot end here below, and that leads nowhere else but to God, without any detour." As for the question of Labre's deprivation, what is often emphasized is the physical ruggedness of his road, his poverty, lack of hygiene, the mockery he endured. "All that is true," Louf writes, "but of little significance compared with that other despoilment that is much deeper: knowing that the road leads nowhere, and that his vocation consisted in not having a country in view, being always on the road, on a quest for something else, on a quest for someone, whom he will only find at the edge of this endless road, at the very heart of the dead end."[57]

56. Louf, JS, 22 April 1962.

57. André Louf, "Prière et contemplation: le chemin de Benoît Labre," conférence donnée à Amettes, ADMC, 31 August 1983.

CHAPTER 13

A Hesychast Abbot

Louf was yet to become the person now known: the great Cistercian abbot, the oracle of the Trappists, the spiritual master—with this secret aspect: the person with no place in this active life, who lived far from his "deep identity."[1] After the refusal of La Chartreuse in 1972, and until his retirement in 1997, he kept to himself that desire of solitude for God that burned in his heart and haunted his life. No one who heard him speak in chapter at Mont-des-Cats, or deliver his viewpoint on the reforms that were being made in the Order's structures, or even illuminate the stages of Christian being in the conferences that drew a public ever more numerous—none could imagine what this great shepherd suffered, or that he had only one longing in his deepest self: to leave behind all public fame and to flee to reclusion in a hermitage, living there in sweet intimacy with Jesus.

Living beside Himself

"My concrete life with its many cares and distractions," Louf wrote, "has become in a way insupportable."[2] People

1. André Louf, Presentation to the chapter of Mont-des-Cats, ADMC, 24 April 1972.

2. André Louf, *Journal Spirituel* [hereafter JS], 21 August 1971.

came to consult him from all over. His books were translated into every language. But he aspired to be unencumbered, living in simplicity, and he suffered from being out of place: "My particular grace is not, despite appearances, one of activity and renown. It is the weight of love that makes me sink in the deep life of God; it is a grace of prayer that makes me whisper in my heart in spite of myself; it is Jesus' face haunting me and dwelling in me, in whose shadow I would love to stay unceasingly."[3] He was persuaded that solitude, solitude alone, was the key that opened the door of his real personality. "Lord Jesus, what can I do to live always on that level? Four full days of complete solitude would be necessary . . . and my life as abbot is what it is: running with utmost urgency, knowing that I will always be insufficient for the task. It is not to do more than you ask, but to do it at a deeper level, drawing from a source to which I do not have habitual access."[4] At bottom he had the impression that he was not himself, that he was not living his deepest life. Like a knife in a wound, every new retreat caused the wound to reopen:

> Yesterday I wept at the thought that I have to return to this Cistercian milieu when I feel that I am so much in accord with La Chartreuse. And at the same time you know to what extent I am happy and pleased to be abbot in Jesus' service, whom I love, and in the service of an Order with which I sense myself thoroughly identified. And there is also at times a temptation to pastoral life and to bear witness to your word. Who am I? What is my identity? Perhaps it is only belonging to you and being deeply available for your perfect will: *Christo quietus*.[5]

3. Louf, JS, 7 June 1975.
4. Louf, JS, 26 March 1976.
5. Louf, JS, 18 Dec. 1981.

Months and years passed, but the pain, mixed with incomprehension, remained just as keen. Why had the Lord let him feel such a desire for solitary life but at the same time kept him from realizing it? Louf tired himself out trying to decipher this mystery. During a retreat at Portes he considered it in his journal:

> To peacefully settle down in solitude. To reach the bottom of my heart by the kindness of this silence. To experience something of the Father who attracts and of the Spirit who urges me. To remain there. I still keep living with that "unreality" of a vocation hesychastic and eremitical. It is only by love that the enigma of this double vocation will someday be solved. I am at my place here at Portes and there at Mont-des-Cats at the same time.[6]

And a few days later: "Lord, you have given me the grace to experience a little bit of what hesychasm is, and at the same time you ask me not to live that way, but to remain with the cares that are its exact contraries. I must accept it as your will, as the design of love. I must not be surprised at this functional ambiguity of my being, of my vocation."[7]

Louf kept in his journal an excerpt of a book by the founder of the Spiritans, Fr. Francis Libermann, in which Libermann developed the idea that certain vocations, even if they come from God and are useful for the soul's progress, are not meant to be fulfilled as vocations. In his journal Louf considered that view:

> Père Libermann realized that, under the influence of grace, desires awake in us that should not be fulfilled. Nevertheless, those desires that would remain in God's

6. Louf, JS, 19 Jan. 1975.
7. Louf, JS, 23 Jan. 1975.

> intention on the level of desires have a salvific efficacy. Their purpose is to maintain fervor in the soul. Their truth lies not in their fulfillment, but in the psychological state they create. Such was the case with the Curé of Ars who desired to enter La Trappe; his desire did not correspond with his vocation, but it was a sign of the depth of his union with God and an expression of his wish to make reparation. Saint Thérèse of the Child Jesus desired the life of a missionary—a desire that would never be fulfilled; she was inspired with this desire in order to deepen her ecclesial experience and to reveal to other people the apostolic function of contemplation. It is then a question of false vocations that serve real ones.

This position is clearly how Louf ended up envisaging his impossible eremitical vocation, as a horizon that maintained the flame of his fervor, establishing his life on the axis of his profound desire.

"Blessed reclusion with you"

Louf learned to walk in the night of this incomprehensible situation. Grasping God's hand, for which he had groped in the darkness, he pursued his pastoral service day after day with a faith that was more and more naked. If his dream was broken into a thousand pieces, he thought, it was so that the Lord might express his own through Louf's, that God might loose all his creative power in the poor life of his abbot: "To agree, O Lord, to be your work, to be only your work, the work you are patiently constructing with the ruins of the masterpieces of our dreams. Whatever is left of these ruins in our lives, we can only have trust that it is you who are at work!"[8] Since he could not become the hermit he wanted to

8. Louf, JS, 16 June 1977.

be, Louf felt called to live his abbatial service differently, entirely given up to the divine will in a way that was "poorer and more solitary."[9] In order to be this "hesychast abbot,"[10] he arrived at some new resolutions: changing his lifestyle, devoting more time to prayer and to *lectio* of Scripture and of the monastic fathers, arranging for himself a quieter rhythm with large intervals of solitude. With the support of grace he strove in this way to exercise his pastoral service in connection with his interior life, always recollected in that life: "To try to live from *quies* in an interior cell from which nothing should go out or be external. It is done with the presence of Jesus, the presence of his sweetness and of his cross, with complete abandonment to his will, so that he may renew his marvels. To meet everyone and all possible contradictions together with all eventual responsibilities from that interior cell, *Christo quietus*."[11]

To recover his interior breath, the abbot also formed the habit of claiming ten days every five or six months for himself at La Chartreuse, usually at Portes. It was in the course of these retreats secured from the excitement of his active life that he wrote the finest pages of his journal on union with God in solitary life. For example, in 1977, addressing God, he wrote while at La Chartreuse de Portes,

> Blessed reclusion with you. Blessed headache that obliges me to be with you in a different way from thinking about you. You fill me like this silence that I breathe in. Solitude has its own value that belongs to it alone. It reduces, it quiets, and it brings back. It also exposes us to love, and at the same time to all our weaknesses. Its fruit is not striking or upsetting, but it is secret and deep,

9. Louf, JS, 2 June 1973.
10. Louf, JS, 2 June 1972.
11. Louf, JS, 2 June 1972.

> often unknown to us. It is not without evildoing or without frightening. But those are the conditions of espousals: I will lead her out to the desert, and there I will speak to her heart. Embrace solitude or embrace Jesus? Marry solitude or marry Jesus? For a certain quality of solitude perhaps they amount to the same thing, solitude has to such an extent been marked by Jesus and filled by the Spirit.[12]

Ten years later he was again at Portes:

> In the peace and action of grace. Nothing sensational except intimate joy, albeit very discreet, to be with Jesus, captivated by him, his own captive. There is nothing else to be or to do. My impression is that it might continue endlessly in order to emerge in his presence and eternal vision. Such should be the vocation of certain people at the heart of the church. Since this solitude has only you for its breath, I wish never to breathe any air but you, your sweetness, your perfume, and the sweet, soft unction of your Spirit. So to wait, detached from everything, so you can accomplish your whole desire in me.[13]

These paragraphs reveal Louf's deepest self, the secret identity of this active, beaming abbot, his insatiable quest for *hesychia*, for that interior silence where Christ is revealed. In his spiritual journal Louf often makes use of the formula invented by Saint Bruno to describe the orientation of the hermit's heart: *Christo quietus*, silence oriented toward Christ.[14] For want of the ability to honor the term *quietist*, ambiguous because of the quarrel between François Fénelon and Jacques-Benigne Bossuet, Louf chose *hesychast*, a fruit of the Byzantine

12. Louf, JS, 13–14 Sept. 1977.
13. Louf, JS, 20 March 1988.
14. André Louf, "Saint Bruno," *Documents épiscopat* no. 12–13 (2001): 5.

tradition, to describe the interior experience to which he felt profoundly called: the solitary search for peaceful repose in God, for a form of idleness through unceasing prayer.[15]

Among the diversity of monastic vocations, the hesychast is distinguished by intense interior activity joined to a precise exterior framework—a place of retirement:

> At the side of hesychast monks who went out to the desert, there have always been city-dwelling monks living in the towns, educated monks more devoted to sacred studies, monks more particularly attached to the person of a bishop; they might be called "cathedral monks"; later on in the West they would be called "canons." And don't forget the impressive cohorts of missionary monks in both East and West. It is obvious that the monastic sweep is broad, and the hesychasts represent only a small curve, certainly minor, but they have always existed, and they continue to exist today. In the East they are called "hesychasts," in the West "contemplatives."[16]

Lovers of Beauty

Louf also searched for this silence with Christ through beauty. It is necessary to say that he had a consuming passion for art. In the archives of the abbey there is a dossier containing letters he wrote to Parisians who owned art galleries and to antiquarians all over the world, seeking to authenticate an icon or to solicit advice on a recently acquired painting. He had the abbey subscribe to two antiquarian reviews and was known as "the white wolf" in the area of art galleries near the Seine in Paris. His quick eye for pictures, his ability to

15. Louf, "Saint Bruno," 13.

16. André Louf, "Quelques constantes spirituelles dans les traditions hésychastes en Orient et en Occident," *Irenikon* 74 (2001): 485.

uncover mastery of technique in various painters, won him the esteem of those specialists who recognized his expertise, especially on the subject of primitive Flemish art.

During Louf's abbatial tenure the cloister walls at Mont-des-Cats were adorned with masterpieces and covered with beauty.[17] Outside of his refined taste, what surprises us in the canvases acquired at his initiative is that they all depict countenances that are very kind, with peaceful traits, interior, radiant with serenity and a kind of simple majesty. They are paintings that rest the eye, pacify the spirit, and release a quiet feeling. All this shows that behind his interest in painting and art in general, his quest for *hesychia* spurred him on.[18]

Louf employed museum-quality art to make it serve the life of prayer, the life of the church, and the life of faith. For him canvases were aids for meeting Christ and visible supports of his presence: "I suffer no wrong from representations of Christ that help me to find him. Such are the Russian icons, but also Western works of art. How great is Christ: this Flemish Christ," he explained in a documentary that features a visit to his hermitage.[19] When he started to use icons in the liturgy of Mont-des-Cats, it aroused the criticism of certain brothers who found it not in conformity with the Western tradition. Behind the altar of the abbatial church he had Josse Van Cleve's *Salvator Mundi* installed, admiring its kind face and its beauty of execution. When he performed the censing of this masterpiece during the Office, the brothers whispered among themselves to tease him, "He is censing his passions."[20]

17. Today certain works acquired during his abbatial tenure are deposited in the Museum of Art and History of Cassel, Flanders (Belgium). A great many of the icons are still used in the liturgy.

18. Dom Jacques De Lesalle, Homily for the funeral of Dom Louf.

19. *Paroles d'ermite*. Father André Louf, documentary, CFRT/KTO Sunset Presse, 52 minutes, produced by Laurence Chartier, 2009.

20. Dom Marc-André Di Péa, conversation with the author.

Louf's collecting side sometimes became a cause of discord in the community. Certain brothers saw this intrusion of art, paintings, icons, and especially contemporary images into the abbey critically; these works, they said, detracted from the Cistercian tradition of simplicity. Louf took this criticism seriously, devoting an article to it that is also a defensive plea *pro domo*. In it he shows that in Saint Bernard's eyes images were a way of meeting God, that Bernard never objected to a holy image. In fact, he said, Bernard allowed their veneration and wanted them respected, the only condition being that their form be sober and discreet, kept to what was essential.[21]

Other brothers stigmatized Louf's taste in art as a worldly passion, a kind of relaxation or pleasure apart from the spiritual life. But for Louf beauty was never an addition to his search; it was central. In his infancy at Bruges he had been surrounded by masterpieces, which awakened in him a kind of nostalgia or desire for beauty. In another context, he reflected on this fact:

> The beauty that we find in an icon is of the order of presentiment. It causes a desire to arise in us for our long-lost homeland, the country that we long for, that we have never seen. In this sense the icon plucks us away from the present time, and it projects us toward a future that still escapes us, except when beauty allows us to have a presentiment of it. But beauty is also a daughter of remembrance. There are memories of splendor and of happiness that belonged to the primeval paradise, deep memories buried in our hearts, that the icon manages to awaken for a brief moment, to slip out in a way.[22]

21. André Louf, "Saint Bernard, fut-il iconoclaste?" in *Saint Bernard et la recherche de Dieu* (Toulouse: Institut catholique de Toulouse, 1992), 64.

22. André Louf, Introduction to *Cherche Dieu et son coeur revivra: Hildegarde Michaelis, 1900–1982* (Paris: Cerf, 2006), 19.

These sentiments were sown in his heart when he was still very young, and they urged him all his life to seek absolute beauty hidden beneath the ephemeral beauty of art, to predict the splendor of Jesus, "the most handsome of the sons of men" (Ps 45:2), beneath every work of art. Animated by this "throbbing nostalgia of God's beauty," Louf tracked down its traces and flashes everywhere, convinced that "wherever Jesus passed he left behind objects covered with beauty."[23] It is certainly no accident that Enzo Bianchi called Louf a "tenacious searcher for beauty."[24] Louf ended his life at the Abbey of Sainte-Lioba, surrounded by love of wisdom, by works, and by monks and nuns who were artists and artisans, in whose journeys toward God art had an important place.

In addition to painting, music also played an important role in Louf's life. Every night at around 11 o'clock, when the Abbey of Mont-des-Cats was fast asleep, he filled the vaults of the church with organ harmonies. According to him the organ was much more than a support for prayer. Organ chant was "a revelation of God in sound. God speaks through harmony, in its tones and in the subtle inflection of its intensity."[25]

What then is art? A manifestation of God, a revelation of his beauty. Louf was convinced that the Lord speaks to humans through paintings and through sonatas, and that frequent exposure to the Lord's masterpieces allows us to know him. In the course of a retreat, he wrote, "An important grace of your radiant countenance in an icon. A growing presence that sweetly masters me. Color, form, and line speak to me

23. André Louf, Homily for Christmas, ADMC, 1977.

24. Quoted from Alessandro Saraco, *La Grâce dans la faiblesse,* trans. Jean Perez (Nouan-le-Fuzelier: Éditions des Béatitudes, 2013): "Enzo Bianchi définissait André Louf comme 'un homme sans frontières, chercheur tenace de la Beauté et de ses reflets dans la réalité.' "

25. André Louf, Homily for the benediction of the organ, ADMC, 13 May 1990.

about your sweetness and your love, and they are for me an inexhaustible source of joy. Beauty is a daughter of your love!"[26] Having discovered the religious inspiration of Western art thanks to a detour through Oriental iconography, he exclaimed, "It is great joy to come into contact with the full Christian iconographic tradition: especially the Western half. It is a constant revelation of your face for anyone who knows how to look with faith. It is a treasure of Jesus always at our disposal. To remain tenderly in the joy of your countenance here below while waiting for the full revelation of your splendor in the hereafter: the glory of God in the face of Christ."[27]

Privately, Louf wrote similarly about the power of iconography: "I have been deeply touched by Oriental iconography, to the extent that at a certain moment, I even started to consider that only the Easterners succeeded in carrying over into their sacred images a veritable religious spirit. In fact, the frequent viewing of Russian icons allowed me to rediscover along the way the religious inspiration that always quickened Western religious art."[28] In the same way, it was thanks to his interest in Oriental hesychasm that he slowly rediscovered the treasures of Western mysticism, especially the spirituality of Ruusbroec.

In every voyage Louf, thirsty for beauty, interposed an unplanned stop to see a monument, contemplate a picture, or discover a masterpiece. His letters to the community are adorned with the works of art about which he writes. For example, he reports during a stop in Belgium,

> The cathedral of Gand has a reredos, "Mystical Lamb," by Van Eyck. At the cathedral of Anvers there is the "Taking down from the Cross," by Rubens. They are two

26. Louf, JS, 10 Dec. 1976.
27. Louf, JS, 28 April 1979.
28. Louf, *À la grâce de Dieu*, 170.

> different worlds, as different as they can be: on the one hand the splendor and interiority of late Gothic, and on the other the shining exuberance and splash of Counter-Reformation Baroque. But in both cases, attempts that resemble each other—two attempts to render transparent on earth something of God's beauty.[29]

During another voyage he stopped at the house of the painter Michel Ciry, some of whose canvases still decorate the abbey. He reveals his love for art in the story of this visit at his workshop:

> The painter settled us in armchairs prepared in advance for the meeting. Yes indeed, it was a meeting, and unforgettable. Michel stood at an easel in front of us, and he set up about thirty of his latest canvases. He announced their titles briefly: a disciple at Emmaus, a dormition, a visitation, some *mater dolorosas*, a country pastor in Bernanos's sense, a doubting Thomas, a prodigal son, some harlequins, and some souvenirs of a recent trip to Mexico. It was an extremely packed moment. In beauty we touch a divine reality. And what can we say other than express our astonishment, detailed by infinite reverence, about Elizabeth with two shaking hands holding the swollen belly of her cousin Mary? Both of them are humbled by the event that God has just accomplished. We silently behold it.[30]

Louf's bewilderment evokes that of a child finding his Christmas presents underneath the tree. His enchantment was repeated in 1985 when a general chapter was held in Spain at the Monastery of El Escorial, near Madrid. He forced himself to get away from it for a little while. His truancy led

29. André Louf, Letter to the community, ADMC, 16 August 1982.
30. André Louf, Letter to the community, 5 June 1979.

him to the Prado Museum in Madrid, along with some other monks and nuns. "For me they were emotional hours," he wrote in a passage where his fascination with beauty shines more brightly than ever:

> As long as color reproductions exist, we can trace from them a history of art, but how emotional it is to find such works in flesh and bone! We recognize them immediately, as if they were old friends. The Prado Museum is one of the richest and most complete in the world. All the Flemish, Italian, and Spanish painters are represented. I will spend hours in front of Christ and the Virgin by the Flemish masters, Jean Van Eyck, Rogier Van Der Weyden, Girard David, Quentin Metsys, Adrien Isenbrandt, and so many others. But what has surprised me more this time has been the Spanish religious painters from the second half of the sixteenth century through the whole seventeenth century. If there has ever been real religious painting after the primitive ones of every country, it is surely there that it should be sought. Simplicity of form, solemn sobriety of color, subtle equilibrium, but peaceful and even severe, between light and shadow: all these elements succeed in creating an environment of depth and interiority that is unforgettable.
>
> Monastic themes abound. Saint Jerome has an intense stare: his cardinal red is completely stunning; Saint Anthony and Saint Paul of the Desert, penitent Magdalenes, lactations of Saint Bernard. There is the unforgettable Christ descending from the cross to embrace Saint Bernard, the work of Ribalta. That name is among the best ones. Others are Murillo, Zurbaran, Ribera, Cano, Morales, Velasquez especially great among the great ones. Three hours are hardly enough to walk among the splendid ones. A sister told me, 'I cannot believe God will destroy all this beauty at the end of the world. But if he does, it will be because he alone infinitely surpasses all his attributes that art has been able to represent. It is

certain that we will have absolutely nothing to regret. And we will never stop thanking him for every reflection of his beauty that he has granted us to have a presentiment of here below."[31]

The Company of Saints

For accompaniment in his quest for *hesychia* Louf was also surrounded by the best of guides: spiritual ones—the saints. The authors from whom he found honey were not chosen randomly. Pearls of Syriac thought (Isaac of Nineveh and Symeon of Taibouteh) or of Flemish mysticism (Ruusbroec): all were masters of interior life who exerted a kind of spiritual paternity on him, marking out for him the road to his deepest heart.

For Louf the saints were elders in the faith. They had already traveled that road, and from beyond the tomb they revealed the risks and the direction. That is how, for example, he speaks about Ruusbroec: "I am glad to have the friendship of Ruusbroec the admirable, the dazzling—He teaches me to live in mysterious proximity with that extraordinary life that is already mine and will be mine, as if it were there quite near and ready to hand, behind a curtain hardly opaque, so that one has only to pull a cord for the curtain to open."[32] In another testimony he goes further: "It is part and parcel of these authors that on the long haul they become real fellow travelers and friends. I have had frequent recourse to their writings for nearly fifteen years already, and that has allowed me to recognize my spiritual aspirations better, and to persevere in tending toward the object of my desires without losing patience. The mystics attract us, because they tell us about something of which we have an obscure presentiment at the

31. André Louf, Letter to the community, 11 May 1985.
32. Louf, JS, 20 March 1988.

very root of our being."[33] Elsewhere he talks about Saint Nil Sorskii as his "invisible staretz,"[34] and he qualifies Isaac of Nineveh as "prince of solitude, of humble charity, and of interior prayer,"[35] who guides him to "the higher stages of spiritual experience."[36] At the end of his life, at his hermitage at Simiane, he said of Isaac, "He wrote for hermits, and I have learned much from him."[37]

Louf felt that he was close to the saints, that they populated his solitude, helped him to live, stirred his ardor, and kept him fixed on the point: to see and know God. Like humble signals in the night, they lit his road. They were for him like icons of Christ, "very much like" Jesus, as the Russians painted them, and especially like the meekness and humility of the heart of the Son of God. They were meek and humble of heart, along with all the chroniclers of the interior life who teach the ways of prayer—the Flemish and the Syrians, but also Elizabeth of the Trinity, and even Etty Hillesum[38]—those are the saints with whom Louf felt immediate partnership, the poor in spirit, the little ones, those with a transparent heart, grounded in the mercy of God. Among them of course went his preference for Saint Bernard and little Thérèse.

The love for the figure of Saint Bernard on Louf's part is certain. Louf had to identify himself with Bernard. Most of

33. Louf, *À la grâce de Dieu*, 155.

34. Louf, JS, 11 June 1961. Saint Nil Sorskii was a Russian Orthodox monk (?1433–May 7, 1508) venerated as a saint by the Russian Orthodox Church.

35. André Louf, "Le pardon," unedited chapter talk at Mont-des-Cats, ADMC, 11 Feb. 1970.

36. André Louf, "Temha-Stupore et tahra-maraviglia negli scritti di Isacco il Siro," in *La Grande Stagione della Mistica Siro-Orientale (VI–VIII secolo),* ed. Emilio Vergani and Sabino Chialà (Milano: Centro Ambrosiano, 2009), 93–119.

37. André Louf, Letter to a Dutch friend, ADMC, 26 May 2006.

38. He later wrote a preface for the book introducing her life: Frère Michael Davide, *En Carême avec Etty Hillesum: Itinéraire en quarante Étapes* (Paris: Salvator, 2016).

the portraits he wrote of Bernard reveal a similarity between their trajectories and their personalities. The two men shared certain traits of character, such as ascendancy over others connected to a personal charisma and a gift for dispensing the word, a great sense of psychology, the absence of a taste for practical matters, and a diffuse affectivity. Their spiritualities are quite close, with an emphasis placed on God's mercy, as are their *curricula vitae*, as both were elected abbot while still young. Their vocational urges were also similar: in each case the taste for contemplative silence pulled against an attraction to pastoral service that their great fame in the church also inclined them to. They both conceived the abbatial charge in such a way that their pastoral teaching rested on their own experience of faith.

Many of Louf's articles on Bernard can also be read as self-portraits.[39] In an article that has been misconstrued, he also tried to trace a bold parallel between the abbot of Clairvaux and Thérèse, the Carmelite of Lisieux, playing on their common insistence on weakness as a way to God. "Today," he writes, "while being a Cistercian and glad of it, I am not far from considering myself a spiritual son of both Saint Bernard of Clairvaux and Thérèse of Lisieux."[40] These two figures express the heart of Louf's spirituality, which is also that of Jesus' message: "I have come not for the righteous, but for sinners" (Matt 9:13). Also, "unless you become like little children, you will not enter the kingdom" (Matt 18:3).

Finally, why not mention Saint Benôit-Joseph Labre, for whom Louf also kept an invisible tenderness? In a homily he spoke of him "as a beloved brother" and added, "We admire

39. For example, André Louf, "Bernard, abbé," in *Bernard de Clairvaux: Histoire, mentalités, spiritualité*, Sources Chrétiennes 380 (Paris: Cerf, 1992), 349–79.

40. André Louf, "Saint Bernard et sainte Thérèse de Lisieux," *Carmel* 3 (1997): 4.

him, and sometimes we even end up envying him a little."[41] Neither should we forget the "patriotic" reasons for this love. Like Louf, Labre was originally from the north, and Louf often went on pilgrimage to that area, which was near the home of his paternal grandfather. Doubtless he was acknowledging his vagabond side, carried on the roads of this life like a leaf blown by the wind. But it was above all the impossible vocation of this vagabond of God, condemned to the abasement of perpetual instability, that he acknowledged in himself: "From one monastery to another, from La Trappe to La Chartreuse, and from La Chartreuse to La Trappe," he said in a passage that could also be applied to himself, "he obstinately searched for that abasement that would lead him to God.

"He searched in vain, however, because this poverty was nowhere to be found, and yet it was everywhere. But he never found it in a stable way during his lifetime, because that abasement was in the search itself and in instability, but above all in the fact that, among all those devoted to God, he was properly unable to be classified. On the side of that abasement, his material poverty undoubtedly counted for little."[42]

41. André Louf, Homily for Saint Benoît-Joseph Labre, 1981.
42. Louf, Homily for Saint Benoît-Joseph Labre.

CHAPTER 14

Toward the One Undivided Church

July 1961. A young Orthodox Romanian monk unknown to the host was staying at the guest house at Mont-des-Cats for a week. His name was André Scrima, and he had requested permission to sojourn there and to share the Divine Office and the common table. At that epoch the act of receiving an Orthodox monk for such a stay was quite bold. So the abbot, Dom Achille, had previously armed himself with all the necessary authorizations before leaving the monastery. "Our father abbot of holy memory was away at the time of the Orthodox monk's visit," Louf confirmed. "He was slightly timorous and excessively prudent, and he would hardly have been eager to grant him a larger audience."[1] But that was not the case with his prior, who was more intrepid, and who profited from the superior's absence to invite this monk, whose mild disposition, accent, and bookish French covered up a crazy charm, to make a speech before the community gathered in the chapter room. The Romanian monk was expected to

1. André Louf, "En marge d'un pèlerinage," *Collectanea Cisterciensia* 1 (1970): 44–46; repr. in *À l'école de la contemplation* (Paris: Lethielleux, 2004), 121.

speak once, but his presence was so edifying that he spoke again for the whole week.[2]

Father Scrima and the Shock of Unity

Father Scrima was an engaging personality and very original. Born in Transylvania in 1925 to a family of intellectuals, he was brilliant and accomplished in all branches of knowledge. At Bucharest he had studied not only philosophy and theology, but also the mathematical and physical sciences. After 1944, in Stalinist Rumania, a great spiritual leader, John the Stranger, had begun to acquire fame; he was a bearer of the spirit of Optina Poustyne, a famous Russian monastery that had been a source of a spiritual renaissance in the nineteenth century. At the same time, a group of intellectuals discreetly gathered, calling themselves "the Burning Bush." From that movement a formidable renewal was born, concerned to have Orthodoxy return to their roots, to hesychasm and to prayer of the heart.[3] André Scrima was a member of this group.

After Scrima was appointed librarian at the patriarchate of Bucharest, he met the Indian minister of culture there, who was fascinated by Scrima's encyclopedic knowledge of Hindu spirituality. He proposed to him an exchange study at Benares, where Scrima could sketch out a dialogue between Christianity and Hinduism, with hesychasm as a start. On his return from India in 1959, Scrima found it impossible to return to Romania, which was by then caught in the Communist vise. Instead he found a place in Lebanon where he became the spiritual father of a monastery.

2. Daniel Curely, conversation with the author.

3. Olivier Clément, "Note biographique," *Contact* no. 23, July–Sept. 2003 (titled "*André Scrima, 1925–2000. Un moine hésychaste de notre temps*"): 243.

In 1961, by chance, Scrima met Athenagoras the First, patriarch of Constantinople, who made him his personal representative at Vatican Council II. Certain decisive formulations of the Council were due to him. After the closing of the Council, Scrima became the privileged intermediary between Paul VI and Athenagoras, being present when Athenagoris and Paul met in Jerusalem in 1964, and working on the text that did away with the mutual anathemas of 1054, making clear the meaning of the Pope's kneeling at Sancta Sophia in June 1967.[4]

With ecumenical cooperation in view, Scrima was later sent to visit Western religious milieux, arriving in France at the beginning of the sixties. In Paris he resided for some time at the Dominican ecumenical center "Istina," later at "Saulchoir," deploying intense teaching activity, giving conferences, and writing some famous articles.[5] In his concern to share his enthusiasm for the philocalic renewal[6] that was flourishing in Communist Romania, he made numerous visits to Catholic monasteries, whether Carthusian, Benedictine, or Cistercian; he initiated communities into the practice of the Jesus Prayer through his conferences on Romanian monasticism and on *The Adventures of a Russian Pilgrim*, that masterpiece of Orthodox spirituality.

It was at this time then, in 1961, that Scrima visited Mont-des-Cats for the first time. Many have reported the seduction exercised by this person who was so unusual and favored with so many gifts. "What was so surprising," remembered a Catholic female hermit, "was his exceptional intelligence,

4. Clément, "Note biographique," 244.

5. André Scrima, "L'avènement philocalique dans L'orthodoxie Roumaine," *Istina* 3 (1958): 295–328; "La Tradition du père spirituel dans L'Église d'Orient," *Hermès* 2 (1967): 79–94.

6. *Philocalia*, Greek "love of the beautiful." Applied to a movement for spiritual renewal in Eastern monasticism and Orthodox devotional life in general.

matched by an excellent memory. His extensive knowledge and his polyglot culture could have been intimidating, but it was not, because he presented himself simply and courteously in his relationships with others. The refinement of his soul, above all, and the qualities of his heart won for him the spontaneous sympathy of those who approached him—a sympathy that was often transformed little by little into friendship."[7] With certain monks and nuns Fr. Scrima also entered into more extensive relationships, guiding them along the ways of prayer. The same hermit bears witness to these facts: "We sensed that he was inhabited by the Spirit, but experiencing the grace of God, whose power acted in him, and he was accompanied by an acute awareness of his own fragility and a deep sense of his own unworthiness."[8] However discreet and little known, Scrima had an exceedingly great influence in contemplative circles in France, particularly Sélignac and Bellefontaine, and also in the life of André Louf.

Among the religious who underwent Père Scrima's influence was Père Séraphim of the Abbey of Bellefontaine, whom Père Scrima guided in his development toward Orthodoxy. Séraphim later assisted Père Deseille in his foundation at Obazine.[9] After the breaking of the Russian wall, Scrima returned to Romania, where he died in 2000; a specialist in Orthodox spirituality, Paul Ladouceur, described his life as one of "Voluntary exile for thirty years." Ladouceur continued,

> Père André Scrima was an example of a new form of monachism, "monachism in the world," "the desert in the city." He saw himself as a "pilgrim" and a "stranger"

7. Soeur Noëlle Devilliers, "Ce qui fut dans ma vie la rencontre du père André Scrima," *Contacts* no. 2 (July–September 2003): 263.

8. Devilliers, "Ce qui fut dans ma vie," 264.

9. Placide Deseille, "Une vie monastique en quête de la vraie lumière: Entretiens," *Lumière et Vie* no. 298 (April–June 2013): 11.

> in the footsteps of Paul the Stranger, his first spiritual father. The call of Christ, the universality of the Christian vocation can have no more frontiers; that is the spiritual meaning of the "secularization" of the end of the twentieth century. Heirs of the centuries of hesychast tradition of Romania, Scrima was a precursor and a powerful witness of monachism in the world.[10]

In July 1961, the young Scrima with his hesitant French stood in front of the Mont-des-Cats chapter. The theme he chose for his address to the chapter did not cause his originality to shine: Monastic Life. Nevertheless, as Louf later recalled,

> From his first phrases the event took place. We were one. There was no longer "he" and "we," he the Orthodox and we Catholics. There were only some monks who shared a single experience. We knew ourselves in the strongest sense of the word to be touched by a grace that was absolutely identical on the part of each one, a grace that had touched them and led them by paths that were very similar toward a completion and a fullness whose nostalgia we all bore in our hearts: the transfiguration in glory of our beloved Lord Jesus Christ. Nothing nor any person could have altered or compromised the intense feeling of communion that had been so abruptly laid on this Latin monastic community.[11]

On the following day, as Louf was walking through the monastery with his Romanian guest, many of the older monks kneeled as they passed to ask his blessing. The door of his cell was also besieged by a squad of brothers asking for a word. But a few days before this shock of unity came about,

10. Paul Ladouceur, "La sainte Roumanie," *Lumières du Thabor* no. 27 (June 2006): 20.

11. Louf, "En marge d'un pèlerinage," 122.

sweeping away in a moment all prejudices and misunderstandings, such changes in attitude would have been unthinkable. "The event that I have just described," Louf recounted, "was for me the first of a whole chain of events. It was repeated time and again in the course of various meetings with Oriental monks. There was always the same wonder."[12] Louf shared his enthusiasm with his friend Merton: "Every evening he had a meeting on monastic life. His visit was a great good. During the last days his room was besieged. How these contacts have united us in the same monastic life!"[13] There is also an echo of this visit in the abbey *Chronicle*:

> Fr. Scrima edified us very much with his daily meetings and his classes with the students and novices. But how can we sum up the seven and a half hours of his talks that were so warm and dense? Here are just a few ideas we have retained: There are not two monasticisms. There is only one monastic population. Between Eastern and Western monasticism there are only nuances. Every Eastern monk should rediscover his Western side, and each Western monk his Eastern side. We are at the peak of the church. The unity of monasticism in the mystical body should be a powerful help towards remaking the unity of the church.[14]

The conviction had been forged in Louf's mind that monachism was the terrain where ecumenical exchanges were destined to take place. During his studies at Rome he had had that same presentiment when he spoke with Protestant and Orthodox brothers.[15]

12. Louf, "En marge d'un pèlerinage," 124.
13. Letter to Thomas Merton, CTM, 26 July 1961.
14. *Chronique du monastère*, ADMC, 28 August 1961.
15. André Louf, *À la grâce de Dieu: Entretiens avec Stéphane Delberghe* (Namur: Fidélité, 2002), 161.

In 1966 Louf asked Père Scrima, whom he had seen several times, to be his spiritual father "in the strict sense of the word."[16] Scrima at once accepted the relationship. It is necessary to picture the boldness of this gesture: the Roman Catholic abbot of one of the flourishing houses of Latin contemplative life was by this act asking to be taken as a son in the spiritual life by a monk of another confession. In the context of that time it was a veritable transgression! Monks of the East and monks of the West were then separated by a wall of offense, rumor, and prejudice that made them two worlds, strictly partitioned. For Louf this relation of paternity that he had initiated was a way of transcending the barriers and of touching with his finger the existing undivided church. After that he went further, to become the untiring promoter of a kind of ecumenism of accompaniment: "There is a place," he wrote, "for a veritable intercommunion of a spiritual nature between brothers who are still separated by the structures of the churches they belong to, but between which a spiritual spark can suddenly dart."[17] "Where, then," he goes on, "could it be stronger or more vital than in this mystery of spiritual begetting, where life is transmitted from one person to another in common and total obedience to the Lord and to his Spirit?"[18] Spiritual direction becomes this "possible ecumenical place that allows a birth to divine life from one confession to another, where the mystery of spiritual paternity that is at the heart of the church is realized."[19]

In Romania, Scrima was the spiritual son of the Russian monk Fr. John the Stranger, survivor of the Soviet Gulag,

16. André Louf, *Journal Spirituel* [hereafter JS], 5 July 1966.

17. André Louf, "Moines et Oecumenisme," *Collectanea Cisterciensia* 3 (1982): 179.

18. Louf, "Moines et Oecumenisme," 180.

19. André Louf, "La paternità spirituale," in *Abba, dimmi una parola!* (Magnano: Qipajon, 1989), 184.

from the monastery of Optina Poustine. Scrima received from this Fr. John a special blessing that Fr. John had received from his own spiritual father at Optina, a blessing that he believed gave him the charism of spiritual paternity. Scrima had consented to transmit this charism to Catholic monks and nuns whom he judged ready for it. Soeur Devilliers remembered having received it: "When he discerned that it was time, he imposed his hands and blessed me, in order that my heart might be filled with the Holy Spirit. That was how—by a living communication from one person to another—he transmitted to me the 'spiritual inheritance' that he bore."[20]

Is this the blessing that Louf received? Two clues allow that conclusion. First, his spiritual journal: he mentioned revealingly that Père Scrima had started him on the road of spiritual paternity in 1966.[21] Then a passage full of modesty in one of his articles: "Are we allowed to think that through Père Scrima's words and prayers, and through this blessing, he consented at times exceptionally to transmit to spiritual sons in the West some of the grace of Optina Poustine, bearing fruit even today in Latin monachism?"[22]

"An Orthodox Corner in the West"

In March 1968, at a suggestion from a friend, Louf invited an archimandrite and a young Russian hieromonk to make a tour of French monasteries. For two weeks the group plowed a furrow through contemplative France, beginning with Mont-des-Cats, with stops at Trappist, Carthusian, and Benedictine abbeys, and at one Carmel. In August 1968 Louf repeated this monastic tour, this time with three Greek archimandrites led by Père Élie Mastroyanopoulos of Athens. Each of these visits

20. Devilliers, "Ce qui fut dans ma vie," 264–65.
21. Louf, JS, 5 July 1966.
22. Louf, "La paternità spirituale," 184–85.

aroused in Louf the same sense of wonder: the spiritual ties that were formed among the separated brothers in the context of their experience of ascesis and prayer, and of the sharing of icons, of the crucifix, and of relics caused him to perceive the extent to which they shared the same grace.

The chief attraction of this tour was the interlude at the Carthusian house of Sélignac. Louf reported it to his brothers:

> Thanks to the welcome beaming from the Carthusian fathers, our Greek brothers were literally among the angels. The prior knew the Eastern monastic spirituality in a wonderful way, almost better than they knew it themselves. But above all it was lived at Sélignac. The person who assisted at the Offices and detected on the monks' faces something of the recollection and joy that lit them up had no need of any further description. For them Sélignac was Eastern hesychasm in its purest form. After a few days Père Élie repeated wherever he went that it was not with theologians or with active religious that Orthodox ecumenists should consort, but rather with contemplatives. It was prayer and the vision of God in pure hearts on one side and on the other that would find the deep unity of the church and through them some external formulation.
>
> The interest in the fathers of Eastern monachism on the part of Westerners surprised and confused them. When we visited the library of Sélignac I noticed a French mimeographed translation of the books of Isaac the Syrian. Such a text is extremely rare in French even at the present day. The prior saw a certain desire in my eyes. At the moment of our departure he offered me the only duplicate there was at Sélignac, telling Élie, "See, Father, how much we talk about the Eastern fathers in the West."[23]

23. André Louf, Letter to the community, ADMC, 17 August 1968.

On leaving the Carthusian house, one of the archimandrites whispered this confidence in Louf's ear: "See, now how I have discovered an Orthodox corner in the West!" "It was neither," retorted Louf, "the West nor Orthodoxy that he had discovered, but rather something higher than both, something belonging to Jesus' church, even today still undivided, certain signs of which sometimes appear here and there, more especially among those who are descendants, whether Eastern or Western, of those whom we call *sancti patres nostri*,"[24] that is, the fathers of the monastic life, the reading of whom Saint Benedict acclaims in his Rule, who constitute the common patrimony of both Byzantine and Latin monks.

The Voyage to Athos

In the first half of the twentieth century Western religious who undertook the voyage to Mount Athos were guided by an educational concern. Most of the time they were patristic scholars or Byzantinists in quest of unpublished manuscripts. Beginning with the sixties, however, the focus of Latin pilgrims' interest shifted. They turned East less to browse in the libraries than to find spiritual fathers, that is, a living spiritual tradition.[25] A Benedictine brother of Fleury, Br. Anselme Davril, who sojourned on the peninsula during this period, has recounted how impressed he was by the climate of prayer that held sway there:

> Among the memories that crowded in upon me on the mere repetition of the word "Athos," one idea was prom-

24. André Louf, "Influssi orientali nella Regola di S. Benedetto," in *Il ruolo del monachesimo nell'ecumenismo,* ed. Giodarno Donato, *Studia Olivetana* 7 (2002): 80.

25. Antoine Lambrechts, "Pélerins bénédictins au mont Athos," *Irenikon* 71 (1998): 287.

> inent; it remained and dominated everything: prayer. We met men of prayer, men who live in order to find God in prayer, who have deliberately and radically eliminated from their lives everything that might risk turning them away from this absolute aim. This life of prayer is the life of Athos, where everything is organized in terms of and for prayer; prayer is the atmosphere that bathes the monks; it is the reason for being and the purpose of the rude ascesis that is imposed on these men.[26]

Further on Frère Anselme marveled at an encounter with some practitioners of the prayer of the heart:

> These men had succeeded in fashioning an extraordinary unity in themselves; that is, their whole being, body and soul, never ceased to pray, since they made every one of their breaths into a prayer. Prayer in this way entered into their vital rhythm and descended into their hearts. So true was this that the old monk could say with concrete realism that during his sleep, even if his mouth could not pray, he continued to pray through the nose. So it was given us to find on Athos such men, for whom prayer had become a reality of every moment. Such encounters are never forgotten.[27]

With this end in view, of finding experienced monks who were spiritual men, Louf set off for Athos in August 1969 at the instigation of Père Elie, who in this way paid him back in the same coin for their earlier monastic journey together.[28] This pilgrimage constituted an essential stage in Louf's development.

26. Frère Anselme Davril, "L'impressions de l'Athos," *Renaissance de Fleury*, no. 76 (1970): 19.

27. Davril, "L'impressions de l'Athos," 24.

28. Louf was accompanied by Frères Nivard and Curely.

Thanks to Dimitris Kaimakis, a young interpreter from Salonika who had studied at Paris, in the course of long conversations at the Holy Mountain Louf met its most eminent persons. After an exchange with Éphrem, spiritual father of the hermits of Katounakia, the French monks visited a small hesychast community whose superior, Père Kharalambos, was well known for his wisdom and the quality of his spiritual life.[29] But the chief attraction of this pilgrimage was the crossing to Stavronikita, a monastery that was profiting from a promising recruitment, where the French monks visited Père Basile Gondakakis, the hegumen, and also the hermit Païssios, who was considered the spiritual father of the community.

Père Païssios (1924–1994) was one of the greatest Orthodox spiritual teachers of the twentieth century. Some ten thousand men and women had come to seek counsel, consolation, support, and strength from this man, who was endowed with a great many charisms, including the ability to read hearts. His mere presence had the gift of giving peace to visitors and of healing or enlightening them, as Hieromonk Isaac, from the Orthodox communion, testifies: "When they came near him, people were purified and pacified; they felt that the saints of old were still living among us."[30] A visitor from the West had the same experience: "He was quiet, but his silence spread out around me like a magnetic field. I sensed a mysterious peace invading me progressively. This unknown something, by the mere profundity of its silent but attentive

29. All these visits are detailed in André Louf, "Les moines d'occident et le Mont Athos," in *Vivere il regno di Dio al servizio degli altri: miscellanea in onore del p. Olivier Raquez osb*, ed. Mihai Frățilă (Barcelona: Galaxia Gutenberg/Lipa Edizioni, 2008), 113–33.

30. Hieromonk Isaac, *L'Ancien Païssios de la Sainte-Montagne* (Lausanne: L'Age d'Homme, 2008), 10, 13.

presence, became in a few moments more intimate to me than my own parents could ever be."[31]

Païssios's little hermitage was located a half-hour's walk from the foot of the monastery of Stavronikita. On the way there Louf had plenty of time to imagine the hermit about whom he had heard so much. He pictured him as a rough, harsh, obdurate person with an air of severity, an emaciated countenance, heroic ascesis and solitude, and reticent with regard to all human contact. The reality was altogether different. "If someone had told me," he recalled, "that I was going to see Saint Isaac the Syrian in person, having arisen in our midst, I could not have imagined him with any characteristics other than those of Père Païssios. The very meekness, the very kindness toward us, the very humility, the very lucidity of his lowly, lively stare, even the silences that regularly punctuated the conversation like pauses in a liturgical celebration, rendering the words that continued to fall more profound, were all impressive."[32]

After their conversation Païssios insisted on breaking his Catholic guests' long journey by leading them himself through the bushes to the dusty side road that led to the monastery. Louf was full of joy. "We had discovered," he said, "a man of such kindness and affection as I could never have imagined. He was a man of God, overflowing with love, who ought surely to have been at the heart of the mystery of the world and of the church."[33] Louf's impression of this meeting was so vivid that in his hermitage at Simiane he pinned a photo of this spiritual man, who was for him like an icon of humble love.

31. Alain Durel, *La presqu'île interdite: Initiation au mont Athos* (Paris: Albin Michel, 2010), 136.

32. André Louf, "En marge d'un pèlerinage," *Collectanea Cisterciensia* 32 (1970): 136.

33. Louf, *À la grâce de Dieu*, 164.

Louf often testified to this fact. Before any meeting could take place, Latin monks had to undergo criticism that was at times virulent from Orthodox monks, criticism that attacked one by one the import of the beard, the length and color of the habit, the validity of baptisms and Catholic sacraments, the role of the pope, the procession of the Holy Spirit, and created grace. The term "Anti-Roman" was the preliminary requirement for any exchange to take place, even if such reserve did not affect the hospitality that was always offered with a great deal of courtesy. Louf often mentioned the example of the monk who, by way of introduction to a conversation that would turn into a violent diatribe against Rome, offered them cucumbers with this delightful commentary: "Take them. They are all I have to offer you, but they are rich with my love. He who eats them becomes my brother."[34] Then, once the storm had passed, the exchange could take place and the miracle could be produced. Then the Roman Catholic and the Orthodox monks could recognize each other as brothers in the same vocation; they could feel themselves moved by the same Spirit in the same search for God. "There is mutual edification and slow but continuous erosion of prejudices, reciprocal acknowledgement of a grace that inhabits one side and the other of a wall of separation: these are beyond any doubt the first fruits of such encounters," Louf testified.[35]

At the time of his trip to Mount Athos Louf pushed his experience of communion further. That event occurred during a meeting with Père Théoklitos of the monastery of Dionysius, a theologian noted for his conservatism and his criticism of Roman Catholicism but considered one of the oracles of the Holy Mountain. Louf had just translated a chapter of one of

34. Louf, "En marge d'un pèlerinage," 127.

35. Louf, "Les moines d'Occident et le mont Athos," 127.

his books for a French journal,[36] and he expressed a desire for an audience with Père Théoklitos to place before him a personal problem, linked to his eremitical vocation, that troubled him. This initiative did not lack boldness, since the abbot was presenting himself as a disciple coming to seek a word of advice from his spiritual father when they were representing churches that were officially separated. The Orthodox priest accordingly hesitated for a long time, and Louf guessed the reason: "Had he the right to enter into closer communion with someone he surely considered a heretic?"[37] He continued:

> I saw that he was upset by my question. He felt that he was taken seriously by a Latin monk in his role as spiritual father, as if there were nothing between us, as if we really lived by the same Spirit. He hesitated for a long moment, then I suddenly felt that he swung to consent. He took me seriously in turn regarding my spiritual request, and by so doing he evaluated the movement of the Holy Spirit in me. A wall of prejudice had collapsed. Communion had again been established between the one and the other. I will never forget the word of light that he then transmitted, fully aware of the responsibility to which I had appealed, aware also of the consent that he made thereto, not to me personally, but to the Lord and to the Spirit, and in the last analysis to the mystery of the church in which both of us had a share.[38]

Undaunted, Louf had been reached in his deepest self, in his personal vocation, by the word of a brother from a different

36. The whole book was translated later: Théoclète Dionysiatis, *Entre ciel et terre* (Lausanne: L'age d'homme, 2011).

37. Louf, *À la grâce de Dieu*, 166.

38. André Louf, "Moines et Œcuménisme," *Collectanea Cisterciensia* 44 (1982): 173.

confession. This intercommunion "at the very source of life, at that place where separation between Christian confessions has not yet started or has been mysteriously surpassed, separation from now on deprived of any relevance,"[39] confirmed what he had already understood with Père Scrima: at a certain deep level the churches are one, and communion is granted. Truly this word of life received from a "separated" brother enabled Louf to touch "the subsistence, beyond or away from every visible separation, and the surface of the one and only church, still in reality undivided and undoubtedly never separated."[40]

The Road to Spiritual Ecumenism

After the ten days spent at Athos, the voyage continued with a week's interlude in Romania, at the heart of hesychast Moldavia, contemplative and eremitical.[41] There again Louf measured the extent to which at bottom monastic grace is the same in the East as in the West. Raised up by the same Spirit, it is directed toward the same search. Beyond the cultural adaptations, there are characteristics that are shared and are dominant; these go back to the beginning, to the body of teachings and usages inherited from the Fathers who represent the common store of the entire church.

From this voyage to Orthodoxy Louf returned with the conviction that when the monk is present to his heart, he touches the undivided church. In his very deepest self there is, as it were, "a fullness that external schisms have not impaired, a point where the undivided church has never been violated."[42] So it is by being present in their heart of hearts, at God's place in them, that monks will become pioneers of

39. Louf, "Les moines d'Occident et le mont Athos," 133.
40. Louf, "Moines et Œcumenisme," 180.
41. Louf, "En marge d'un pèlerinage," 139.
42. Louf, "Moines et Œcumenisme," 175.

what Louf called "the intercommunion of hearts,"[43] that interior ecumenism that renews, beyond surface divisions, the vein of indivisibility. He wrote more on the subject:

> The path of spiritual ecumenism is privileged to take as a point of departure a preceding communion, so to speak, that is already experienced clearly, although all the consequences have yet to be explored. Beginning with such an experience, the ecumenical worker possesses from the first a criterion of discernment that will allow him to go ahead boldly, but with perfect fidelity to the Holy Spirit. There has never been any evidence that ecumenical dialogue should make steady progress from the start by way of a rational clarity that would be more and more convincing. Rather, experience proves the opposite. Dialogue proceeds from life and follows life closely. It moves ahead by successive slippings behind that are unforeseeable and irresistible; they can suddenly modify the theological or ecclesiastical landscape and cause new configurations to appear in the terrain that no one would have dared to predict. These backslidings happen on the surface crust of the church, and they are beyond any doubt caused by a new subterranean equilibrium that is always caused by a growth in holiness and love. It is in this way that monks remain open and available for ecumenical grace. Their contribution is not spectacular. But it would like to cling to the church's resources, that is to say to its heart of hearts.[44]

Architect of Unity

Louf experienced true suffering because Christians had not reached the high level of this grace of unity and could not yet formulate theological terms to express this communion, which

43. Louf, "En marge d'un pélerinage," 149.
44. Louf, "Les moines d'Occident et le mont Athos," 132.

had been given for all eternity. Beyond a work of translation destined to make known the spiritual riches of Orthodoxy in the West, as an architect of unity he stirred himself to build bridges to reveal, in large part by his studies, the family traits uniting Roman Catholic and Orthodox spirituality.

The brethren of the Reform were not left behind. Living monastic life to the hilt was for Louf a way to meet the separated brethren and to transcend the doctrinal quarrels of past centuries. Protestants in fact played an important role in Louf's personal itinerary. It was his reading of Karl Barth that opened up for him the way of *lectio,* and the figure of Luther that helped him to live the Gospel ascesis. His dialogue with Protestants often focused on this question of ascesis, which should be an ascesis of fragility, conformable to Luther's intuition concerning the respective roles of human action and grace.

As regards the Orthodox, Louf's abundant bibliography contains a whole litany of articles initiating a dialogue between East and West, illuminating their relationship, and pointing out their common viewpoint on certain themes: mercy in Saint Bernard and Isaac the Syrian,[45] the relationship of action and contemplation in Ruusbroec and Saint Silouane,[46] interior prayer in Saint Nil Sorsky, the Russian hermit, and in Blessed Paul Giustiniani, Italian reformer of the Camaldolese.[47] In addition, by studying these parallels he little by little rediscovered his own tradition: by making the effort to read the spiritual teachers of Orthodoxy in order to relate them to those of Latin Christianity, he alerted himself to all those in the heart of his own church who had borne witness to a similar quality of interior life. "It was surely my

45. André Louf, "Le repentir, clé de la vie en Christ," *Buisson Ardent* 9 (2003): 9–47.

46. André Louf, "Le cœur brisé," *Buisson Ardent* 3 (1997): 48–60.

47. André Louf, "Quelques constantes spirituelles dans les traditions hésychastes en Orient et en Occident," *Irenikon* 74 (2001): 486.

interest in hesychasm," he confirms, "that led me to the discovery of Ruusbroec."[48] Elsewhere he wrote, "It is sometimes salutary to detour by way of the East to rediscover the West with its patrimony, which is just as unique. In fact it has frankly often been beneficial to choose the East to help the sons of the West become aware of their own tradition, which they had quite simply left fallow."[49]

Louf traced the nostalgia of that epoch upstream from the doctrinal quarrels of the Middle Ages, when no ecclesiastical barrier separated those who were spiritual. "From East to West, by passing through Jerusalem, men of God were known and recognized," he said. "They knew they were sons of the same spiritual traditions. Their way of life was similar, and their ministry in the church identical."[50] Well, he remarks, despite the separation that forced them to make their own way singly from that point, each parallel to the other and often in the most complete ignorance, the Latin and Byzantine monks really never stopped being close, because they drew wisdom from the same sources, which led them to the same experience: the Desert Fathers, their apophthegmata, the writings of John Climacus, John Cassian, and still others, all of them going back to the first centuries of our era. "The marvelous Church of Jesus Christ," he concludes, "has always stayed undivided at a certain depth, despite appearances, and she undoubtedly remains so today. It is up to us to perceive it!"[51]

48. Louf, *À la grâce de Dieu*, 170.

49. André Louf, "L'évolution de la vie monastique en France depuis le Concile," *Documents épiscopat* no. 12 (June 1981): 2.

50. Louf, "Quelques constantes spirituelles," 483.

51. Louf, "Quelques constantes spirituelles," 486.

CHAPTER 15

Oracle of the Trappist Order

In the archives of the Abbey of Mont-des-Cats a dossier of photographs presents Louf in all the aspects of his life as abbot: surrounded by novices, presiding at the Eucharist, standing in the midst of an Orthodox delegation, speaking the Word in a monastic gathering, or leading the community through the cloister with the monks following in a straight line. What is most surprising is the number of shots linked to events of Christian life. He is distinguished by his height and by his joy in life, as betrayed by a contagious smile. He is shown at the side of many popes, but also on many decisive occasions for the Order, at various general chapters, and in many of the world's abbeys where Rome sent him to visit (or to listen, in common parlance). The whole life of the Order of Cistercians of the Strict Observance (OCSO) in its geographical extension and its post-Conciliar evolution passes in review through these photographic documents. They illustrate the foremost role that he played in Trappist politics, in the noblest sense of the word, in the course of the second half of the twentieth century.

Secret Powers

Louf was elected abbot of Mont-des-Cats at the time when Vatican II was in full session. He was a member of that generation of abbots who were charged with the duty of making the breath of the Council felt, not only in their own abbeys but also in the very structure and life of the Order. Many of the texts in fact that redefined the Cistercian vocation and remodeled its structures in the light of the intuitions of Vatican II bear his stamp. In a recent history of La Trappe, however, where his role has been passed over almost in silence, he is mentioned along with Thomas Merton among the handful of monks who contributed to "the great work of spiritual renewal in the Order" in the twentieth century.[1]

For Trappists the General Chapter, meeting every three years, holds the authority of the Order, decides its important evolutions, and traces its perspectives. When it meets, the general chapter elects the abbot general for an undefined term; the abbot general's role is to assure the unity of the Trappist family. The abbot general is assisted by a council of five members who reside in the Generalate at Rome, the abbot general's house. The general chapter is prepared by a General Commission, whose members are proposed by the various regions of the Order, because the Order is structured by its geographical and linguistic areas. Because of political acumen and willing care to serve Cistercian life, to help advance its evolution, and to stamp a certain contemplative sensitivity upon it, Louf was often invested with secret powers. He was in fact suspicious of his attraction to that role, where his self-love could always slip in, writing in his journal, "Avoid as far as possible all 'political responsibility,' and all obligation to put myself forward, which is contrary to *sancta simplicitas* and the one thing necessary: the simple eye that wounds the gaze of the Bridegroom. Pay special attention to every kind

1. Dom Mariano Ballano, "À mi-parcours du xxe siècle: bilan et perspectives," in Marie-Gérard Dubois, ed., *L'Ordre Cistercien de la stricte observance au xxe siecle,* ed. Marie-Gérard Dubois, with Augusta Tescari and Maria Paola Santachiari, 2 vols. (Rome: OCSO, 2008), 2:20.

of choice, but without forcing anything; suspect above all interior haste (ambition) for functions only slightly important; try for self-effacement."[2]

Among the innumerable posts Louf held, one was particularly visible: between 1974 and 1993 he was what is called "promoter" at the General Chapter, otherwise called the working agent of that organ of supreme power. From 1969 to 1988 he was also the president of the region of Central Europe. He was a member of the Central Commission for the General Chapter of 1969, a member of the commission that directed the plenary assemblies of the General Chapter of 1971, and the abbot general's vicar from 1974 to 1984.[3] As promoter of the General Chapter, a strategic post that he occupied for nearly twenty years, he was able to pull certain strings, and he built a reputation of being a diplomat and a brilliant orator.

During the conflicting debates that agitated the chapter, Louf often figured as a providential influence. His intelligence, clear thinking, and ability to synthesize allowed him to identify the issues that were bogging down the discussions. The abbess of Les Gardes, who had often been present in those situations, remembers, "I have always appreciated his lucid mind and his well-considered ideas, which he strove to express, perhaps too forcefully, in the eyes of certain people."[4] Louf was endowed with a mastery of the art of oratory and was very charismatic; his "personality was brilliant and engaging."[5] He exercised an ascendancy whose political objective could easily captivate his audience and influence the discussion. One abbot remembers, "Confronted by him,

2. André Louf, *Journal Spirituel* [hereafter JS], 14 March 1973.

3. Soeur Danièle Levrard, advisor to the abbot general, in correspondence with the author; and Dubois, *L'Ordre Cistercien,* 2:205.

4. Danièle Levrard, correspondence with the author.

5. Placide Deseille, correspondence with the author.

no one could remain neutral. His personality was seductive, and he often banked on this advantage."[6]

Louf was known for his formidable skill in upsetting a settled proposition with the aid of arguments cleverly chosen and distilled. "He was often reproached for it," one expert confirms. "Certain abbots, particularly Americans, whose culture was more based on consent, did not subscribe to this way of acting, and they reproached him for being too much a manipulator."[7] Dom Armand Veilleux, who was the abbot of Mistassini in Canada, and who had lived through all the general chapters since 1969 at Louf's side, nicely pinned this eccentricity on him:

> There was no lack of tension between us, but I believe there always remained a certain friendship. The tensions were above all revealed during the meetings held at the General Chapters, where he had for a long time been moderator of the discussions. At almost all of these chapters I was a member of commissions charged with the drafting of the Constitutions and the various statutes of the Order in the spirit of Vatican II. André Louf was brilliant, and he knew the monastic tradition very well. He seemed to conceive his role as moderator in the sense of leading the assembly to make the decisions that he thought were the right ones . . . . My position was that we should present to the assembly all the possibilities that existed and let the assembly choose among them.[8]

Roaming Abbot

During the thirty-five years of his abbatial tenure, Louf was regularly occupied by the demands of his office and his many

6. Jean-Marc Thévenet, conversation with the author.
7. Jean-Marc Thévenet, conversation with the author.
8. Armand Veilleux, correspondence with the author.

responsibilities in the Order; he spent his life very much "outside the walls," on the road, far from his stability, torn between two abbeys, two meetings, two regular visitations. In an engaging book Régis Debray called on historians to note the material underpinning of the spiritual life and the concrete modalities of the Spirit's movements.[9] From this point of view it is important to remember that Louf's generation preceded the TGV.[10] As a young abbot, except for trips to other continents, including Africa, Asia, and America, he never traveled by air. He plowed the roads of monastic Europe by car, trips that sometimes amounted to veritable epics.

A quick overview of Louf's correspondence with his community reveals the high frequency of these trips.[11] Sent during his voyages, these letters tell of his "gyrovague" manner of life and show that while traveling he carried out a spiritual fatherhood from a distance. "They played an enormous role," recalled Dom Jedrzejczak. "They were read in the refectory, and the community was enthusiastic."[12] The letters were crammed with humor, spirit, and life, and they give an idea of Louf's abbatial style and his joyful life. One example among many is the account of a visit to Fille-Dieu: "An old bicycle from the time of the patriarchs was dug out of the trash in the attic. It was repainted and fixed up, and it now serves as Père Jacques's conveyance on his rare walks. Neither the horse nor the rider was among the most aerodynamic of the species, so their maximum speed was rarely surpassed. The thorniest problem, however, was not that of relearning the maintenance of balance, once lifted up over the two

9. Régis Debray, *Dieu, un itinéraire* (Paris: Odile Jacob, 2001).

10. TGV (Trains à Grande Vitesse): French high-speed trains, introduced in September 1981.

11. Letters inventoried in the category "FA35 Lettres à la communauté (1963–1997)," ADMC.

12. Dom Jedrzejczak, conversation with the author.

wheels. Instead it was the ability to avoid soiling the robe."[13] Here is another story that evokes a conference given to the Swiss nuns: "After None Dom Firmim gave a conference on Maromby.[14] He was quite frank and minced no words. In that holy dovecote he exposed the matrimonial morality of mid-Malgache with all its concubinage and adultery. Mother Abbess seemed to be sinking beneath her veil."[15]

But after 1990 the tone of his letters became more factual and lost briskness. His pastoral obligations put him on the continental roads an average of every two months, either to carry out visitations to his daughter houses, to preach retreats, to clear up problems for communities, or, more often, to attend meetings in some event of the Order. For example, in April 1972 he was at Cîteaux for a meeting of the Order. In May he went to Italy to the daughter house of Frattochie. From June to July he sojourned at Rome to prepare the following General Chapter. On his return, he went to Fille-Dieu in August; from there he went on to Bornholm, Denmark, in September, then returned to Frattochie to supervise an abbatial election. In October he was at Maromby, a foundation of Mont-des-Cats. Then he returned to Europe for another interlude at Fille-Dieu, and then he had a clear passage to Myrendale in Scandinavia. Except for the trip to Madagascar, all these voyages were made by ground conveyance.

Although Louf was abroad and attending all kinds of meetings, this life on the road was not without torment for his conscience. "You know," he wrote in his journal, "how much I suffer from being away from the brotherhood at Mont-des-

13. André Louf, Letter to the community, ADMC, 26 Nov. 1964.

14. Dom Firmim Deboes was one of the founders of the abbey of Maromby in Madagascar and served as superior from 1958–1960 and 1967–1996: https://ocso.org/monastery/maromby/.

15. Louf, Letter to the community, ADMC, 10 May 1965.

Cats."[16] He stuck to his aim "of accepting [his] many departures with simplicity and without dramatics."[17] Like Saint Bernard, Louf felt that he was at fault for not giving his brothers an example of that cloistered life of which he was the advocate, that of reclusion in silence and solitude.[18] His absences led him to rethink the meaning of his vow of stability: "I am taking a more accurate account of what has up to now been a small aspect of my vocation: only passing through without staying fixed at all except in the will of God."[19]

The trips that Louf narrated with a sure sense of drama were veritable odysseys. He delighted in driving the abbey's Peugeot 204, which loosened him up to a large extent. He was not afraid to share his automobile passion with the brothers, proof that this great man of spirit never posed as a saint: "The new little green car is very good. Its roadworthiness is still good, and we keep from pushing it too far. Yet it is strong on the uptake, especially on flat roads. On the hills she quickly runs out of steam on the fourth gear."[20] The trip from Mont-des-Cats to the Dutch abbey of Tilburg that he was narrating had particular problems. There was a bad snowstorm, and at midnight the car was immobilized by a flat tire, as he explained:

> Among the dangers of the road that Paul enumerated in his epistles, he certainly did not include those caused by modern traffic. I hope they too will be crowned in heaven. I had a frightful time of it last night. I had the grace of a flat tire. But the Lord has a father's kindness, even when he teases us a bit. Where the accident took place, right on the highway at an obscure corner of the

16. Louf, JS, 21 Jan. 1966.
17. Louf, JS, 5 April 1968.
18. André Louf, "Le Cîteaux de saint Bernard," *Collectanea Cisterciensia* 61 (1999): 77.
19. André Louf, Letter to the community, ADMC, 16 Sept. 1963.
20. André Louf, Letter to the community, ADMC, 4 Nov. 1968.

> countryside, there was a red light at the circle boulevard of Eindhoven. It was not my first blowout and patch, thanks be to God, but at that time of night it was impossible to take it apart. If I had not already had one, I would have gotten a sprain in the back. Well, there was, not far from the streetlamp, with this abbot sweated up in the snow, a gas station with a lay employee who took the business out of my hands with a hammer and jack.[21]

Sometimes, under the old regime of money, it was the customs house that cast a curious eye on this abbot wandering about with currency issued by all the monastic countries. In one case, as he reported,

> A slight misadventure happened to me at the Swiss border. I was en route for more than ten hours from Mont-des-Cats to our Swiss daughter house, Fille-Dieu. The customs officer who asked to see my billfold would have had to be intrigued by the diversity of bank notes included therein. There was French, Swiss, Italian, Dutch, Belgian, and Danish money. There was even a note from Madagascar without any monetary value. There was no vast sum of money, but it had to pique his curiosity. I had to pull the car over. And then there was a legal inspection. Books were opened, including the breviary. Pictures were inspected. Even my itinerary was checked by means of telephone calls. Happily there was nothing suspect. I passed quickly and could continue my journey.[22]

The Renowned Visitor

Cistercian abbeys are autonomous, but they are also united as one common entity, with each father immediate in charge

21. André Louf, Letter to the community, ADMC, 4 Dec. 1966.
22. André Louf, Letter to the community, ADMC, 2 Oct. 1982.

of its realization. The superior of a given monastery is responsible for making a regular visitation every two years to the abbeys dependent on his or her supervision, with the purpose of supporting the pastoral action of the local abbot or abbess, to amend it if necessary, and to revive the spiritual fervor of the monks and nuns. As abbot of Mont-des-Cats, Louf was father immediate of five communities: the monks' abbeys of Tilburg in the Netherlands, Frattochie in Italy, and Maromby in Madagascar, and the nuns' abbeys of Belval in the Calais region of France and La Fille-Dieu in Switzerland.

Louf also carried out visitations at the community of Myrendal, the small foundation on the island of Bornholm in Denmark, located midway between Sweden and Poland in the diocese of Copenhagen. This small community had been founded in 1966 by Cistercian brothers from the abbey of Achel, intending to allow them to experience "an original foundation with less rigid structures, where poverty could be more strict and separation from the world less absolute." The Order named Louf the community's head or overseer, and after December 1965 Rome considered him juridically "as the abbot of these six religious." He visited the community once a year until the mid-eighties. He had great sympathy for the initiative:

> Among the numerous attempts at "simplified monastic life" that arose during the Council, it is one of the rare ones to have survived until the present day. It is of course not perfect in all respects, but the attempt has still succeeded in many important aspects that remain valuable for the Order today. The brothers have succeeded in transplanting Cistercian life on a small scale, emphasizing certain qualities that are essential for any Cistercian life. They live by the work of their hands (bookbinding), but very simply and poorly. They are satisfied with little in every domain. Their elementary regime is very "frugal." Their liturgy is profound, and the atmosphere thereof is "interior" and contemplative. They live a veritable solitude, and because of their

> geographical situation, in real isolation. The superior has always been biased in favor of an evangelical climate of spiritual freedom.[23]

In 1997 Louf made his last regular visitation at Tilburg, a few months before his retirement. From there he wrote a letter to Mont-des-Cats, in which he recalled a past pilgrimage:

> When the car passed through the gate at the abbey of Tilburg, I remembered my very first Visitation as a very young father immediate, which took place exactly thirty-four years ago. Dom Willibrord was then abbot of Tilburg, and he awaited me, as was then obligatory, wearing the long clerical overcoat, with his great plush hat in his hand, decorated with cords and the three black tassels that Benedictine and Cistercian abbots of Benelux then wore. It was a solemn reception, as was the custom in that era. The church's two bells began to ring. Then the new father immediate was conveyed in procession up to the church, while a Latin responsory, reserved for the occasion, was being sung. I still remember the impression made on me by the community, when the double doors of the enclosure were opened and I saw them forming two lines extending all the way to the church entrance. The lines were at least fifteen meters long, half wearing the white cowl and half the brown cloak. There were almost a hundred monks. I was breathless.[24]

After the Council many observances were simplified. There was no more pomp, and visitations could be confined to

23. Report of André Louf on the community of Myrendal at Bornholm (Denmark), October 1996; http://gerarddesaintmars.pagesperso-orange.fr/Les_Six_dAchel/les_six_d_achel.html. [As the domain "Pages perso" ceased operation on Sept. 5, 2023, this site is no longer available. For current information about Myrendal, see https://ocso.org/monastery/myrendal/. BK]

24. André Louf, Letter to the community, ADMC, 18 July 1997.

functional meetings. The important thing was private meetings with the brothers and sisters.

In fact the important ministry of the father immediate was the act of listening. During a Regular Visitation he received visits from ten to fifteen brothers or sisters a day, occasions when they opened their hearts to him. When Louf made the visitation at the abbey of Zundert in 1966 because of an abbatial vacancy, he described in a detailed letter to the community how he spent his time: "My schedule was full. This morning the council met for four hours. In the afternoon there was an uninterrupted sequence of visits. The ability to hear the Holy Spirit speaking in each one is a subtle craft. For that it would be necessary that I be familiar with his voice myself and with his action. It is not difficult to give counsel out of common sense or out of acute politics. But to be radiant with the Spirit and to communicate that to others is something else."[25] At the end of a visitation at Myrendal a few days later, he wrote, "The day has been spent in exchanges with the brothers, first one by one and afterwards with the whole group. I like it very much, listening in that way and trying to remain listening to God's grace, the grace that is hiding behind their difficulties, and that is suddenly revealed in unexpected light, and in peace and joy more stable than usual."[26] From the Dutch abbey of Nazareth, which was not in his filiation but which he covered as father immediate, he wrote,

> A regular visitation is a form of fraternal co-responsibility. Every Christian community is co-responsible for all the other communities. Well, there are certain services that a community, even if autonomous and independent, cannot render for itself. There is a need for a viewpoint and a hand to come from outside. A certain recourse should still

25. André Louf, Letter to the community, ADMC, 24 July 1966.
26. André Louf, Letter to the community, ADMC, 3 Jan. 1969.

> be possible, when a local situation is jammed. And where is there a human community where relationships or everyday matters do not get jammed from time to time, without any person's real fault on one side or the other?
>
> But the special purpose of a visitation is the common life of a community and the position of every one of the sisters with regard to the whole community. It is important to be precise, above all toward those nuns who often, more or less, are expecting something else, whether it be a meeting or a retreat or some spiritual counsel. That is a legitimate desire, but it is clearly not the primary purpose of a visitation. So what do we expect from a visitation? Changes or improvements? Instead we expect great clarity. We want to see more clearly, in the tensions of a group and in its own needs and frustrations, and that is already a great step forward, an indispensable step to be on the right track for someday attaining a true maturation of matters and of situations.[27]

Right after his abbatial election, Louf expressed his state of mind to the sisters at Belval. He anticipated his caution not to interfere too much with their business affairs: "The father immediate should not intervene much, but he has to keep a long-range view."[28] "Being abbot of one of his daughter houses," the former abbot of Tilburg has confirmed, "Dom André always gave me full confidence when he had to make any difficult decisions. He always respected the autonomy of his daughter houses. We are still appreciative of all he did for us."[29] With that said, the contacts were not always so peace-

27. André Louf, Letter to the community, ADMC, 16 August 1982.

28. André Louf, First meeting with the community of Trappistines of Belval, ADMC, 6 Feb. 1963.

29. Korneel Vermeiren, former abbot of Tilburg, correspondence with the author.

ful, especially when Louf had to face abbesses with a strong temperament. His stormy relations with the superior of Fille-Dieu are legendary. Mère Hortense was called Mère Atomique, since she had a doctorate in nuclear physics and was endowed with an explosive temper. She knew how to cope with Louf, and the latter did not necessarily appreciate that, even if he did treat her with severity. Still he often returned to Fille-Dieu with pleasure: "Spiritual contact with this community renews me," he wrote in his journal."[30]

Besides visitations in the abbeys of his filiation, Dom André was also invited by communities that wanted to benefit from his experience. In this way he helped many Belgian and Dutch abbeys to get over the hump of the difficult secularization of the 1960s. "I am convinced that it is thanks to him that a whole generation of monks and nuns in our Netherlands—Holland and Flanders—were able to persevere in their vocation and deepen it,"[31] confirmed the abbot of Tilburg. Frère Aerden, a monk of Westmalle in Belgium, agreed: "It is thanks to him," he added, "that I remained a monk."[32] The Belgian abbey of Saint-Sixte also owed a part of its awakening during the 1970s to the benign paternity Louf exercised through the intermediary of Dom Remi Heyse, who was novice master at the time.[33] His charism of discernment did not escape the notice of the Curia, and numerous delicate missions were entrusted to him in order to correct monastic communities that were experiencing difficulties.

Louf was also president of the monastic conference of France at the time, and he was in one case ordered by Rome to accompany Dom Calvet and the community of Barroux at the time when this community was trying to get around the

30. Louf, JS, 2 April 1968.
31. Korneel Vermeiren, correspondence with the author.
32. Guerric Aerden, correspondence with the author.
33. Benoît Standaert, correspondence with the author.

Holy See. Louf was working behind the scenes during the years that preceded the promulgation of the canonical statute that marked the re-integration of this abbey in the bosom of the Roman Church. Père Basile, a monk of Barroux, remembered this episode: "Dom Louf came in November 1983, at the request of the archbishop of Avignon, to write a report on our community for the attention of the Congregation for the Institutes of Consecrated Life at Rome. In order that he might question us in all freedom, our founder absented himself part of the time. The second time Dom Louf came, on October 2, 1989, he participated in the dedication of our abbatial church, during which he consecrated one of our altars."[34]

These public visitations were preceded by more discreet exchanges with certain brothers whom Louf received at Simiane. Masterful worker at reconciliation that he was, he initiated the dialogue with Dom Gérard Calvet, either by letter or by face-to-face encounter.[35] "Dom Gérard met Dom Louf at Simiane on January 8, 1985. At that time it was convenient for our monks to be able to visit other monasteries and to receive other monks here. Dom Louf encouraged that, in order for us to get to know each other better," recalled Père Basile in correspondence with the author. "With Calvet and Louf the conversations were sometimes stormy. The brothers at Barroux mentioned, in the course of a meeting in September 1985, a discussion on the crisis in the church that lasted four hours."[36]

Frère Benoît Standaert, a close friend of Louf, remembers: "He emerged from these exchanges in great distress. He found no spirituality, properly speaking, but much that was juridical in their conception of the monastic life and of the problems

34. Père Basile, of the Abbaye Sainte Madeleine du Barroux, correspondence with the author.

35. Dom Gérard Calvet was the founder of the abbey of Sainte Madeleine du Barroux and was its abbot from 1989 to 2003.

36. Père Basile, correspondence with the author.

of relationships with 'the others.' "[37] As Louf was cultivating discretion, Standaert said, he was not very open, using obscure words with regard to these contacts with integralists in his article on the topic:

> I took the opportunity, since I was asked to do so, to dialogue with some traditionalist circles of monks. I was surprised at their undeniable generosity, but I noticed as well that the Council's message had by no means been received. I think the fundamental problem is culture. The traditionalists represent a culture that is humanly respectable but that has not yet perhaps been sufficiently evangelized. In every one of us, you see, culture has a need to be wounded and healed by the Word of God to avoid being darkened with ideology. But the difficulty is also deeply spiritual. There is undeniably in some of them a problem of discernment, of sensitivity to the Spirit, of capacity to see what is happening today in the church. The rediscovery of tradition does not mean to turn around and go back, but it means to become aware of one's sources and roots. It is not a question of repeating what was done in the past, because repetition is a sign of death. Instead we must look at tradition as a living reality that lets us live more in communion with the world of today.[38]

Along with so many other missions entrusted to him by Rome, Louf assisted the sisters at Bethlehem at a difficult point of their history, but he had also, beginning in 1978, been appointed apostolic visitor for the monastic family of Sainte Lioba.[39] This community had been founded by a Dutch nun,

37. Benoît Standaert, correspondence with the author.

38. André Louf, "La tradition ne regarde pas en arrière," *La Croix* 14 January 1989.

39. Mère Eláiaé Bollen, "L'ermite de Sainte-Lioba," in André Louf, *S'abandonner à l'amour: Méditations à Sainte-Lioba*, ed. Charles Wright (Paris: Salvator, 2017).

Mère Hildegard Michaelis, who was a very spiritual person, though a bit odd, and the community found it difficult to be fitted into the diocese of Aix. Louf assisted in this process. He reinstated the community at the deep center of its vocation. Still today the brothers and sisters of this still flourishing abbey keep a fond remembrance of him. Louf wrote in his journal, "At the very time of the concelebration I received a precious grace of complete detachment. It was like a full and sweet uprooting of all my attachments. This uprooting was accomplished by Jesus himself, and he left only a great peace and a total availability. The sweetness was marvelous. Jesus does not wrench, and he does not cut off the plant, leaving only the roots. He uproots sweetly without tearing a thread, but he leaves absolutely nothing in the ground."[40]

That description is about the way Louf proceeded in his accompaniment of communities: sweetly, without violence to anyone. "Careful to support people," recalls the abbess of Sainte-Lioba, "to never hurt them or to cut short their enthusiasm. He gave evidence of an infinite patience. I remember his meeting a sister who unloaded on him a pile of reproaches for some hours. And at the end, without flinching, he was content to answer in a meek and gentle voice: 'Have you anything else to tell me?' His capacity to allow the other to express himself or herself taught me much. Thanks to his listening without judging this sister, who was very fragile, she did not feel guilty, and she was freed from her bitterness, leaving the way open before her."[41]

Crossing the Desert

Since he was considered "the Order's Mouthpiece"[42] during the 1980s, Louf had a place on the list of possible monks who

40. Louf, JS, 29 Sept. 1971.
41. Mère Elaié Bollen, conversation with the author.
42. Jean-Marc Thévenet, conversation with the author.

could be elected abbot general at the 1990 general chapter. That would have been his way to lay down his ministry as abbot after twenty-five years of good and loyal service, and a part of his community wanted that to happen. The chapter, however, did not decide as was expected. Instead of Louf, it was his "best enemy" who was elected, Dom Bernardo Oliveira, abbot of Azul, in Argentina. There are many reasons to explain this defeat. Many of the abbots, and especially of the abbesses, at first feared the slightly personal style of Louf's administration, and his habit of imposing his viewpoint on other people. "This tendency," submitted a witness, "was above all the bristling witness of the monks who originated from the American continent, whose culture was founded upon free trade, transparency, and concerted action."[43] This geographical logic emphasized opposition to Louf, who appeared to be a representative of a European monasticism that was a bit paternalistic and tended to block certain evolutions arising from the extension of the Order to new continents. Armand Veilleux has explained: "It is necessary to say that at the time André Louf was one of the spokesmen of a European monasticism that remained very paternalistic with regard to all the developments in other parts of the world. I represented the monasticism of North America (which included Canada as well as the United States). This viewpoint looked toward new possibilities for the Cistercian charism to flesh out (and the end of colonization was a trauma for all Europeans)."[44]

Even if Louf did not show it, the election of Dom Bernardo affected him deeply. An odd rivalry put these two monks in opposition to each other, developing for the first time at the General Chapter of 1984. Dom Bernardo had just been elected abbot. The unfriendly attitude between the two was as sudden as it was violent. "Dom André, who was moderator,

43. Jean-Marc Thévenet, conversation with the author.
44. Armand Veilleux, correspondence with the author.

immediately displeased Dom Bernardo," remembers an eyewitness. The latter was irritated by what he perceived as condescension on Louf's part.[45] The animosity between Dom André and Dom Bernardo perdured until after 2000, when an affair linked to the economic government of a Belgian monastery in 1995 became a point of contention. From 1984 on, every new encounter fed their mutual antagonism. They were there face-to-face at the chapter of abbesses in 1985 at the Escorial. "It was during the time of the updating of the Constitutions," recounts one participant, "and ardent questions divided the meetings. Bernardo and André were almost always on opposite sides. During certain sessions theirs were the only voices to be heard, as if it were a sort of game. The abbot general at the time even had to ask them to leave the room, to calm down the abbesses. They were two strong personalities, spiritual authorities as well as intellectual, but their sensitivities were quite divergent."[46]

Of course the weight of their interpersonal animosity should not be underestimated, but their different ways of conceiving the religious life also had its weight, which crystallized in a struggle for influence in the Order. At bottom it was a struggle of sensitivities. Louf stood for a monasticism that was more strictly enclosed, with the interior desert experience emphasized. Olivera's emphasis was on the community dimension, where the apostolic character was more striking. The latter was triumphant over the years. Louf had a presentiment of that. That is why, after the defeat in 1990, he retired little by little from the Order's public life and contented himself with sending a few warnings out against the evolution he regretfully saw coming about.

45. Dom Augustine of Spencer, former abbot of Azul in Argentina, conversation with the author.

46. Jean-Marc Thévenet, conversation with the author.

Such was the case with certain articles that summed up the changes after the Council, so that one could re-read the road traveled, articles that in their examination of the past are quite enthusiastic. Monastic life, Louf wrote, was showing itself globally rejuvenated by its *aggiornamento*, stripped, simplified, "more clarified, and more attractive."[47] But there remained some reasons for anxiety. With the passing of time he at first considered that the *aggiornamento* of the liturgy had too quickly abandoned certain aspects of its patrimony, especially Gregorian chant, and he regretted the loss of its interior beauty. At the end of the 1980s he wanted to reintroduce some Gregorian selections into the abbey's liturgy, but he aroused the hostility of a part of the community that had made the use of French a sanctuary. So he made himself the leader of a group to compose a whole office in French (both music and texts) inspired by Gregorian modes.

The relaxing of the discipline of silence and the emphasis put on fraternal relationships also seemed to Louf to be detrimental to the contemplative quality of the monastic life,[48] so that an important effort remained to be made to rediscover the meaning of *ascesis*. "Will we someday be able," he quasi-defiantly asks, "conveniently to demonstrate to our consumer society the rather piteous remains of the ancient monastic *ascesis*, as an authentic path to interior life?"[49]

But what above all alarmed Louf was the growth of a sensitivity encouraged by Dom Olivera that he saw as deviating

47. André Louf, "L'évolution de la vie monastique en France depuis le Concile," *Documents episcopat* no. 12 (June 1981): 1.

48. André Louf, "Vue d'ensemble sur la situation présente," in *L'Ordre Cistercien de la stricte observance au xxe siecle*, vol. 2, *Du concile vatican II a la fin du siècle,* ed. Marie-Gérard Dubois (Rome: OCSO, 2008), 2:206.

49. André Louf, "Quelques leçons d'un centenaire," *Collectanea Cisterciensia* 60 (1998): 223.

from the special grace of Cîteaux, a grace that consisted in a strictly cloistered and contemplative observance, a monasticism lived in a desert without compromise with the external world:

> With regard to that which was the central intuition of our fathers and of Saint Bernard, are we still lovers of contemplative repose, as convinced of it as ever, and still willing to pay the price? The inherent fragility of the marvelous gifts of God is unceasingly threatened by so many particulars of modern culture to which monks and nuns themselves have been led to sacrifice little things. The thing is especially obvious in our monastic economies, which are always at risk of seeing themselves dragged along into busy affairs. Our fathers applied themselves to "invent" a new economy that would keep the monks away from the world, in order to guarantee them the benefit of contemplative tranquility.[50]

Another temptation lay in wait for monks, Louf thought: that of looking for social or ecclesial justifications for preaching and for missions that led them to reduce the conditions of their enclosure, and in this way to lose their reason for being. More and more communities he said, were in this open break with the traditional separation from the world. Regretting this development, he described it as amounting to grave infidelity to the charism of Cîteaux, to "the *quies* favored by the early fathers,"[51] and to the DNA of the Cistercians, who in Saint Bernard's time were called "lovers of the desert."[52] So, to let his brothers take their bearings among these changes and to evaluate the "inculturations" that were underway, he entrusted one simple criterion to them: "Have these *aggiornamento*(s)

50. Louf, "Quelques leçons d'un centenaire," 224.
51. Louf, "Vue d'ensemble sur la situation présente," 207.
52. Louf, "Quelques leçons d'un centenaire," 221.

really improved the conditions of our solitude, in order to free up for us more and more space to favor our contemplative *quies*, that pearl of great price of our Bernardine Cistercian patrimony?"[53]

53. Louf, "Quelques leçons d'un centenaire," 225.

CHAPTER 16

Renunciation

January 10, 1988, was a feast day at the abbey of Mont-des-Cats. The twenty-five years that Louf had spent at the head of the community were being celebrated in an atmosphere joyous and fraternal. In the minds of so many monks this anniversary was a turning point, a transition. After so many years of an abbatial tenure that had fashioned a community and shaped its style and spirituality, Louf would soon retire. The moment had come. The monks sensed in a confused way that there was a need for a new start, and they seemed to be ready for a change, even if they knew that being separated from Dom André, then at the peak of his greatness, would be a tearing away. The election of 1990 was in everyone's mind. He was expected to be chosen abbot general. That would be a fitting crown for his career in the service of the Order, to which he still had much to give. But in fact he was not elected abbot general of the Trappists, and his resignation, which had kept being put off, would not take place until December 1997, almost ten years after this anniversary.

The Final Breath

From 1989 to 1990 the abbey's climate became heavy; the younger generation required air. The lost election of 1990 claimed attention. Dom André would have had to leave Mont-des-Cats if he had been made the supreme head, but now he returned to the monastery and no longer seemed pressed to give notice. The community was more and more openly divided between those who wanted to keep him and those who wanted him to go. Tension mounted to a crescendo. He sensed himself exposed to the hostility of certain cliques, and he lived painfully through a situation that he considered rejection of his own person. He then became slightly closed in upon himself, his trips became more frequent, and he turned his energies more and more to externals. Some of the brothers acted as if the government of the abbey were now without leadership, as though the abbot had quit; he neglected his chapter talks and abandoned his ministry. The atmosphere became suffocating and painful.

In 1994 the father immediate of Mont-des-Cats noticed this choked atmosphere and advised Louf to give up his charge. But Louf opposed him with all sorts of arguments: he was victimized by a clique that wanted to undermine his authority, he had not yet reached the limiting threshold of age seventy-five prescribed by the Constitutions, the time was not yet ripe, in two or three years the community would be better prepared to pass this point. But the question of his resignation was on the table from that point on. Louf suffered a pressure more and more regular and insistent, but rather than giving in to it, he waxed stubborn and kept putting off the date, as if he neither wanted to nor could turn the page. In July 1997, in the course of the regular visitation, when his retirement was confirmed, he tried to obtain a final delay of six months, before the visiting abbots of Tamié and Sept-Fons gave him to understand that this time it was no longer possible.[1]

1. Jean-Marc Thévenet, conversation with the author.

Maturation of a Decision

Nevertheless, Louf had for years been thinking about this renunciation. Already in 1989 he had written in his journal, "When I think of the ten or fifteen years of active life ahead of me, I often think of five years of ministry at Mont-des-Cats followed by resignation and old age: a humble, studious, solitary, and prayerful life. Such is my project, and such, I believe, are my deepest longings. But I place all that in Jesus' hands."[2] In 1994 he wrote,

> My stay at Portes in a Carthusian cell made the prospect of a possible retirement seem more pleasant. I could then live more or less as though on retreat and devote myself to *lectio* and prayer. I could feel myself to be in God's hands and abandon both initiative and choice to him. Concerning the future, two desires live in me. First I desire not to wait for my seventy-fifth birthday before resigning my abbatial charge. I even desire to resign without waiting too long a time. Then I desire that my departure should happen with the community's good pleasure.[3]

The following year, 1995, Louf wrote, "I was at Portes again by God's grace. After two regular visitations all is clear. Plan for my resignation in two or three years. Today I would say: Easter 1998; after the Centennial celebration for Cîteaux."[4] These entries prove that the prospect of departure did not find him unprepared. He saw it coming a long time beforehand, and he prepared himself for it with a concern for his community; he did not want to offend his brother monks by an excessively rushed departure or one that was too hasty.

2. André Louf, *Journal Spirituel* [hereafter JS], 16 July 1989.
3. Louf, JS, 22–23 June 1994.
4. Louf, JS, 13 Sept. 1995.

In June 1994 Louf received a letter from his close friend, Dom Denis Huerre, the former abbot of La Pierre-qui-vire, who had experienced this trial:

> I know you envisage giving up your charge. You confided that to me when I visited Mont-des-Cats. This is a brotherly message with a confidence that I place in you, having lived through those transitions, strong and lovely, that mark our road to God. For an abbot the giving up of his charge should be an act of love for Christ and for his community. If I were you I would send in my resignation before the regular visitation, leaving the community free in this way to choose its new father abbot and avoiding the mixed feelings—reasonable or affective—that can paralyze anyone's choice. Then you will avoid those useless pangs.
>
> If I were you, I would go to Latroun for a year, in order to have a community at Jerusalem to pray there and study the Bible. You would be free and comforted by God in that first phase (grief) that can be rough. Then you would be like a new man, able to render service, and to take on a responsibility here or there. You perhaps think me bold? But I have seen bruised abbots, after a long fruitful tenure, who were under constraint to efface themselves. Forestall going through a departure of that kind. You will see, Mont-des-Cats will be still freer, and you as well.[5]

Louf always kept this letter with him in his journal, proving that the question troubled him, and that he reflected on it unceasingly. He was anxious to accomplish his leave taking in a way that was comforting both for himself and for his community. Why, then, did he wait so long to do it?

5. Dom Denis Huerre, Letter to Dom Louf, ADMC, 30 June 1994.

The Intoxication of Solitude

To explain these delays, some people promoted the notion that Louf had completely identified himself with his abbatial charge and that he could no longer exist without it, all the more so as his election had taken place at a time when an abbot was still elected for life. The man and his office were henceforth one and the same. Louf was fully aware of the risk. Already in 1962, when he reluctantly gave up *Collectanea*, he wrote, "It is so hard to detach oneself from an employment, because we unconsciously identify ourselves with it. The function is for us a saving plank that we unconsciously cling to, to save ourselves from our own weakness, from our misery, and from our inferiority, in fact from the sin within us."[6] That is, he had a presentiment of the extent to which the giving up of a charge that had occupied his mind for more than thirty years would constitute a crucifying trial. He had written at length about this struggle:

> For years the abbot has progressively identified himself with a ministry that Saint Benedict himself intended to be the keystone of the community. The function has ended up forming the one who performed it, and neither the brothers nor he himself would be able to detach themselves from that "person" without some interior displacement. When all these links are found to be cut roughly, it is necessarily the person himself who collapses. He who had been covered by it in the desire to be helpful to others finds himself suddenly deprived of all the nourishment that had sustained his life and experience. He is then reduced to its barest expression, in other words to himself. That is to suppose that he still existed outside or above that personality. That is an event that is much easier to describe than to live. The

6. Louf, JS, 22 August 1962.

> abbot then runs the risk of falling into a void that he had neither foreseen nor expected.[7]

It is necessary not to underestimate this psychological dimension in Louf's difficulty in getting past a roadblock. If he kept putting off the decision to leave, was it not because he experienced a certain fear of the void, because he trembled at the vertiginous prospect of losing with one blow his whole social exterior, together with the stimulating solicitations that were part of it, of finding himself totally naked, with no support or space to maneuver? In the course of a retreat at Portes in 1996, he wrote in his diary, "To live the rest of my life with Jesus, devote all my time to this intimacy, and let Jesus himself grow in my heart."[8] God knows at what point he expected this loving face-to-face encounter to take place. But behold, all of a sudden the event happened! What he had so long desired and hoped for like a dream he had now to live out. Who would not be seized by panic at this prospect?

This reaction was all the more true now, since he knew by experience that before being a paradise, solitude is a cross. Far from removing obstacles, the hermitage accumulates difficulties, makes the heart naked, scatters illusions, robs the person of false images of God, and confronts the solitary with his truth, with flight being impossible. "The desert," he writes, "makes a man small; it is a poor road, deeply evangelical."[9] His journal reflects this ambivalence, awareness of solitude as the place of both God's presence and God's absence, blessing and despoilment. Consequently it both attracted and

7. André Louf, "Autrement la grâce n'est plus la grâce," in Andre Louf, Denis Huerre, and Marie-David Giraud, *Dieu intime: Paroles de Moines* (Paris: Bayard, 2003), 89–90.

8. Louf, JS, 15 Sept. 1996.

9. André Louf, "Gouvernement et accompagnement dans les communautés contemplatives," *Vie consacrée* 58 (1986): 345.

frightened him. At one point he wrote, "On the horizon there is hope of a brief but true time of solitude in two months. As usual, it both attracts and frightens me. Oh, I must really get over that someday. Anguish is a trial for our trust, but always a joyful symptom. It is a cry of alarm uttered by the sin that is in us and that is on the point of seeing the abandonment of a part of ourselves."[10] Again: "I experienced solitude at Belval. There was at the same time deep joy and anguish, because it required a despoilment that can no longer be avoided. It is the true desert. It is impossible to be distracted from Jesus and our inability, linked to our sin, to pay attention to Jesus alone."[11] Of course such an experience causes hesitation. The life of solitude, he wrote, is, citing Merton, "an exploration of that desert region where one is completely alone with God."[12] It plunges the hermit into the abyss of his nothingness and burns him in the furnace of temptation:

> Without fail solitude starts to weigh down the hermit like a leaden cape. The gray monotonous days that pass will give birth to weariness. The lack of external distractions will throw the solitary person back upon himself and upon all the desires that still swarm in his heart, till then unacknowledged. In the hubbub of worldly life they only sleep. Now they awake and hurl themselves out into the occupation of territory unoccupied until then. The diabolical monsters that painters like Hieronymus Bosch or writers like Gustave Flaubert have depicted in scenes of Saint Anthony or his rivals are nothing more than projections of what the solitary person finds in himself—sin and frailty. The postulant in solitude is quickly convinced of the fact that he is no better than

10. Louf, JS, 17 July 1960.

11. Louf, JS, 8 December 1961.

12. Thomas Merton, "La vie solitaire," *Collectanea Cisterciensia* 2 (1973): 138.

> the others. Solitude teaches him that he is a weak and unarmed person; he is prey to all the passions, from the most carnal to the most subtle and mental, a person henceforth uniquely exposed to the power of God's grace, if God so wills. And any provisional assurance of that is denied him.[13]

Louf continued to express his understanding of the way the solitary person experiences incapacity to persevere in the desert, short of a miracle for which one cannot hope, and he is uncertain how far God prepares him at a distance:

> It was to describe this crisis that Evagrius Ponticus coined the term *acedia*. It is a feeling of weariness touching on despair, which then settles in the solitary person's heart. Evagrius's description lets us catch a glimpse of the depth, both psychological and spiritual at once, of this purification that happens in the hermit's heart. It follows the heart down to its very roots. Sometimes the depression does not seem long, and *acedia* can show us some of its symptoms: physical and moral weakness, inability to feel pleasure, tearful crises, shooting pains of despair.[14]

What does this trial mean? He continued:

> By not immediately answering impatient dreams of contemplation, the Holy Spirit gently draws the solitary person toward the deeper regions of the heart where God awaits and where the solitary person has perhaps long been conspicuous by his absence. Solitude and silence will purify his experience of God there. On condi-

13. André Louf, "L'acédie des cénobites et des ermites," in *Triestesse, acedie, et medicine des ames: Anthologie de textes rares et inedits (XIIIe–XXe siecles)*, ed. Nathalie Nabert (Paris: Beauchesne, 2005), 173–74.

14. Louf, "L'acédie des cénobites," 174.

> tion of his watchfulness over this solitude that it may always remain true, the solitary person will end up there as if gropingly in the presence of his Lord, there where he abides in the depths of his being.[15]

Solitude is a paschal tomb. Before being reborn and transfigured, the postulant in the hermitage has to consent to suffering a death there, immersed in the night of faith. Who could reproach Louf for having delayed the falling due of this event, which after all he longed for with all his heart?

Finally one can understand none of these hesitations without taking into account the strong personal relationship that bound Louf to the brothers of Mont-des-Cats. "There is," he had already written in 1972, "a very strong tie between the abbot and his community. I believe that very deeply. Even if this tie is sometimes more or less unconscious, it is not for all that any less real, and it stamps us internally, the brothers just as much as the abbot. The abbot has no right to break unilaterally a mutual engagement of such high quality. If he acts in this way he runs the risk of deeply wounding his community."[16]

This deep tie shines out from Louf's correspondence full of warm affection, as in this letter written from Frattochie: "My absence is almost over, and I can even foresee that this is the last community letter that I will start. God knows how much joy those brief notes written on paper intended for you have brought me every day. They relieve my heart with all the affection that I feel for every one of you."[17] He also wrote from the United States to his brothers: "I received your letter this morning, and it brought me the atmosphere of

15. Louf, "L'acédie des cénobites," 177.

16. André Louf, Address to the chapter of Mont-des-Cats, ADMC, 24 April 1972.

17. André Louf, Letter to the community, ADMC, 28 April 1964.

Mont-des-Cats. I feel less an exile because of it."[18] Louf was abbot of a community, and he lived out his connection to that community as though it were an indissoluble claim. Did he not dread, even unconsciously, that his departure would strain their relationship?

Leaving La Trappe

The decision to resign was taken during the regular visitation in June 1997. Louf officially reported it to the abbot general in September, and Dom Bernardo accordingly sent one of his counselors to Mont-des-Cats: Dom Loys Samson, the former abbot of Cîteaux. Samson had Louf's confidence to smooth the way with the community. "I have received Dom Louf's resignation," Dom Bernardo had written to the community. "Before accepting it, I thought it would be opportune to know the thoughts of each one of you on the matter. So I decided to send you my permanent counselor, Dom Loys, to meet each one, hear your thoughts, and let me know them."[19] A month later the abbot general accepted the resignation: "My initial response is a feeling and a conviction of great recognition for all that Dom André has done during his long service for you, for his community, for the Order, and even for the whole monastic life."[20] From Louf's decision to lay down his charge in June until the election of his successor, Dom Guillaume Jedrzejczak, in December, six months passed in a heavy, suffocating, and slightly sad atmosphere.

Dom Louf left the abbey secretly one Thursday in October, while the conventual Mass was in full swing. "That act hurt

18. André Louf, Letter to the community, ADMC, 21 Jan. 1983.

19. Bernardo Olivera, Letter to the community of Mont-des-Cats, ADMC, 29 Sept. 1997.

20. Bernardo Olivera, Letter to the community of Mont-des-Cats, 10 Oct. 1997.

the community very much," Dom Guillaume testified. "I recall that I told him, 'No one should leave like that. People have a need to tell you goodbye.' He left us in the worst way possible, at a moment when no one could be there, even to close the gate when he passed. I sensed that he just could not face that goodbye."[21] But Louf had created that community. He had given it his own prestige, and he had exerted an uncommon human and spiritual influence upon it. Could his separation from it take place in any other way? It was the conclusion of a love story. Like all loves that are rudely interrupted, it could not be ended without tears and strong feelings.

After his sudden departure in October 1997, Louf spent six or seven weeks uneasily wandering in quest of a place to stay. To those who met him during this short time, he presented the figure of a fallen man coming down from Mount Tabor. It was undoubtedly the most trying of times for this man who had been so recently famous. Another abbot who had also passed through the crisis of this trial of retirement reported, "You have the impression of facing an enormous emptiness. It is all over, and you have nothing left. I think that at such a moment all the remaining time seems like a kind of deep chasm that you have to cross."[22] For Louf the experience must have been all the more difficult because he had barely prepared for his departure.

Concerning these six weeks when he had no fixed abode, opinions differ. Some say he spent time at Belval, others at La Fille-Dieu. One thing is sure: he visited his friend, Dr. Ronse de Craene, at Bruges. Then in December he stopped at the Abbey of Simiane in Provence, where the abbess proposed that he fulfill his dream of living as a hermit behind her abbey in a hermitage, which she could build for him if that was his wish. Louf accepted her proposal on the spot.

21. Marc-André di Péa, conversation with the author.

22. Citation not provided in the French volume.

While waiting for the work to proceed, he spent seven months at the Carthusian house of Portes, from February to August 1998, returning to Simiane in September. Since the hermitage was not yet finished, he took up provisional quarters in a painter's studio used by Frère Muban. In December 1998 he was permanently installed in his little house, where some sheep and a donkey had previously lived.[23]

Information about this transitional year comes from a letter Louf wrote to Dr. Ronse de Craene:

> It has now been more than a year since I visited you to say my goodbyes at your Chartreuse, where you were so admirably hidden in the greenery. That was a rather painful day for me. A year later I celebrated its anniversary with a heart full of thanksgiving, which signifies that so many things have happened since. Six months passed in the Carthusian house, then in September I stayed on the fringe of a Benedictine monastery where a hermitage (or a villa) was built for my use. Once I was an apostolic visitor of this community, and the sisters have kept a strong memory of me from that occasion. God is certainly a genius. I would never have dared even to dream of such a gift! One phrase you spoke last year, "It is a beautiful thing to realize in one's old age a dream of his youth," has been a great support for me.[24]

Except for the handful of weeks that passed between October and November, when he was looking for a resting place, Louf does not seem to have greatly suffered from his departure or foundered in a depression of any kind. "For the whole

23. Mère Elaié Bollen, "L'ermite de Sainte Lioba," in André Louf, *S'abandonner á l'amour: Meditations á Sainte Lioba*, ed. Charles Wright (Paris: Salvator, 2017).

24. André Louf, Letter to Dr. Ronse de Craene, 19 Dec. 1998, Personal archives of the Ronse de Craene family.

length of his life," wrote an Italian Benedictine, "P. André was convinced that an abbot who has not prepared his resignation runs the risk of falling into a serious crisis. He told me one day, 'I have met many abbots who fell into depression after their resignation, but that has not happened to me, thank God. I do not know how to put it into practice, but I have a great desire to retire.' "[25] If he suffered pain, it was the pain of going adrift. But once the ties were broken, he quickly found his equilibrium again in his profound desire. His friend, Dom Jacques Dupont, procurator general of the Carthusians, bore witness to his recovery:

> After he had to retire he spent some time at the Carthusian house of Portes. After some days had passed, the prior asked him how things were going, since generally speaking abandoning an office like that of abbot after so many years results in some bitterness. But Dom André answered him, "Everything is going well; I do not need to be sorry for myself." The meaning is clear, especially from the lips of a man experienced in psychology: "I have no need to groan internally for having accepted this being put aside." We can see in the episode a clear sign of the spiritual standard of Dom André: He was completely detached from himself, from his office, from its title, and from the attitude of others toward himself. His heart and his spirit were in God.[26]

At Mont-des-Cats Dom André had missed his goodbye. He was aware of it. His departure was too long drawn out, and it left wounds and tensions that bruised the community. He regretted it sharply for the sake of the brothers. But he also saw it as a certain mark of grace. Was not this failure a

25. Roberto Loi, "Alla Scuola della Grazia. Il Percorso Spirituale di P. André Louf," *La Scala* 70 (2016): 39.

26. Dom Jacques Dupont, correspondence with the author.

way of being configured to Jesus' passion? His departure was in human eyes without splendor. "Whether we like it or not," he would avow, "the idealized image that we construct for ourselves of our future 'resignation' has always given up much to the narcissistic image that each one of us unconsciously fashions for himself. The applause thereof has been anticipated. The reality is something else. It has too much resemblance to Jesus' passover. And that too is much better."[27]

In November 1997, a few days after his resignation, Louf wrote in his journal, "At last fulfilled, if I may say so. For long years I have prayed every day for this moment. Now here I am, upheld by your grace from moment to moment. Thank you for these thirty-five years of abbatial tenure. Thank you also for my ability to offer them to you. It is an offering whose total importance I cannot yet weigh, nor its suffering, nor its joy. It could have been terminated with more panache, but a little something like me had to show a greater resemblance to you. It is better so, O Jesus."[28]

27. André Louf, "Autrement la grâce n'est plus la grace," in André Louf, Denis Huerre, Marie-David Giraud, *Dieu intime: Paroles de moines* (Paris: Bayard, 2003), 92.

28. Louf, JS, 21 Nov. 1997.

CHAPTER 17

The Hermit of Saint-Lioba

One morning at sunrise in December 1970 Louf was in in Rome. Sitting in the foremost stalls, he watched the rising of the sun: "The colors slowly succeed one another in the sky. Violet becomes purple, purple changes to scarlet, which turns into orange, then to golden yellow. Then suddenly a point of bright light seems to flash out over the mountain top like a tangent between heaven and earth: the top of the solar disk appeared as pure gold. In a few seconds the Tiber valley was inundated with light, and the belfries and cupolas of the Eternal City lit up like a solemn liturgy."[1] He loved the Flemish light, which he said "possesses an intimacy, an interior power of meditation, almost a modesty that excavates a depth in the landscape and in hearts," but Provence, with its midday sun and its dazzling heat, was where he chose to end his life. The sun's vivid red was the shining image of this incandescent ardent God, "consuming fire" (Heb 12:29), in whose presence he desired to warm himself.

When Louf was dispatched in 1978 by Rome to aid a community to get beyond a difficult point, he discovered the abbey of Saint-Lioba at Simiane. He was enchanted at first sight by this corner of Provence. Everything seduced him: the velvet

1. André Louf, Letter to the community, ADMC, 3 Dec. 1970.

landscape, the light that reminded him of Tuscany and Umbria, the odors of cypress trees, vineyards, lavender. But he also appreciated the quality of community prayer and contemplative beauty, the complementarity of masculine and feminine voices that made for a splendid harmony in choir. "The liturgy at which I assist is always rather refined," he wrote. "The vestments are ample and colorful. The musical instruments succeed one another. One day there is a harp, another day a flute and a viola da gamba, the next day a lute. Everything is lovely, dignified, and harmonious, and at the same time very expansive."[2] Then, in this community founded by Hildegard Michaelis, a woman from the Netherlands, where Dutch was still spoken, he felt himself at home, in his own northerly climate: "It is really and rather curiously a corner of Holland in Provence."[3] But what he loved above all was the originality of this community and the quality of its artists: painters, potters, and philocalic weavers, "lovers of beauty," who gave importance to art in their journey to God.

Ever since the 1980s Louf had been a close friend to these brothers and sisters of Saint-Lioba. His ties with them continued to grow stronger, and especially with the abbess, Mère Elaié, with whom he shared an attraction for Carthusian life. So when he reached Simiane after his resignation in 1997, slightly disoriented, not knowing well what he was doing, he accepted on the spot Mère Elaié's proposition to transform the former donkey's stable into a hermitage where he could finally realize his deepest desire: enclosure for the love of God in a life of solitary prayer.[4]

2. André Louf, Letter to the community, ADMC, 3 Dec. 1970.

3. André Louf, Letter to the community, ADMC, 3 Dec. 1970.

4. Mère Elaié Bollen, "L'ermite de Sainte-Lioba," in André Louf, *S'abandonner á l'amour: Meditations á Sainte-Lioba*, ed. Charles Wright (Paris: Salvator, 2017).

"A Youthful Dream come True at a Mature Age"

On a visit to Chartreuse de Portes in 1975 Louf wrote,

> Vigil of love with a humble density. Through silence and even the absence of any feeling, something happened like a mutual presence of one person to another. Perhaps it was an intense gaze by God directed towards me. I had to stay there with joined hands without losing anything of this darkness or of this great sweetness. The Lord always gives me the same attraction for the hesychast way of life, so I should not be surprised if someday he fulfills it in my life. Will he perhaps very suddenly and unexpectedly be there to offer it to me, not necessarily as a repulse or a catastrophe, but by a path not yet presently imaginable?[5]

Again, at Abbey of Mont-des-Cats, 1977:

> When I think of the future, an intuition remains very strong: The Lord will someday grant me the trial of a solitary life with all the deprivations implied by such a life. The older I get the more a certain fear grips me that my time will run out. And I would love to have this solitary trial marked as well by a certain length of time as being necessarily part of it, it seems to me. I do not know where or how this can happen. One thing is sure: I should not abandon the place I presently hold. Nevertheless I have the confidence that the Lord will show me what to do.[6]

At the end of 1998, the moment so long awaited and hoped for arrived: "Since yesterday I entered into solitude. Thank you, Lord Jesus, endless thanks. These days before Christmas,

5. André Louf, *Journal Spirituel* [hereafter JS], 24 Sept. 1975.
6. Louf, JS, 5 July 1977.

I have the impression that this whole life of solitude will pass like a long waiting period before great happiness."[7]

Throughout his life the abbot lived a kind of "second vocation"[8] that never stopped stealthily keeping him company. It lived with him in the cloister of his thoughts, alone with God, identified with God's will, available for whatever God wanted, as he devoted all the moments of his day to this prayer that would in principle be uninterrupted. After these desires had continued to spring up around him for thirty years, they had finally been heard. His psychiatrist friend, Dr. Ronse de Craene, told him one day, "A successful life is a youthful dream come true at a mature age."[9]

The Eremitical Life

Situated at the back of the abbey's enclosure, the hermitage resembled a small shed, with walls of ochre and a tile roof. Its surroundings were the countryside of Provence: olive and cypress trees, holm oaks, blue sky, and in front the massive Pilon du Roi. The barriers of trees hid the hermitage from curious eyes and served as the borders of a small garden. The inside of the hermitage was divided into three rooms: the first served as an office, the second was a modest refectory, and the third screened a humble chapel where the solitary also put his bed. In this slender oratory was a small table that held candles, a chalice, and four pieces of stone—one from Jerusalem, one from the monastic desert of Judah, and the other two from Mount Athos and La Grande Chartreuse. There

7. Louf, JS, 23 Dec. 1998.

8. André Louf, "Autrement la grâce n'est plus la grace," in André Louf, Denis Huerre, and Marie-David Giraud, *Dieu intime: Paroles de moines* (Paris: Bayard, 2003), 92.

9. André Louf, Letter to Dr. Hubert Ronse de Craene, Archives of the Ronse de Craene family, Ronse.

was also a face of Christ painted by an early Flemish painter. Night and day Louf recited the Divine Office in front of that painting. On the left was a magnificent iconostasis holding ancient Russian icons.

There reigned in this little house such clutter that one could hardly clear a path all the way to the door. Everywhere were piles of books heaped up, correspondence, articles, dictionaries, DVDs, CDs. On the walls were photos of the Mont-des-Cats community, the pictures of certain monks of Mount Athos, including the hermit Païssios, and pictures of young monks whom Louf had accompanied as spiritual father. In his office, beside the organ, was a small portable computer connected to the Internet, some icons, some masterpieces of sacred art, some selections from Bach, and even an iPod. Finally there was a radio receiver on which Louf could hear the news during mealtime, when he did not activate the CDs for sacred music.

From the first months of his occupancy, Louf was faced with a dilemma. "There were," he realized, "proposals for apostolic activity. Requests for the preaching of retreats and the giving of conferences, as well as missions, were not lacking. Could I have continued to devote myself to them?"[10] He wrote to the new abbot of Mont-des-Cats that Mère Elaié "knew very well the life I wanted to live, and she jealously watched over my enclosure."[11] His spiritual father was Dom Gerard Marie Meneust, abbot of Melleray from 1995 to 2017, whom he called every Sunday afternoon for a telephone rendezvous. To this routine he remained faithful until the end of his life. It restored his facing up to his long-standing desire to lead a contemplative life in a profound, solitary way. Mère

10. André Louf, *À la grâce de Dieu: Entretiens avec Stéphane Delberghe* (Namur: Fidélité, 2002), 43.

11. André Louf, Letter to Guillaume Jedrzejczak, abbot of Mont-des-Cats, ADMC, 12 April 2001.

Elaié drove him on in the same way and invited him to make a clear-cut choice: "Either to become rooted in an experience of true solitude in order to find peace in it progressively, or to become an 'abbot on retreat' but just as busy as before (or even more so) and no longer living on anything but nostalgia."[12]

Louf was grateful to these two friends, who made him aware of the risk that requests from outside would militate against the intention that ought to be his witness from then on: silence, separation from the world, joyful repentance, and continual prayer in waiting for the world to come. So he radically broke away from the world in favor of the solitary life, and he settled on this line of conduct: "Among the many invitations that I still receive regularly, I accepted only two or three a year, in order not to run the risk of retiring within myself in my solitude. Such was the advice of my spiritual father, and it seemed sound to me. But how was I to choose among these requests? What I needed was a 'token.' So I made an agreement with the Lord only to accept those meetings that had a certain ecumenical component. That was my token."[13] He answered a Cistercian abbot who asked him to preach a retreat,

> I would love to please you, but I do not wish it if my silence is to remain. The important thing is quite simply the way of life that is to be mine from now on, and I believe that way is a special vocation the Lord has given me. In a still more special way it is the wonderful answer to an interior desire that has endlessly grown during the years of my abbatial service. Here I am finally, providentially answered in conditions that are really exceptional. It seems to me that I have no right to give them up without reasons that are really obvious, and without

12. Louf, *À la grâce de Dieu*, 43.
13. Louf, Letter to Guillaume Jedrzejczak, 12 April 2001.

> an absolutely clear sign on the Lord's part. For the moment then I hold myself bound by the rule: two or three regularly scheduled interventions in the course of a year, preferably with an ecumenical flavor.[14]

After making this decision, Louf refused all conferences, retreats, and meetings, even though invitations were not lacking. He made two exceptions to this rule: ecumenical meetings, essentially confined to relations with the Orthodox Church. He had cultivated numerous friendships with the Orthodox. A mutual esteem existed between him and Msgr. Hilarion Alfeyev, who represented the patriarchate of Moscow. Alfeyev was brilliant, and Louf translated many of his works.[15] Alfeyev also paid many visits to Louf at Simiane. In addition Louf participated in the large ecumenical gatherings concerning Orthodox spirituality that were held annually at the Italian monastery of Bose, where he became the quasi-spokesman for Western spirituality. At the meeting on Russian spirituality in 2001, he gave a talk on hesychasm,[16] and the following year he spoke of spiritual paternity.[17] In 2003 his contribution was a treatise on spiritual accompaniment in Palestinian monachism in the seventeenth century.[18] In 2007

14. André Louf, Letter to Jean-Marie Couvreur, ADMC, 23 Oct. 2000.

15. Louf translated the following two works from Russian: Hilarion Alfeyev, *L'univers spirituel d'Isaac le Syrien* (Bégrolles-en-Mauges: Abbaye de Bellefontaine, 2001), and *Le nom grand et Glorieux: La vénération du nom de Dieu et la prière de Jésus dans la tradition orthodoxe* (Paris: Cerf, 2007).

16. "Alcune costanti spirituali nelle tradizioni esicaste d'oriente e occidente," in *Vie del Monachesimo Russo,* ed. Adalberto Mainardi (Magnano: Qiqajon, 2001), 33–36.

17. André Louf, "La paternità spirituale," in *Abba, dimmi uns parola*! (Magnano: Qiqajon, 1989), 75–85.

18. "Barsanufio e Giovanni: Un Accompagnamento Spirituale Concertato," in *Il Deserto di Gaza: Barsanufio, Giovanni e Doroteo,* ed. John Chryssavgis (Magnano: Qiqajon, 2004), 179–284.

he spoke on Guigo the Carthusian,[19] and in 2009 on the theme of prayer in Isaac the Syrian.[20]

Louf also participated in Interconfessional International Meetings on Religion (EIIR). In July 2004 in Finland he gave a conference on the link between prayer and ecology,[21] and in July 2006, speaking to some German deaconesses, he gave an as-yet-unpublished conference on a similar topic titled "Transfiguration as an Icon of the Consecrated Life." These yearly meetings, where Christians belonging to all confessional traditions met to pray and reflect together, were for Louf a "form of prophecy."[22] Louf loved the community at Bose, where he was always received with a warm welcome. He was much attached to the founder, Enzo Bianchi, with whom he shared the same vision of monastic life. "I have always felt on the same wavelength with all that Enzo could publish, and the reverse must be true as well," he wrote to his brothers during a visit to Bose.[23]

Louf's second exception to his rule of strict solitude was openness to the Carthusian way of life. Each year he spent Lent at the Italian Carthusian house of Serra San Bruno, and twice a year he went to La Grande Chartreuse, where he did duty as the extraordinary confessor for the monks. "This year," he wrote to a friend, "I again spent the season of Lent at the Carthusian house of Serra San Bruno in south Italy,

19. "La Trasfigurazione nella-Scala dei monaci di Guigo II il certosino," in Ilarion Alfeyev, et al., *Il Cristo trasfigurato nella tradizione spirituale ortodossa* (Magnano: Qiqajon, 2008), 263–76.

20. "Isacco il siro e la lotta della preghiera," in *Lalotta spirituale nella tradizione ortodossa,* ed. Enzo Bianchi and Sabino Chialà (Magnano: Qiqajon, 2010), 75–93.

21. "La vie de prière: engagement pour la sauvegarde de la création," *Collectanea Cisterciensia* 66 (2004): 260–74.

22. André Louf, Préface to Mario Torcivia, *Enzo Bianchi et la communauté de Bose* (Paris: Salvator, 2005), 5.

23. André Louf, Letter to the community, ADMC, 25 August 1997.

where Bruno spent the last years of his life, and where his relics rest in the church. I find the Carthusian rhythm quite suitable, and I have very good relations with the monks there. The prior is French, and there are also a Swiss, a Slovak, and an Argentinian. The rest are Italian, twelve monks."[24] "He came to Serra San Bruno," confirms Dom Jacques Dupont, former prior of that Carthusian house, "every year until 2010, the year of his death, to live with us during Lent and to celebrate Easter. It had become a tradition.[25]

To avoid repeating himself or letting himself be drawn by his impressions, Dom André drew up a horarium for himself, based on the Carthusian horarium. It prescribed what he was to do at each moment of the day: go to bed at 8 p.m., rise at midnight, keep vigil for three hours of prayer (the Office of Vigils with readings from the monastic fathers), sleep again at 3 a.m., and then get up at 5:15 for Lauds. He celebrated Mass alone each morning except on Sunday, when he joined the community of Saint-Lioba. Then he continued his *lectio divina* until 8:30. After briefly reviewing the news on the Internet, he worked until noon. Dinner was followed by a short siesta, then by another session of work until Vespers, celebrated at 5:00. He celebrated Compline at 8:00, and then it was time to go to bed.[26] Every Monday afternoon Louf found it agreeable to space himself.[27] He often used this time to walk to the village of Simiane.

24. André Louf, Letter to a friend, ADMC, 26 May 2006.

25. Jacques Dupont, correspondence with the author.

26. Roberto Loi, "Alla Scuola della grazia: Il percorso spirituale di p. Andre Louf," *La Scala* 69 (2015), and 70 (2016): 40–41.

27. The term, "to space," explains Dom Jacques Dupont, "means the act of taking space or of moving into a broader area. The monk lives during the week in a cell of limited dimensions. From there he moves out on Mondays to enlarge his horizon in the space of a world that surrounds him" (*Seul devant l'unique: Entretiens avec un chartreux* (Paris: Parole et Silence, 2016), 169.

Louf followed this time division rigorously, but also flexibly, and he knew how to isolate himself to be free for the care of the soul. "In the beginning," he wrote, "when the novice is initiated into solitary life, he needs a relatively strict horarium, which he is asked to follow literally. . . . But in this matter, more perhaps than elsewhere, the external rule only plays a pedagogical role on the path of spiritual freedom, and it should render him progressively attentive to the internal rule, that is, to the Holy Spirit in the depth of his heart."[28]

Ora et Labora

Louf's prayer was nourished by the celebration of the liturgy, the monastic Divine Office, which he usually read in solitude. He recited this prayer according to the cycle of hours. It created a climate of recollection, a musical background that accompanied his day like a mysterious presence. So that these Offices might remain living, he regularly changed his language. In front of his bed, a small bookcase held the books needed for the liturgy of the hours in Latin, Syriac, Russian, Italian, English, etc. He changed language as often as he wished, so for example Spanish if he considered it best for the chanting of the Office on a particular day.

As the years passed the prayer became ever more simple. Already in 1992 Louf had written in his journal, "The words I say at prayer are now reduced to what is essential: 'Into your hands I commend my spirit—let your will be done in me—thank you for your marvelous deeds, renew your marvels in me—you are my love—Guide me to your love—Take me for your love.' "[29] For the Carthusian Dom Porion, with whom Louf used to have frequent conversations, such simplicity is the secret of prayer. "The more complicated we are,"

28. André Louf, "Saint Bruno," *Documents episcopat* no. 12–13 (2001): 14.

29. Louf, JS, 13 March 1992.

he says, "the further we are from God. To chat with his father, does a child need to use a manual on correspondence or a code of polite behavior? No. The child talks simply and does not search for perfect phrases. He does not end with any formal construction. We should act in that way toward our heavenly Father."[30]

That is how Louf's prayer at Saint-Lioba developed: it had a childlike simplicity and was often confined to what is called in the Christian East the prayer of the heart, that is, the slow repetition of the name of Jesus. Louf often added some verses of the Word of God recalled from his day's *lectio*, what John Cassian calls the *voluntatio cordis*, the act of "turning over," revolving and returning a word of Holy Scripture in the heart. "We might call it," he explained, "the rolling waves of the heart. In other words, it is the beating and rocking of the name of Jesus within oneself."[31] Louf remained faithful to this way of prayer, sometimes with consolations to be felt, at other times with interior dryness. But he was indifferent to these changing feelings. As he explained,

> All that depends on God's will. I abandon myself to that will. I abandon myself to whatever he wants to do with me today. The rest does not concern me and is unimportant. I find a great deal of peace by exposing myself in this way to the holy will of God in the very moment of prayer. It is a peace that is very deep, beyond all power of sensation. I think I am in God's hands and abandoned to him. It is a story of love, persevering, humble, and abandoned to all that the Lord wills. I love him, and he loves me. I feel happy and fulfilled.[32]

30. Jean-Baptiste Porion, *Amour et silence et autres textes* (Paris: Ad Solem, 2010), 40–41.

31. André Louf, *Initiation à la vie spirituelle* (Paris: Parole et Silence, 2008), 63.

32. André Louf, "Paroles d'ermite," unpublished papers: archives.

Louf had composed a prayer that he recited every time he entered his cell:

> Holy Mary, virgin recluse in the temple, Mother in whose womb the Son was enclosed, tenderness of the Father, sweetness of the Spirit, gateway to heaven! Receive me in this beloved solitude as if it were the hidden abyss of God! Hide me there as in the hollow of his Face. Let me be conceived by the Holy Spirit in the womb that bears and brings forth the new man, the church of the first-born, and the coming kingdom. Grant that I may endure there meekly, fighting the angel of God until daybreak, persevering in humble patience and faith, keeping vigil in prayer, growing mature at the will of grace. Grant that I may remain there until he comes, abiding in Jesus and abiding in love, rooted in his word, reposing in the blessed womb, recollected in the quietness of God, breathing the name of his tenderness, satisfied with the beauty of his face, gathering the fruits of his love, exulting with joy and overflowing with thanksgiving. Seed of Easter for this passing world, distraught expectation of his return, but witness already of the assumption of all things into the light and peace of the unending day of eternity.[33]

To declare his communion with the community of Saint-Lioba that had welcomed him, Louf chose to celebrate some hours of the Divine Office with them. He was a recluse in his cell, from which he only emerged to be with the brothers and sisters at Vespers every evening. He came down limping with halting steps along the little path that connected his hermitage with the abbey church, like Jacob after his wrestling match with the angel. He had retained a slight limp after an operation on his hip in 1978, so he gave an impression of hesitation

33. Louf, "Paroles d'ermites."

when he walked. On Sundays he also celebrated the Eucharist with the community and gave a homily on that occasion, taking turns with Frère Muban, the community's chaplain. "They were homilies full of light," recalled Mère Elaié, "that showed us a way of life: how to place all our confidence in another Person, Jesus, stronger than our weakness, and to consent to always become smaller, following the Lord's example."[34] For the brothers and sisters of Simiane, having Louf stay with them was a grace. "He shone with God," confirmed the abbess, "by his presence, his words, and his homilies, which reflected his interior life and became as the years passed always shorter, simpler, and more lovely. Dom André reminded us of our deepest desire that we wanted to live out. He was like a reminder, a horizon, and a lantern for our road."[35]

In Louf's life prayer alternated with work, allowing him to attain a certain interior stability. Although he devoted himself slightly at first to the cultivation of a garden, he soon abandoned this manual activity to concentrate on intellectual work. In this way he contributed some articles on Isaac the Syrian[36] and Syméon de Taibouch,[37] and participated in some meetings, particularly on Elizabeth of the Trinity[38] and

34. Mère Elaié Bollen, conversation with the author.

35. Mère Elaié Bollen, conversation with the author.

36. André Louf, "L'Homme dans l'histoire du salut selon Isaac le Syrien," *Connaissance des pères de l'Église* 88 (2002): 44–54; "Pourquoi Dieu se manifeste, selon Isaac le Syrien," *Connaissance des pères de l'Église* 80 (Dec. 2000): 37–56; "Isaac le Syrien, La grâce, non pas les Œuvres," *Proche-orient chrétien* 5 (2001): 243–46.

37. André Louf, "Introduction à Syméon de Taibouch," *Collectanea Cisterciensia* 64 (2002): 30–33.

38. This meeting was held in 2006 at Venasque during the celebration of the centenary anniversary of the death of Elizabeth of the Trinity. It resulted in the publication of *Élisabeth de la Trinité: L'aventure mystique*, ed. Jean Clapier (Toulouse: Éditions du Carmel, 2006), to which Louf contributed "Elisabeth de la Trinité et Ruusbroec" (53–69).

acedia of monks.[39] But he remained above all an exceedingly active translator. It was at Simiane in fact that he completed the rendering in readable French of the works of Ruusbroec. Volume IV of the *Écrits de Ruusbroec*, translated and presented by André Louf, was published by Éditions de Bellefontaine in 1999. The first volume appeared in 1990, the second in 1993, and the third in 1997. The only existing translation before then dated from the 1930s, and as Louf explained, "it was not made from the Dutch language of the original, but from a Latin translation of the sixteenth century, which was unfortunately marred by the 'Thomist' formation of the team of translators, and Ruusbroec's vocabulary is a stranger to Saint Thomas's."[40] "It is the best French translation I know," opines Paul Verdeyen, a specialist on Flemish mysticism,[41] and the judgment pronounced by the theologian Adolphe Gesché is that Louf "has contested with Maeterlinck the honor of rendering the acoustics of a language in such a way that the indefinable Flemish and the Latin are familiarly weighed against each other."[42]

But above all Louf was beating a path that would occupy him for the rest of his life: the translation of the unpublished sermons of Isaac the Syrian, collaborating with Sabino Chiala,

39. After a meeting held in 2005 at the Institut Catholique de Paris, Louf published "L'acédie des cénobites et des ermites," in *Tristesse, acédie et médecine des âmes: Anthologie de textes rares et inédits (XIIIe–XXe siècles)*, ed. Nathalie Nabert (Paris: Beauchesne, 2005), 165–79.

40. André Louf, *À la grâce de Dieu: Entretiens avec Stephane Delberghe* (Namur: Fidelité, 2002), 152.

41. Paul Verdeyen, in a conversation with the author. During this period Louf also translated a thesis by this same Flemish Jesuit: Paul Verdeyen, *Guillaume de Saint-Thierry: Premier auteur mystique des anciens Pays-Bas* (Turnhout: Brepols, 2003).

42. Adolphe Gesché, [? Discours pour la remise du titre de Docteur honoris causa à André Louf, Université catholique de Louvain, 2 Feb. 1994]. [The French volume provides no citation, but the words seem likely to have come from this address. BK.]

a monk of Bose, along with the works of Syméon of Taibouteh. Many of these writings had been published during Louf's lifetime,[43] but many others saw daylight only posthumously. The work began with the translation *Sur les monts du Caucase*, which appeared in 2016, a masterpiece of philocalic spirituality.[44] At Sources Chrétiennes three volumes on William of Saint-Thierry translated by Louf will soon be published. Treasures of Syriac spirituality, notably unpublished works by Syméon de Taibouteh and others by Isaac, along with a text by Dadisho on quietness should also appear soon.[45]

Louf also became entranced by the memoirs of a Flemish mystic rediscovered at Simiane, Maria Petyt. He wrote to a friend about his reading of her work:

> I began the autobiography of Maria Petyt, a Flemish mystic who lived in the seventeenth century. She was born at Poperinge, and she grew up at Hazelbrouck. She led the life of a semi-recluse at Gand and Malines. She writes a Flemish that is absolutely delightful, whose vocabulary shows the strong influence of Ruusbroec. I had a photocopy done years ago (made from a seventeenth-century edition) with the intention of translating it into French someday, certainly after Ruusbroec, and undoubtedly concurrently with Isaac and other Syrians.[46]

Separated from All and United with All

A celebrated desert father of the fourth century, Evagrius of Ponticus, described the position of monks at the heart of

43. Isaac le Syrien, *Oeuvres spirituelles* II and *Oeuvres Spirituelles* III (Bégrolles-en-Mauges: Éditions de Bellefontaine, 2003, 2009).

44. The dedication of this book reads, "This version of the book is dedicated to the memory of Dom André Louf, the originator of the project" (Paris: Éditions des Syrtes, 2016), 6.

45. None of these books has yet appeared. BK.

46. André Louf, Letter to a friend, ADMC, 6 Feb. 1999.

the church with this aphorism: "The monk is a person who is separated from all and united with all." Louf lived this mysterious presence to the world intensely at Simiane. He was persuaded that beyond his material enclosure he was rejoining the assembly of the people of God and even of all humanity whom he upheld by his intercession. That is how he conceived of his vigils of prayer. "During Vigils," he wrote in his diary, "I bear on my eyelids all the heavy sleep of the world, and in that way I keep some part of it awake for God."[47] "When we arose for the night office at 1:00 in the morning," wrote Mère Elaié, "on desert days we noticed that the light was on at the hermitage. It was still on when we returned at 2:30. We then realized his faith and loyalty that kept him awake every day, praying for the people in this world."[48]

Hermits are apparently good for nothing. They retire from the world to live alone, and they cannot pay their respects to the Gospel precept that calls all Christians to announce the good news. But Louf relied upon Saint Thomas Aquinas, believing that hermits' outreach belongs to a different order, and that hermits abide at a depth that is beyond visibility. It is not necessary for them to be seen or known; it is enough for their existence to be acknowledged somewhere. In fact, the more invisible hermits are, the better the witness that they bear. They are united to the Lord and to the Eucharist, and they bear witness to a reality that is essential for the life of the church. Louf wrote of the hermit, "He is united in a privileged way to the church's Bridegroom, and he represents the whole church in some way, which in turn is identified with him."[49] Like a question mark, hermits are a sign for the world. The solitary invites believers and all humanity to go

47. Louf, JS, 11 Sept. 1964.

48. Bollen, "L'ermite de Saint-Lioba."

49. André Louf, "La solitude monastique: Séparé de tous et unis à tous," *Christus* 180 (1998): 429.

beyond what is visible and reminds them that an interior dialogue with God can fill one's life.

Louf often cited Saint Peter Damian, a tenth-century theologian who coined the phrase "plural solitude." The phrase is a way of saying that the most solitary hermit is found to be in permanent contact with the church, that the hermit's solitude is always inhabited and linked to other people, that it opens out upon a fullness of communion. "What the hermit celebrates," Louf explained, "is echoed in the whole church. In prayer no gesture can be strictly solitary anymore. Peter Damian goes so far as to say that the hermit can be called a *minor ecclesia* or a 'micro-church,' a miniature church, which is in communion with all the other members and already possessing in itself all the essentials of the church's mystery."[50]

There is then an apostolic fruitfulness in contemplative solitude. For Louf it was of the highest importance that twenty-first-century Christians should rediscover that fruitfulness, and that they should also remember that the church should always be supported by the desert. "Her roots," he argued, "must be buried in the desert as in God's soil. The desert is her home ground, from which her works begin. She is not afraid to withdraw or retreat to it at certain times, to stay at a distance, to collect her thoughts, and to let her word grow rich, the word that she will proclaim in the sight of men, which will be spoken the more forcefully the more surely it has been heard from God's mouth."[51]

In the desert, solitaries rejoin the world by being present to their own heart. Because the desert robs them of their contingency, it makes them face their alienation, their sin, and their great need for God. By doing so they discover the

50. André Louf, "Solitudo pluralis," *Solitude et communion* 28 (1990): 42.

51. André Louf, "Saint Benoît, homme de Dieu pour tous les temps," *Collectanea Cisterciensia* 42 (1980): 18.

plots that are hatched in all human hearts. "The most hidden depths of human beings," Louf wrote, "remain unexplored as long as the human being has not yet been led to go all the way to the goal of solitude. There in his solitude, in his own heart, the monk becomes a brother of men and of poor sinful humanity. His heart bears the sins of the universe."[52]

But the solitary's communion with the world also takes a more direct approach. "The one who retires attracts" is a common saying that has been often verified in monastic history. Whenever one becomes spiritual and is able to share something of God's inbreathing, with which he or she has been endowed, people are sensitive to that fact. They then hasten to the threshold of the desert, even to the center of his solitude. At Simiane Louf knew of this immense popularity of spiritual seekers. Bishops, priests, monks, simple Christians, and, in a wider context, people suffering trials, who had particular needs: all came to see him and to hear from him a word of life. "He listened to them with all his heart," recalls Mère Elaié, "and with his complete attention. Emerging from a meeting with him, people felt that they were loved, some of them for the first time in their lives. Dom André shone with a humble love, and his power to attract people was enormous. Our guests were eager for his presence. It was a time when spiritual guides were in demand, and he was for our guests one of those beacons that light up the road to God."[53]

"A Handsome Old Man"

One Monday afternoon in 2007, as was his custom during his time of spacing, Louf walked to the village of Simiane. At around five o'clock the telephone rang at the abbey. It was Louf, asking Frère Muban to meet him in the village. While

52. André Louf, "Solidaires," *Collectanea Cisterciensia* 2 (1973): 144.
53. Bollen, "L'ermite de Saint-Lioba."

eating some ice cream he had lost his false plate. Muban quickly joined him, and together they began the search. At the village everyone knew and loved Louf, and the people were not slow to speak to them. "Can we help you?" "Did you lose something?" With a big smile Louf answered, "Yes, I had ice cream, and I lost my teeth." All Simiane was soon in an uproar over the news. People ran up from all over to help him in his search. On his return to the abbey, after the object was found, Louf presented himself to Elaié, and she burst out laughing: "All is well with the Order!" There was simple joy, humanity, absence of serious attitude, self-forgetfulness, humble love noised abroad, spiritual childhood—all Louf's being was in this *fioretto,* which was retold for a long time about the man he had become during twelve years in the hermitage.[54]

There is an old proverb that says, "Where there is nothing, the king loses his rights." By the same token Carthusian Jean-Baptiste Porion comments, "Over him who agrees to be nothing, the Prince of this world loses his power. The demons of pride, impatience, and jealousy no longer attack the one who has abandoned all that those powers could claim."[55] Such was the abandonment that Louf lived at Simiane. Week by week, from one day to the next, he who had known honor and been familiar with the heights had become nothing. Then his road of deprivation had begun in earnest with the following of Jesus. His life at Sainte-Lioba was a conformation to the poor and forgotten Christ that deepened every day. Louf had nothing more to lose, because he had already given all, consenting on his part to suffering and humiliation, and accepting being put aside and abandoning himself to God's work, pronouncing an amen to all of that without reserve. "At the end of his life," recalled Elaié, "he had really become

54. This little story comes from a conversation with Mère Elaié.
55. Porion, *Amour et silence*, 154–55.

a beggar of mercy. He was one of those 'little ones' who gave up everything to put their trust in God alone, who had emptied themselves completely."[56]

In this period Louf in fact resembled those poor people Luke mentions in his gospel, the humble-hearted who were hungry for God and had no riches other than God. Vexation seemed no longer to have a hold on him. He was a branch of his own heart. He was established in that interior cell in which he lived, breathed, and celebrated the uninterrupted wedding with Jesus. He really radiated the meekness and humble love of Christ; he seemed happy with everything, and endlessly thankful. His brothers at the Italian monastery of Bose called him "the handsome old man." To amuse himself he signed the letters he wrote to them with the same title: "Your *kalogiros*" (Greek for "handsome old man"). When Louf died Enzo Bianchi spoke of him in a message as "an old man, a *kalògheros*, a *staretz-pneumatikòs*, much loved by the brothers of the Orthodox churches for his capacious teaching, for his humble wisdom, and for his profound peace that transcended all divisions." In one of his books the Orthodox theologian Olivier Clement applied the sense of this phrase in a passage that speaks to Louf's elderly years:

> In the Christian East, the elderly are loved, because they are thought to be ready to pray. When a person is old, and when one senses that God is near, because biological life is getting more and more tenuous, the person becomes like a conscious child, sent back to the Father, lightened by the proximity of death, and transparent to a different light. A civilization where there is no more prayer is a civilization where old age has no meaning anymore. We walk on to avoid death. We copy youth. It is a heart-breaking spectacle, because of a possibility

56. Bollen, "L'ermite de Sainte-Lioba."

> that is offered, prodigious through the ultimate dispossession and what is not seized. We need old people who pray, who smile, who love with a disinterested love, who can be astonished. Only they can teach the young that life is worth the trouble, and that nothingness is not the final word. Every monk whose ascesis has borne fruit is called in the East, however old he may be, a "handsome old man." He is handsome with the beauty that rises from the heart. In him the different ages of life are adjusted, we might say "symphonized." Nevertheless the original is rediscovered: white with transfigured brightness, the "handsome old man" with the eyes of a child.[57]

"Christus, Christus, Christus"

After 2008 Louf's intellectual and physical powers were curtailed little by little. Was he affected by Alzheimer's Syndrome? In any case, he began to lose his memory. Like many people of advanced age, he scrutinized his past and immersed himself in books about war that reminded him of the period of his youth, the liberation of Bruges, and undoubtedly the figures of his father and grandfather.[58] All those who met him during this period reported that he had begun to be a bit out of touch, without ever losing his smile or lapsing into bitterness. "The greatness of his life as a whole was such that, whether willingly or not, his way of life had brought him that peace of mind and poverty of spirit that his writings had

57. Olivier Clément, "La prière du coeur," in Olivier Clément and Jacques Serr, *La prière du coeur*, Spiritualité Orientale 6 (Bégrolles-en-Mauges: Abbaye de Bellefontaine, 2011), 60–61.

58. His grandfather Léon had helped many people between 1940 and 1944, hiding fugitives and feeding them. His father André, for his part, doted upon wartime cemeteries (Lieve Louf, correspondence with the author).

proclaimed over the course of forty years," witnessed the Benedictine Benoît Standaert.[59]

In April 2010 Louf returned from the Carthusian house Serra San Bruno, where he had spent the season of Lent. On the way to the church one day he suffered a severe fall. After this accident he spent a few weeks at the hospital in Aix-en-Provence. His doctors' diagnosis was without appeal. He could not walk any more, nor could any hope of recovery allow a return to the hermitage. So it was decided to send him to a clinic in the north, at Bailleul, very near the abbey of Mont-des-Cats, for rehabilitation. He allowed himself to be led, arriving there at the beginning of May. His last conversation with Mère Elaié took place at the end of June, when he was preparing to leave the clinic. Over the telephone he confided to her about his twelve years at Simiane: "They were the happiest years of my life."[60] On June 25 he arrived at the infirmary of Mont-des-Cats. "It was not with enthusiasm," recalled a witness, "that we felt that something was wrong. He suffered from stomach pains. From time to time we heard his cries." A doctor visited but did not see anything abnormal. On July 12 in the morning a loud cry resounded in the corridor. The abbot received a call from the infirmarian: It was over! Even now no one knows the cause of death. Some say it was a neglected urinary tract infection. One thing is sure: the last words that he uttered just before his death were "Christus, Christus, Christus," the name of Jesus repeated three times, like an *ostinato* of hope at the moment when the great symphony of his life was seeking its final harmony. Or

59. Benoît Standaert, "In memoriam André Louf, ocso (1929–2010)," unedited, 2010.

60. Mère Elaié, conversation with the author. André had already let that be understood in confiding to the press, "I am a truly happy man, and I am thankful, because I have always desired to live like this" (*La Croix*, 29 August 2005).

like the sigh of a lover who wanted to hasten the hour of his meeting: "the stake of a whole life condensed into one word, one solitary sound, the last syllable of the prayer endlessly repeated, the last beat of a self-giving heart," according to the abbot of Mont-des-Cats.[61]

Louf's burial took place two days later, on July 14. The beautiful homily given by the abbot of Mont-des-Cats, Dom De Lesalle, ended with these words: "May the Lord deign to lead Dom André in this dark silence where all lovers of God will be lost." These words came from Ruusbroec's *The Spiritual Marriage,* which ends just afterward with these last sentences: "Let us ask Divine Love to grant us this. He does not refuse any beggar."

Then came the burial. At the moment of arrival at the cemetery a torrent of rain fell on the worshipers. "This is no burial," exclaimed one abbot. "This is a baptism."[62] We were submerged," confirmed Mère Elaié, "by spouts of water, as if heaven was sending us a sign!"[63]

61. Jacques de Lesalle, *Homélie pour les funérailles de Dom Louf*, 14 July 2010.

62. Jean-Marc Thévenet, conversation with the author.

63. Mère Elaié Bollen, conversation with the author.

Epilogue

Chronicler of Grace

André Louf's disappearance passed almost unperceived. The day after his burial only one French daily paper did him homage, presenting him as one of the last witnesses of contemplative interiority, "One of the great spiritual figures of the contemporary epoch." "His experience of faith," wrote the author, "Dom Louf shared unceasingly with a large public in numerous works on the spiritual life. It was associated with a renewed vision of the monastic life, sometimes doubled for his epoch, which put him forward as one of the great spiritual figures of the contemporary epoch."[1]

There was also no abundant homage in the church, except from Louf's close friends. The Metropolitan Hilarion Alfeyev wrote in the name of the Orthodox patriarchate of Moscow, "this great monk of the Western Church played a role during the Second Vatican Council that was preponderant in the renewal of the monastic life. Through his books he formed a great number of men and women in the whole world for the spiritual life, for meditation on the Word of God, and for prayer."[2] In a recent letter Alfeyev also spoke of Louf as a father "close to my heart," acknowledging himself to "keep a warm remembrance of my meetings with him, of our conversations, and of the trace

1. Bruno Bouvet, "Dom André Louf, a shared monastic life," in *La Croix* 15 July 2010.

2. Hilarion Alfeyev, correspondence with the author.

he has left in my memory." He hailed the project of this biography as "an important and significant work."[3]

In a communicated message Enzo Bianchi, the founder of Bose, traced the portrait of a mystic, nourished at the sources of the fathers of the East and of the West, but above all a spiritual father with an extraordinary capacity to listen, with discernment and with mercy.[4] Another close friend of the hermit, the Benedictine monk Benoît Standaert, eulogized an "exceptional figure in the spiritual landscape of the West, a light for numbers of people," before adding, "a fatherly friend, abbot, hermit, creative writer, enterprising translator, master of spiritual accompaniment for so many persons, fervent ecumenist, he was like a multi-faceted diamond; with his personality so rich in talents, his fame reached far beyond monastic circles."[5] Innumerable people have acknowledged their debt to him. For example, the Jesuit priest Paul Verdeyen says, "I count it among the great graces of my life when I met Dom Louf."[6] The procurator general of the Carthusians, Dom Jacques Dupont, says Louf "was and remains for me an essential reference in my monastic life, one of my spiritual fathers, as he has been for so many others."[7]

Among Trappists, however, there is silence. His only homage is found in *Collectanea,* in a brief notation accompanying the reprinted version of one of Louf's articles: "This conference was given by Dom André Louf as part of a meeting on the Syrian fathers of the eighth century at the Orthodox parish of the Holy Apostle Andrew at Gand. We are happy to publish it as a homage to Dom André. This conference touches on all

3. Hilarion Alfeyev, correspondence with the author.

4. Enzo Bianchi, communicated message.

5. Benoît Standaert, "In memoriam André Louf, ocso (1929–2010)," unedited, 2010.

6. Paul Verdeyen, conversation with the author.

7. Jacques Dupont, correspondence with the author.

the great themes developed by Dom André in the many books and articles that we owe to him."[8] Until its recasting in 2016, the Order's website still held the eulogy written by the Benedictine Benoît Standaert, but the text has since been lost.

As appropriate as they are, these few acts of homage have insufficient weight on the scale of Louf's merits. His abbatial tenure opened up a new period of prestige for the abbey Mont-des-Cats, which has really shone by the quality of her recruits and the intensity of her spiritual life. Guiding his community along the paths of *aggiornamento*, Louf made this monastery of French Flanders what Adolphe Gesché called "one of the most significant spots of Christian inspiration in the West."[9] In discussions among Trappists about brothers formed in this school, the abbey is said to be a nursery of abbots.

For more than thirty years the Holy See has considered André Louf as one of the brilliant representatives of the Trappist Order. He was the one Pope Paul asked to compose the "Message of Contemplative Religious" for the Synod of Bishops that followed the Council in 1967. During the 1980s Pope John Paul II appealed to Louf's charism of discernment to clear up many thorny issues, including that of integrist monks;[10] afterwards the pope appealed to Louf's spiritual sensibility by inviting him to compose the Way of the Cross at the Coliseum in 2004. In 1980 during a search for a representative of Benedictine monasticism for the solemn opening

8. André Louf, "L'homme intérieur ou la liturgie du coeur," *Collectanea Cisterciensia* 72 (2010): 334.

9. Adolphe Gesché, [? Discours pour la remise du titre de Docteur honoris causa à André Louf, Université Catholique de Louvain, 2 Feb. 1994]. [The French volume provides no citation here, but it seems likely to have come from this address. BK].

10. "Integrism," says Richard P. McBrien, "regards everything in the world as evil or worthless unless and until it is somehow 'integrated' with Christianity" (Richard P. McBrien, *Catholicism,* 2 vols. [Minneapolis: Winston Press, 1980], 2:692). (BK)

of the year of Saint Benedict at Notre-Dame de Paris, Louf was unanimously chosen, and he gave the inaugural conference at the cathedral. In 1990 and 1998 he was found at the outpost of the official commemorations of the birth of Saint Bernard and of Cîteaux.

But Louf's influence radiated far beyond monastic circles. In 1994 he received an honorary doctorate awarded by the Catholic University of Louvain to personalities who "by their choice and manner of life opened up to humanity new traces of hope."[11] With this title the university honored him first as the erudite, the scholar, part of whose work initiated an original dialogue between the Christian tradition and the human sciences.[12] But it especially distinguished the spiritual person, devoted to interior activity. It was one way of reminding the world that mortal life does not consist in production and consumption alone, and that the value of material things is not measured alone by their economic and practical returns. "If it seems legitimate and urgent to us," reasoned the rector, "at this turn of the century to worry about the deforestation of the planet, which threatens the loss of the fruits of the earth, how much more necessary should it be to defend ourselves against the spiritual deficiency of humanity that gravely risks the loss of our souls?"[13] Through Louf, then, the quality of the spiritual life, its gratuity, even its uselessness received recognition at a time when everything conspired against it.

These few examples suggest the immense influence exerted by Louf upon the church of his time, and they emphasize by way of contrast the stunning silence in which his death was enveloped. After his disappearance, but already while he was

11. Reported in a press review established by the external relations of the Catholic University of Louvain, ADMC, 2 Feb. 1994.

12. To initiate this dialogue between faith and critical thought, the philosopher Paul Ricoeur was appointed to sponsor the delivery of the prize.

13. *Vers l'avenir*, 3 Feb. 1994.

still a solitary at Simiane, Louf had become forgotten. There were, however, discrete signals suggesting that he was on the verge of emerging from his purgatory. Outside of France, especially in Italy, theses were devoted to him and books studied his spirituality. He was even on the curriculum of certain universities. In the province of San Domenico in the north of Italy a Dominican friar offered a course entitled "The School of André Louf. Proposition for a spiritual life for men of today." This was a part of the course for a licentiate in spiritual theology. Fr. Festa justified his action by saying that Louf was "one of the most representative, most original figures of contemporary spirituality."[14]

In the Trappist Order too a movement of rediscovery is afoot. In a recent book a former abbot of Mont-des-Cats speaks of André as "one of the foremost spiritual teachers of Christianity."[15] New editions of André's works have been announced, and unpublished ones will appear. "It is time," judges Mère Elaié, "to offer the good seed of André's life to our world. His books are a gift offered to the church."[16]

In the preface of a new edition of *Seigneur, apprends-nous à prier*, Louf recounted the reason for writing the book, which catapulted him throughout the world. It made him one of the goldsmiths of the interior life. It came at the end of the 1960s, when he had been invited to give a conference at a spiritual center maintained by the Carmelites. The priest who would become Cardinal Godfried Danneels was then in the diocese of Bruges, and he assisted on that occasion. He asked Louf's permission at the end of the conference to publish his remarks in the journal of spirituality that he was editing. The article

14. http://s2ew.domenicani.it/provincia_san_domenico_in_italia/studiare_con_i_domenicani/00001290_Alla_scuola-di-Andre_Louf.html#_ftn1.

15. Guillaume Jedrzejzak, *L'extraordinaire originalité du christianisme* (Paris: Salvator, 2014), 34.

16. Mère Elaié Bollen, conversation with the author.

quickly attracted the attention of a Belgian editor, who convinced Louf that the piece could be expanded and published as a book. Louf saw it through but did not make a cent from the success of the book that came out in Dutch in 1971. "For good or for bad," he recalled later, "I thought I was writing above all for the monks and nuns, and I asked myself what my testimony could bring to lay Christians living in the world. The book was the fruit of a personal experience of *lectio* of Holy Scripture, done within the traditional context of cloistered contemplative life. One whole chapter was in fact devoted to the various observances of monastic *ascesis,* concerning which I thought that they could hardly inspire Christians who were pestered by the innumerable concerns of a worldly life."[17] However, the sequel showed that translations multiplied, and the book was accepted as a classic of the spiritual life.

Where did this craze come from? "Monastic spirituality," Louf suggested, "seems to contain some secret treasure of graces that attracts all baptized Christians, even if most of them are not called to apply them concretely in their everyday lives. It is indeed a question of a treasury of graces that are at the disposal of all Christians, among which they recognize something that belongs to their own baptismal vocation."[18] But the author's style and personality obviously counted for something in the book's success. The ancient monks spoke of the spiritual father as a *pneumatophore*, that is a bearer of the spirit. Louf was a person of that kind. The breath of the Spirit can be felt gliding over the pages of his books. He incontestably possessed an apostolic charisma for writing. His works resound with a note more exact than what he describes. He lived it himself, or, in the case of others, he was a witness. He only appealed

17. André Louf, Preface to *Gospodine nauči nas moliti* (Peterborough, UK: Verbum, 2005), 5.

18. Louf, Preface to *Gospodine,* 6.

to inner experience, to what is felt, since he was a pedagogue of spiritual sensitivity, and he believed in a God who touches humans and affects them through interior movements, who works in the human heart through his grace.

In the spiritual life Teresa of Àvila distinguishes three great graces: benefiting from mystical experience, being able to recognize such experience when it occurs, and being able to speak of it.[19] Louf received all three. God had at first marked off the smallest corner of Louf's interior cell by gratifying the abbot with innumerable visits. But God had also sharpened Louf's interior ear, endowing him with the ability to mark and discern the movements of the spirit in his own heart as in that of others. Finally God bestowed on him the art of transmitting spiritual experience, of becoming an educator of the spiritual life by word and by books. That is why it is necessary to read and re-read Louf. We find in his books the invitation to stop being extroverts, living skin-deep on the surface of ourselves, where the spark of prayer cannot be struck. In those books we also find the way by which we may learn recollection: we will learn how to reach the heart and to find joy there.

Dom André marks the road with clear signals, comprehensible to everyone. His books are written in today's language. This solitary monk was persuaded that the Gospel and contemporary culture could stimulate each other, so he had no fear of letting himself be challenged by the human sciences, nor of re-interpreting the Christian tradition in the light of today's expectations. "It is an excellent idea," confirms the Carthusian Jacques Dupont, "to make known this person who knew how to render an ancient inheritance contemporary.

19. "C'est qu'en effet recevoir de Dieu une faveur est une première grâce; savoir en quoi elle consiste en est une seconde; enfin c'en est une troisième de pouvoir en rendre compte et en donner l'explication" (Sainte Thérèse d'Àvila, *Ma Vie*, édition du 4e centenaire (Paris: Fayard, 1962), 157.

He could unite the most authentic tradition with the proven values of today's world."[20]

A letter from Louf explains his approach: "The community is interested in a monastic spirituality that I try to present in a way that is both ancient and modern at the same time, mixing ancient truths with those that are modern. The themes I have chosen are in fact among the most essential ones in the religious life: obedience, prayer, charity, trials, and temptation."[21] The most recent attainments of psychology especially helped him to clear the terrain of spiritual experience, making him, like his master Saint Bernard, a veritable psychologist of the spiritual life. It especially made him one of the shrewdest analysts of the psychology of sin and repentance, able to dislodge the illusions that can hide behind the most pious intentions.[22]

Saint John Climacus spoke of the monastery as a "hospital for the soul," where the great ones of the world could come and have their wounds healed by Christ the Healer. In the same spirit Louf invited people to let themselves be reconciled with their weaknesses, their fragilities, their sins, their depressions, their complexes, their anguish: all those thorns that hurt us and paralyze us, breaking our narcissistic mirrors. God, whose image he reveals, is never discouraged by our failings. Our poverty does not make him flee. He is a God who always returns to the charge and never stops knocking on our door, like the persevering beggar that he asks us to be before our Father's door. His mercy is boundless. His power of forgiveness is ready at every moment, especially in those

20. Jacques Dupont, correspondence with the author.

21. André Louf, Letter to the community, ADMC, 5 Feb. 1968.

22. André Louf, "Repentir et expérience de Dieu," in *L'expérience de Dieu dans la vie monastique*, ed. Denis Huerre (Saint-Leger-Vauban: Les Presses Monastiques, Abbaye Sainte-Marie de La Pierre-qui-vire, 1973), 28. See also Louf, "La faiblesse, un chemin pascal selon Saint-Bernard," *Collectanea Cisterciensia* 65 (2003), 15–16.

humiliating trials that make a mess of our lives but are also full of Easter grace. It is enough, but very difficult, not to run away from them, not to be inflexible, to stay peaceable and humble, to abandon ourselves to the love of God, of him who always intercedes for us when we lay down our arms. All human effort is fated to fail before the marvels of grace. For Dom Louf all spiritual artistry lies in that: remaining open to God's grace, following his urging closely, and marveling at the absolute gratuity of his love.

Sources

Archives

Aside from the personal writings of Dom Louf, this book is supported by the opening of the archives concerning him located at the abbey of Mont-des-Cats. The letters he wrote to the community from 1963 to 1997 are classified FA–35. There are also some boxes of icons, a rich mine that has never been inventoried. It was necessary to remedy a certain disorder to find the unpublished documents that provide the rich material found in this book. The manuscript of Louf's *Journal Spirituel* (cited as JS) is contained in three notebooks running from 1958 to 1997. In addition, the archival materials include his private correspondence, never-published articles, notes for chapter talks, plans for conferences, and a dossier of unedited homilies. The collections of these precious documents are cited in the footnotes to the chapters of this book.

The unearthing of these archives, used here for the first time, was completed by a work of creation of another kind of archives through an oral quest (conversations) and a written quest (correspondence) destined to collect in a methodical way a small part of the "living memory"[1] of the second half of the twentieth century. More than sixty persons who had known Dom Louf at one time or another during his earthly

1. Guillaume Cuchet, "Recueillir à temps la 'mémoire vive' de l'Église," *La Croix* 12 Dec. 2016.

trajectory were solicited for their testimony, which is cited in the book to clarify decisive episodes in the life of the church that he witnessed and carried out, especially the outbreak of *aggiornamento*.

Finally, thanks to the Thomas Merton Center at Bellarmine University in Louisville, Kentucky, which provided access to Dom Louf's correspondence with Fr. Thomas Merton, a correspondence that ran from 1956 to 1965.[2]

Written Works by André Louf

Louf's works are arranged chronologically. Works by other authors are arranged alphabetically.

Books

Seigneur, apprends-nous à prier. Brussels: Foyer Notre-Dame, 1976.

La voie cistercienne: À l'école de l'amour. Paris: Desclée de Brouwer, 1980.

Seul l'amour suffirait: Commentaires d'Évangile pour l'année C. Paris: Desclée de Brouwer, 1982.

Seul l'amour suffirait: Commentaires d'Évangile pour l'année A. Paris: Desclée de Brouwer, 1983.

Seul l'amour suffirait: Commentaires d'Évangile pour l'année B. Paris: Desclée de Brouwer, 1984.

L'accompagnement spirituel. Ottawa, Canada: Éditions de la Conférence Religieuse Canadienne, 1986.

Au gré de sa grâce: Propos sur la prière. Paris: Desclée de Brouwer, 1989.

La grâce peut davantage: L'accompagnement spirituel. Paris: Desclée de Brouwer, 1992.

Heureuse faiblesse: Homélies pour les dimanches de l'année B. Paris: Desclée de Brouwer, 1996.

Heureuse faiblesse. Homélies pour les dimanches de l'année C. Paris: Desclée de Brouwer, 1997.

2. Thomas Merton Center, Section A, correspondence.

Heureuse faiblesse: Homélies pour les dimanches de l'année A. Paris: Desclée de Brouwer, 1998.

L'Humilité. Paris: Parole et Silence, 2002.

À la grâce de Dieu: Entretiens avec Stéphane Delberghe. Namur: Fidélité, 2002.

À l'école de la contemplation. Paris: Lethielleux, 2004.

Les effets de la prière. Ivry-sur-Seine: Éditions de l'Atelier, 2004.

Chemin de croix du Colisée. Namur: Fidélité, 2005.

L'œuvre de Dieu, un chemin de prière. Paris: Lethielleux, 2005.

Cherche Dieu et ton coeur revivra: Hildegard Michaelis, 1900–1982. Paris: Cerf, 2006.

Saint Bruno et le charisme cartusien aujourd'hui. Paris: Parole et Silence, 2008.

Initiation à la vie spirituelle. Paris: Parole et Silence, 2008. New edition, "Point/Sagesse," 2012.

Journal Articles

"Une théologie de la pauvreté monastique chez le bienheureux Guerric d'Igny." *Collectanea Cisterciensia* 20 (1958): 207–22.

"La vie monastique vue par un moine du mont Athos." *Istina* (1959): 9–60.

"Pour une nouvelle édition de la littérature latine médiévale." *Collectanea Cisterciensia* 21 (1959): 262–63.

"Une nouvelle revue monastique." *Collectanea Cisterciensia* 21 (1959): 261.

"Le Congrès de spiritualité monastique à Saint Grégoire in Celio, Rome, 2–3 January 1959." *Collectanea Cisterciensia* 21 (1959): 261.

"Marie dans la parole de Dieu selon saint Amédée de Lausanne." *Collectanea Cisterciensia* 21 (1959): 29–62.

"Exégèse scientifique ou *lectio* monastique?" *Collectanea Cisterciensia* 22 (1960): 225–47.

"Caper emissarius ut typus Redemptoris apud Patres." *Verbum Domini* 38 (1960): 262–77.

"Un grand docteur monastique: saint Pierre Damien." *Collectanea Cisterciensia* 23 (1961): 261.

"Une ancienne exégèse de Phil. 2:6 dans le Livre des Degrés." *Studiorum Paulinorum Congressus Internationalis Catholicus*, 1963.

"Écouter la tradition." *Collectanea Cisterciensia* 25 (1963): 3–7.

"Pour une revue monastique." *Collectanea Cisterciensia* 27 (1965): 3–8.

"The Purpose of a Monastic Review." *Cistercian Studies* 1 (1966): 1–16.

With Jean–Baptiste Porion. "Message des moines contemplatifs au Synode des évêques de 1967." *La documentation catholique* no. 1504 (5 Nov. 1967): 1907–1911.

"La parole au-delá de la liturgie." *Collectanea Cisterciensia* 31 (1969): 169–94. (Spanish: *Cuadernos Monásticos* 7 [1972]: 127–82. English: "The Word beyond the Liturgy [Part I]." *Cistercian Studies* 6 [1971]: 353–68, and "The Word beyond the Liturgy (Part II)." *Cistercian Studies* 7 [1972]: 63–76.)

"En marge d'un pèlerinage." *Collectanea Cisterciensia* 32 (1970): 46–66.

"Das monastische Zeugnis in einer säkularisierten Welt." *Erbe und Auftrag* 47 (1971): 375–92. (English: "Monastic Witness in a Secularized World." *Cistercian Studies* 6 [1971]: 200–18.)

"Y a-t-il une attitude de prière propre au moine?" *Collectanea Cisterciensia* 33 (1971): 41–56.

"Pentimento ed esperienza di Dio." *Subiaco* (1973): 27–39. (Spanish: *Cuadernos Monasticos* 7 [1972]: 25–38.)

"Ascèse et prière." *Collectanea Cisterciensia* 33 (1971): 141–58. (Spanish: *Cuadernos Monasticos* 8 [1973]: 63–78.)

"La obediencia monástica." *Cuadernos Monásticos* 8 (1973): 295–98.

"Solidaires." *Collectanea Cisterciensia* 35 (1973): 143–48. (Spanish: *Cistercium* 25 [1973]: 265–72.)

"The Place of Prayer." *Cistercian Studies* 9 (1974): 385–88.

"L'acédie chez Évagre le Pontique." *Concilium* (1974): 113–17.

"L'expérience spirituelle." *Cistercian Studies* 10 (1975): 127–34. (Spanish: *Cuadernos Monásticos* 11 [1976]: 277–83.)

"La humildad." *Cuadernos Monásticos* 37 (1976): 201–10.

"Solitudo Pluralis." *Collectanea Cisterciensia* 38 (1976): 29–39.

"L'obéissance dans la tradition monastique." *Vie Consacrée* 48 (1976): 197–210. (Spanish: *Cuadernos Monasticos* 12 [1977]: 429–38.)

"À l'École des Psaumes." *Christus* 96 (1977): 419–31.

"Demut und Gehorsam bei der Einführung ins Mönchsleben." *Erbe und Auftrag: Benediktinische Monatsschrift* 54 (1978): 343–64.

"Het gebed bij de Oudvaders." *Benediktijns Tijdschrift* 39 (1978): 85–98.

"Geestelijke begeleiding vandaag." *Benediktijns Tijdschrift* 40 (1979): 122–36.

"Rijping van Benediktus vaderschap." *Benediktijns Tijdschrift* 41 (1980): 69–75.

"Gebed en Genezing." *Collationes* (1981): 131–54.

"Saint Benoît, homme de Dieu pour tous les temps." *Collectanea Cisterciensia* 42 (1980): 81–92. (Italian: *Vita consecrata* 16 [1980]: 179–89. Spanish: *Cistercium* 32 [1980]: 53–64. German: *Erbe und Auftrag* 56 [1980]: 183–93. English: *Cistercian Studies* 15 [1980]: 217–28.)

"L'accompagnement spirituel aujourd'hui (1)." *Vie consacrée* 6 (1980): 323–35.

"La prière dans la règle de Saint Benoît." *La Vie Spirituelle* 134 (1980): 511–29. (English: *Word & Spirit* 2 [1981]: 118–35. Spanish: *Cuadernos Monasticos* 17 [1982]: 123–38.)

"Saint Benoît Aujourd'hui." *Collectanea Cisterciensia* 43 (1981): 234–41.

"L'évolution de la vie monastique en France depuis le Concile." *Documents épiscopat* no. 12 (June 1981): 1–8.

"L'accompagnement spirituel aujourd'hui (2)." *Vie Consacrée* 1 (1981): 32–43.

"Moines et Œcuménisme." *Collectanea Cisterciensia* 44 (1982): 169–82.

"Humility and Obedience in Monastic Tradition." *Cistercian Studies* 18 (1983): 261–82.

"Vivre en communauté fraternelle." *Vie Consacrée* 56 (1984): 135–52. (English: *Cistercian Studies* 21 [1986]: 82–95. Dutch: *Benediktijns Tijdschrift* 47 [1986]: 82–98.)

"Prière et Travail (I)." *Le Lien des Contemplatives* no. 79 (Oct. 1984): 1–16.

"Prière et Travail (II)." *Le Lien des Contemplatives* no. 80 (Jan. 1985): 1–12.

"La dimension apostolique et contemplative de la vie religieuse." *Vie Consacrée* 3 (1985): 147–64. (English: *Cistercian Studies* 22 [1987]: 111–25.)

"La paternité spirituelle dans la littérature du désert." *La Vie Spirituelle* 140 (1986): 335–60.

"Gouvernement et accompagnement dans les communautés contemplatives." *Vie Consacrée* 58 (1986): 341–62. (English: *Cistercian Studies* 23 [1988]: 193–210.)

"Bernard, getuige voor deze tijd." *Benediktijns Tijdschrift* 51 (1990): 135–42.

"Bernard de Clairvaux et les Cisterciens." *Études* 373 (1990): 89–100." Repr. *Cistercian Studies* 26 (1991): 58–71.

"Les Moines dans l'Europe de demain." *Vie Consacrée* 27 (1991): 291–97.

"Un Triptych de Simon Bening commandité par Pierre van Onderberghen, abbé des Dunes (1515–1519)." *Cîteaux* 43 (1992): 221–37.

"Saint Bernard fut-il un iconoclaste?" *Bulletin de Littérature Ecclésiastique* 93 (1992): 49–64.

"Geleid door de Geest, op het spoor van de Geest." *Aggiornamento* 25 (1993): 118–29.

"Pour voir il importe d'aimer." *Les Amis du Monastère* 4 (1993). Repr. in *À l'école de la contemplation.* Paris: Lethielleux, 2004. 228–32.

"Het Contemplatieve Leven." *Benediktijns Tijdschrift* 2 (1994): 82–85.

"La Fonction d'une Revue Monastique selon Thomas Merton." *Collectanea Cisterciensia* 56 (1994): 21–26.

"Le Drame d'un Amour porté jusqu'à l'extrême. Homélie pour la Veillée de prière (Mont-des-Cats, 29 mai 1996)." *Collectanea Cisterciensia* 25 (1996): 197–98.

"Le coeur brisé." *Buisson Ardent* 3 (1997): 48–60.

"Saint Bernard et Sainte Thérèse de Lisieux." *Carmel* 3 (1997): 2–19.

"La Solitude Monastique: Séparé de tous et unis à tous." *Christus* 180 (1998): 421–31.

"Quelques Leçons d'un Centenaire." *Collectanea Cisterciensia* 60 (1998): 216–25.

"Être formé à l'accompagnement spirituel." *Séminarium* 39 (1999): 553–68.

"Le Cîteaux de Saint Bernard." *Collectanea Cisterciensia* 61 (1999): 40–78.

"L'Humilité dans la vie monastique." *Le Lien des Moniales* no. 14 (July 2000): 1–21.

"Salve Regina." *La Vie Spirituelle* 80 (2000): 27–35.

"L'Abbé et l'Accompagnement Spirituel." *Collectanea Cisterciensia* 62 (2000): 214–30.

"Pourquoi Dieu se manifesta, selon Isaac le Syrien." *Connaissance des Pères de l'Église* 80 (2000): 37–56.

"Quelques Constantes Spirituelles dans les Traditions Hésychastes en Orient et en Occident." *Irenikon* 74 (2001): 483–514.

"Zonder te weten waarheen hij ging (Heb. 11:18)." *Aggiornamento* 2 (2001): 98–105.

"Saint Bruno." *Documents épiscopat* no. 12–13 (2001): 1–18.

"Une Expérience de *lectio divina*." *La Vie Spirituell*e 81 (2001): 461–81.

"Isaac le Syrien: La Grâce, non pas les Œuvres." *Proche-Orient Chrétien* 51 (2001): 243–46.

"Violence chez les moines: la transformation spirituelle de l'agressivité?" *Christus* 192 (2001): 427–36.

"Syméon de Taibouch: Discours sur la Cellule." *Collectanea Cisterciensia* 64 (2002): 30–59.

"L'Homme dans l'Histoire du Salut selon Isaac le Syrien." *Connaissance des Pères de l'Église* 88 (2002): 49–54.

"Le Repentir, clé de la Vie en Christ." *Buisson Ardent* 9 (2003): 9–47.

"San Benedetto, Maestro di Sapienza." *Parola, Spirito e Vita* 48 (2003): 223–45.

"La Faiblesse, un Chemin Pascal selon Saint Bernard." *Collectanea Cisterciensia* 65 (2003): 5–20.

"Veilleur, où en est la Nuit." *Christus* no. 200 (Oct. 2003): 418–26.

"L'acédie des moines." *Études* 399 (2003): 35–44.

"Le Discernement dans la Tradition Orientale." *Itinéraires Augustiniens* 30 (2003): 33–46.

"Faire pénitence?" *Sources Vives* no. 108 (March 2003): 81–87.

"La vie contemplative." In *À l'école de la contemplation*. Paris: Lethielleux, 2004. 22–27.

"Un accompagnement spirituel concerté: Barsanuphe, Jean, et Séridos." *Collectanea Cisterciensia* 66 (2004): 35–50.

"La vie de prière: engagement pour la sauvegarde de la création." *Collectanea Cisterciensia* 66 (2004): 260–74. (Spanish: *Studia Monastica* 63 [2008]: 33–49. English: *The Way* 45 [2006]: 119–36.)

"La paternité spirituelle." *Art sacré: Revue de la Fraternité Saint Martin* no. 17 (2005): 11–25.

"Chercher Dieu au temps de la déréliction." *Vie Consacrée* 77 (2005): 219–31.

"'À la recherche du bonheur' dans la règle de saint Benoît." *Vie Consacrée* 80 (2008): 116–24.

"L'Homme intérieur ou la liturgie du coeur." *Collectanea Cisterciensia* 72 (2010): 334–53.

"Saint Bruno (1)." *Cistercian Studies Quarterly* 48 (2013): 213–24.

"Saint Bruno (2)." The Carthusian Charism Today." *Cistercian Studies Quarterly* 48 (2013): 353–67.

Book Chapters

"Repentir et expérience de Dieu." In *L'expérience de Dieu dans la vie monastique*, edited by Denis Huerre. Les Presses Monastiques. Saint-Léger-Vauban: Abbaye Sainte-Marie de La Pierre-qui-Vire, 1973. 28–43.

"Saint Benoît Homme de Dieu pour tous les temps." In *Fraternités monastiques de Jérusalem: Saint Benoît aujourd'hui*. Collection Épiphanie. Paris: Cerf, 1980. 9–35.

"La Dimension Œcuménique de la vie monastique." In *Prière et Retrouvailles: Journée monastique en l'abbatiale de Payerne, 28 juin 1980, à l'occasion du quinzième centenaire de la nais-*

sance de saint Benoît de Nursie (480–1980). Posieux, Switzerland: Abbaye d'Hauterive, 1981. 54–75.

"La paternità spirituale." In *Abba, dimmi una parola!* Magnano: Qiqajon, 1989. 89–117.

"De spiritualiteit van Bernardus naar vandaag toe." In *Bernardus en de Cistercienzerfamilie un België*. Louvain: Bibliotheek van de faculteit der Godgeleerdheid, 1990. 431–45.

"Saint Bernard fut-il iconoclaste?" In *Saint Bernard et la recherche de Dieu: Actes du colloque organisé par l'Institut catholique de Toulouse et l'abbaye Sainte-Marie-du-Désert (25–27 janvier 1991)*. Toulouse: Institut Catholique de Toulouse, 1992. 49–64.

"Solitudo Pluralis." In *Solitude et Communion: La vie érémitique, un lien très fort d'unité entre les différentes confessions chrétiennes*. Vie Monastique no. 48. Bégrolles-en-Mauges: Abbaye de Bellefontaine, 1992. 41–56.

"Bernard, abbé." In *Bernard de Clairvaux: Histoire, mentalités, spiritualité*. Sources Chrétiennes 380. Paris: Cerf, 1992. 349–79.

"L'impossibile umiltà: un criterio certo di discernimento spirituale." In *In Colloquio: Alla scoperta della paternità spirituale*. Centro Aletti. Rome: Lipa, 1995. 115–48.

"Uno sguardo monastico: cosa narra un solitario alla chiesa?" In Paul Beauchamp, André Louf, et al., *La Solitudine: grazie o maledizione?* Magnano: Qiqajon, 2001. 65–78.

"Influssi orientali nella Regola di S. Benedetto." In *Il ruolo del monachesimo nell'ecumenismo*, ed. Giordano Donato. *Studia Olivetana* 7 (2002): 61–80.

"Autrement la grâce n'est plus la grâce." In André Louf, Denis Huerre, and Marie-David Giraud, *Dieu intime: Parole de moines*. Paris: Bayard, 2003. 9–97.

"Alcune costanti spirituali nelle tradizioni esicaste d'oriente e occidente." In *Vie del monachesimo russo: atti del 9. Convegno ecumenico internazionale di spiritualità ortodossa. Sezione russa: Bose, 19–21 settembre 2001*, edited by Meletios di Nikopolis, et al. Magnano: Qiqajon, 2003. 33–66.

"La paternità spirituale nel monachesimo d'occidente oggi." In *Optina Pustyn' e la paternità spirituale. Atti del X Convegno ecumenico internazionale di spiritualità ortodossa. Sezione russa. Bose, 19–21 settembre 2002*, edited by Adalberto Mainardi. Magnano: Qiqajon, 2003. 175–85.

"Barsanufio e Giovanni: un accompagnamento spirituale concertato." In *Il deserto di Gaza: Barsanufio, Giovanni e Doroteo: Atti dell'11. Convegno ecumenico internazionale di spiritualità ortodossa sezione bizantina, Bose, 14–16 settembre 2003*, edited by Sabino Chialà and Lisa Cremaschi. Magnano: Qiqajon, 2003. 179–204.

"Vie commune, École de Charité. Document de travail pour le Chapitre Générale de 1996." In *À l'école de la contemplation.* Paris: Lethielleux, 2004. 28–47.

"L'acédie des cénobites et des ermites." In *Tristesse, acédie et médecine des âmes Anthologie de textes rares et inédits (XIIIe – XXe siècles),* edited by Nathalie Nabert. Paris: Beauchesne, 2005. 165–79.

"I monaci d'Occidente e il Monte Athos." In *Atanasio e il monachesimo al Monte Athos*, edited by Sabino Chiala and Lisa Cremaschi. Magnano: Qiqajon, 2005. 275–95.

"Autour de quelques traductions d'oraisons liturgiques." In *Un bonheur partagé. Mélanges offerts à Dom Marie-Gérard Dubois. Cahiers Scourmontois* 5 (2005).

"Élisabeth de la Trinité et Ruusbroec." In *Élisabeth de la Trinité: L'aventure mystique. Sources, expérience théologale, rayonnement*, edited by Jean Clapier. Toulouse: Éditions du Carmel, 2006. 53–69.

Introduction to *Cherche Dieu et ton coeur revivra: Hildegard Michaelis, 1900–1982*. Paris: Cerf, 2006. 5–19.

"L'homme intérieur." In *Le chant des profondeurs*, edited by Nathalie Nabert. Paris: Salvator, 2007. 55–87.

"Les moines d'Occident et le mont Athos." In *Vivere il regno di Dio al servizio degli altri: miscellanea in onore del p. Olivier Raquez osb*, edited by Mihai Frățilă. Rome: Galaxia Gutenberg/ Lipa Edizioni, 2008. 113–33.

"La trasfigurazione nella 'Scala dei monaci' di Guigo II il certosino." In *Il Cristo trasfigurato nella tradizione spirituale ortodossa.*

Bose, 16–19 settembre 2007, edited by Sabino Chialà, Lisa Cremaschi, and Adalberto Mainardi. Preface by Enzo Bianci. Magnano: Qiqajon, 2008. 263–76.

"Vue d'ensemble sur la situation présente." In *L'Ordre cistercien de la stricte observance au XXe siècle,* Vol. 2: *Du concile Vatican II à la fin du siècle*, edited by Marie-Gérard Dubois, with Augusta Tescari and Maria Paola Santachiari. 2 vols. Rome: OCSO, 2008. 2:205–7.

"Temha-stupore et tahra-maraviglia negli scritti di Isacco il Siro." In *La grande stagione della mistica siro-orientale (VI–VIII secolo),* edited by Emilio Vergani and Sabino Chiala. Milan: Centro Ambrosiano, 2009. 93–119.

"Isacco il siro e la lotta della preghiera." In *La lotta spirituale nella tradizione ortodossa. Atti del XVII Convegno ecumenico internazionale di spiritualità ortodossa*, edited by Enzo Bianchi and Sabino Chiala. Magnano: Qiqajon, 2010. 75–93.

Introductions and Prefaces to Books by Other Authors

La règle de Saint Benoît. Édition du 15e centenaire. Trans. Henri Rochais. Paris: Desclée de Brouwer, 1980.

Saint Bernard. *Sermons divers, tome I*. Paris: Desclée de Brouwer, 1982.

Marie de la Trinité Kervingant. *Le monachisme, lieu œcuménique La bienheureuse Maria-Gabriella*. Paris: Éditions de l'Œil, 1984.

Frère Ephraïm. *Le chemin de croix*. Nouan-le-Fuzelier: Éditions du Lion de Juda, 1984.

Robert Thomas. *Mystiques Cisterciens*. Paris: Éditions de l'Œil, 1985. 9–12.

Robert Thomas. *Prier le Salve Regina avec un moine cistercien du XIIIe siècle*. Paris: La Source, 1987.

Denis Trinez. *L'école de la fragilité*. Paris: Cerf, 2005.

Jean-Marie Howe. *Secret of the Heart: Spiritual Being*. Monastic Wisdom series 2. Kalamazoo, MI: Cistercian Publications, 2005.

Mario Torcivia. *Enzo Bianchi et la communauté de Bose*. Paris: Salvator, 2005.

Joris Van Ael. *Le récit de la Passion en 16 icônes*. Namur/Paris: Fidélité/Cerf, 2007.

Wouter Deruwe. *Gezegend mijn kronkelweg. Een spirituele gids op weg naar je diepere zelf*. Gent: Carmelitana, 2010.

Michael Davide. *En Carême avec Etty Hillesum: Itinéraire en quarante étapes*. Paris: Salvator, 2016.

Editions, Presentations, Translations

Saint Antoine. *Lettres*. Spiritualité Orientale. Bégrolles-en-Mauges: Abbaye de Bellefontaine, 1976. 7–36 (introduction).

Saint Nil Sorsky. *La vie, les écrits, le skite d'un staretz de Trans-Volga*. Spiritualité Orientale. Bégrolles-en-Mauges: Abbaye de Bellefontaine, 1980. 11–14 (presentation).

Lettres des Pères du Désert. Ammonas, Macaire, Arsène, Sérapion de Thmuis. Spiritualité Orientale. Bégrolles-en-Mauges: Abbaye de Bellefontaine, 1985 (presentation).

Jan van Ruusbroec. *Écrits I. La pierre brillante: Les sept clôtures. Les sept degrés de l'amour. Livre des éclaircissements*. Bégrolles-en-Mauges: Abbaye de Bellefontaine, 1990 (presentation, translation, and notes).

Jan van Ruusbroec. *Écrits II: Les noces spirituelles*. Bégrolles-en-Mauges: Abbaye de Bellefontaine, 1993 (presentation, translation, and notes).

Jan van Ruusbroec. *Écrits III: Le royaume des amants: Le miroir de la béatitude éternelle*. Bégrolles-en-Mauges: Abbaye de Bellefontaine, 1997 (presentation, translation, and notes).

Jan van Ruusbroec. *Écrits IV. Les douze béguines. Les quatre tentations. De la foi chrétienne. Lettres*. Bégrolles-en-Mauges: Abbaye de Bellefontaine, 1999 (presentation, translation, and notes).

Hilarion Alfeyev. *L'univers spirituel d'Isaac le Syrien*. Spiritualité Orientale. Bégrolles-en-Mauges: Abbaye de Bellefontaine, 2001 (translation from the Russian).

Isaac le Syrien. *Œuvres spirituelles II: 41 discours récemment découverts*. Bégrolles-en-Mauges: Abbaye de Bellefontaine, 2003 (presentation, translation, and notes).

Paul Verdeyen. *Guillaume de Saint-Thierry: Premier auteur mystique des anciens Pays-Bas*. Brepols: Turnhout, 2003 (translation).

Hilarion Alfeyev. *Le nom grand et glorieux: La vénération du nom de Dieu et la prière de Jésus dans la tradition orthodoxe*. Paris: Cerf, 2007 (translation).

Isaac le Syrien. *Œuvres spirituelles III: d'après un manuscrit récemment découvert*. Bégrolles-en-Mauges: Abbaye de Bellefontaine, 2008 (presentation, translation, and notes).

Hilarion Domratchev. *Sur les monts de Caucasse*. Geneva: Éditions des Syrtes, 2016 (translation).

Guillaume de Saint-Thierry. *Commentaire bref sur le Cantique des Cantiques*. Sources Chrétiennes. Paris: Cerf, forthcoming (translation).

Guillaume de Saint-Thierry. *Discussion contre Pierre Abélard*. Sources Chrétiennes. Paris: Cerf, forthcoming (translation).

Guillaume de Saint-Thierry. *Lettre de Guillaume à Bernard*. Sources Chrétiennes. Paris: Cerf, forthcoming (translation).

Popular

"La tradition ne regarde pas en arrière." *La Croix* 14 Jan. 1989.

"Comme un moine traversant le désert." *La Croix* 25 Dec. 1993.

"Donnons à Dieu l'occasion de se manifester." *La Croix* 25–26 Dec. 1999.

"Pour un cœur de chair. Interview de Dom André Louf." *Unité et charismes* 3 (2001): 28–32.

"Marchons vers notre Pâques intérieur." *Panorama* April 2002: 24–30.

"Le bonheur . . . comme je veux." *La Libre Belgique* 25 July 2002.

"Entre chien et loup." *La Croix* 13 Dec. 2002.

"La prière des heures." *Prier*, hors-série, Oct. 2003.

"On ne possède pas la foi, on est possédé par elle." *La Croix* 29 August 2005.

"Le plus important d'abord." In Luc Templier, *52 méditations pour vivre*, Dervy, 2005.

"Le bon combat." *Prier* March 2007.

"Compagnons de route." *Les essentiels*, no. 3323, *La Vie* (26 Feb. 2009): 43–49.

Paroles d'ermite: Le Père André Louf. Documentary. CFRT/KTO/Sunset Press, 52 minutes. Directed by Laurence Chartier, 2009.

General Bibliography

Adnès, Pierre. "La méthode hésychaste." *Studia Missionalia* 25 (1976): 279.

Aerden, Guerric. "Le portrait spirituel d'un grand moine." Unedited document, 2010.

Ampe, Albert. "Jean Ruusbroec." *Dictionnaire de Spiritualité, Ascétique et Mystique.* Paris: Beauchesne, 1932–1995. 8:659.

"André Scrima (1925–2000), un moine hésychaste de notre temps, I." *Contacts* no. 203 (July–Sept. 2003).

Aubert, Roger. "Organisation et caractère des mouvements de jeunesse catholiques en Belgique." In *La "gioventù cattolica" dopo l'unità. 1868–1968*, edited by G. de Rosa. *Politica e Storia* 28 (1972): 271–323.

Benoît XVI. *Dernières conversations avec Peter Seewald.* Paris: Fayard, 2016.

Bertrand, Dominique. "L'envol de la patristique en France au milieu du XXe siècle (1942–1958)." *Bulletin de l'association internationale Cardinal Henri de Lubac* 7 (2005): 28–49.

Bertrand, Dominique. "Saint Bernard en Français." *Collectanea Cisterciensia* 50 (1988): 46–56.

Bour, Pierre. *Le psychodrame et la vie.* Paris: Desclée de Brouwer, 1976.

Bour, Pierre. *Les racines de l'homme.* Paris: Robert Laffont, 1976.

Bour, Pierre. *L'inconscient et la grâce.* Paris: Levain, 1985.

Bouyer, Louis, *Le sens de la vie monastique.* 1950. Paris: Cerf, 2008.

Cassien, Jean. *Conférences VIII–XVII.* Trans. and notes Eugène Pichery. Sources Chrétiennes 54. Paris: Cerf, 1958.

Caza, Lorraine. "Mon passionnant 'Chantier cistercien.' " *Collectanea Cisterciensia* 50 (1988): 5–45.

Cogent, Louis, "Introduction aux mystiques rhéno-flamands." Paris: Desclée de Brouwer, 1968.

Davril, Anselme. "Impressions de l'Athos." *Renaissance de Fleury* 76 (1970): 19–30.

De Lubac, Henri. *Exégèse médiévale: Les quatre sens de l'Écriture.* Paris: Aubier, 1959.

Deseille, Placide. *Étapes d'un pèlerinage: Autobiographie spirituelle.* Saint-Laurent-en-Royans: Monastère Saint-Antoine-le-Grand, 2015.

Deseille, Placide. "Une vie monastique en quête de la vraie lumière. Entretiens." *Lumière et vie* no. 298 (April-June 2013): 5–24.

Doyère, Pierre. *Benoît Labre, Ermite-pèlerin.* Paris: Cerf, 1983.

Dubois, Marie-Gérard. *Happiness in God: Memories and Reflections of the Father Abbot of La Trappe.* Translated by Georges Hoffmann and Jean Truax. Monastic Wisdom series 58. Collegeville, MN: Cistercian Publications, 2019.

Dubois, Marie-Gérard. *Le bonheur de Dieu: Souvenirs et réflexions du père abbé de La Trappe.* Paris: Robert Laffont, 1995.

Dubois, Marie-Gérard. *L'ordre cistercien de la stricte observance au XXᵉ siècle.* 2 vols. Rome: OCSO, 2008.

Dupont, Jacques. *Seul devant l'unique: Entretiens avec un chartreux.* Paris: Parole et Silence, 2016.

Durel, Alain. *La presqu'île interdite: Initiation au mont Athos.* Paris: Albin Michel, 2010.

Escobar Molina, Alvaro. *L'enfermement: Espace, temps, clôture.* Paris: Klincksieck, 1989.

Gevers, Lieve. "Apogée et fin d'une époque (1926–1961): L'archevêché sous le cardinal Van Roey." In *L'archidiocèse de Malines-Bruxelles: 450 ans d'histoire,* edited by J. De Maeyer, É. Put, J. Roegiers, A. Tihon, and G. Vanden Bosch. 2 vols. Anvers: Halewijn, 2009. 2:172–253.

Gilbert, Maurice. *L'Institut biblique pontifical: Un siècle d'histoire (1909–2009).* Rome: Pontificio Istituto Biblico, 2009.

Gilson, Étienne. *La théologie mystique de saint Bernard.* Paris: Vrin, 1934.

Gribomont, Jean. "Une mission monastique à la Sainte-Montagne de l'Athos." *Collectanea Cisterciensia* 34 (1972): 155–74.

Gueullette, Jean-Marie. *L'assise et la présence: La prière silencieuse dans la tradition chrétienne*. Paris: Albin Michel, 2017.

Guigues le Chartreux. *Lettre sur la vie contemplative*. Sources Chrétiennes 163. Paris: Cerf, 1970.

Guilerand, Auguste. *Silence cartusien*. Paris: Desclée de Brouwer, 1976.

Guillaume de Saint-Thierry. *Lettre aux frères du Mont-Dieu*. Sources Chrétiennes 223. Paris: Cerf, 1975.

Hausherr, Irénée. *Solitude et vie contemplative d'après l'hésychasme*. Bégrolles-en-Mauges: Abbaye de Bellefontaine, 1980.

Isaac, Hiéromoine. *L'ancien Païssios de la Sainte-Montagne*. Lausanne: L'Âge d'homme, 2009.

Jean-Claude, Frère. *Primitifs Flamands*. Paris: Pierre Terrail, 2007.

Lambrechts, Antoine. "Pèlerins bénédictins au mont Athos." *Irenikon* 71 (1998): 281–89.

Leclercq, Jean. *L'amour des lettres et le désir de Dieu: Initiation aux auteurs monastiques du Moyen Âge*. Paris: Cerf, 1957.

Leclercq, Jean. *The Love of Learning and the Desire of God*. Trans. Catherine Misrahi. 3rd rev. edition. New York: Fordham University Press, 1982.

Lekai, Louis Julius. *The Cistercians: Ideals and Reality*. Kent, OH: Kent State University Press, 1977.

Loi, Roberto. "Alla scuola della grazia: Il percorso spirituale di p. André Louf." *La Scala* 69 (2015): 147–64, 244–60; 70 (2016): 38–42.

Mellerin, Laurence. "L'édition des œuvres de Bernard de Clairvaux dans la collection 'Sources chrétiennes.' " *Actes du colloque "Journée culture cistercienne" du 12 juin 2009*. Paris: Conférences du Collège des Bernardins, 2009. 129–48.

Merton, Thomas. "La vie solitaire." *Collectanea Cisterciensia* 35 (1973): 137–41.

Merton, Thomas. "Letter on Solitude and Community." *Cistercian Studies* 25 (1990): 75–78.

Moine, Un. *L'ermitage*. Preface by Jean-François Holthof. Paris: Ad Solem, 2005.

Morales, Xavier. *Dieu est amitié: La spiritualité d'Aelred de Rievaulx*. Paris: Salvator, 2016.

Panofsky, Erwin. *Les primitifs flamands*. Paris: Hazan, 2010.

Parolari, Enrico. "Nel ricordo di André Louf." *Tredimensioni* 9 (2012): 58–69.

Porion, Jean-Baptiste. *Lettres et écrits spirituels*. Paris: Beauchesne, 2011.

Rodenbach, Georges. *Bruges-la-Morte*. Paris: GF/Flammarion, 1998.

Salin, Dominique. Introduction to *L'abandon à la Providence divine*. Paris: Desclée de Brouwer/Bellarmin, 2005. 7–30.

Salin, Dominique. *L'expérience spirituelle et son langage: Leçons sur la tradition chrétienne*. Paris: Éditions Facultés Jésuites de Paris, 2015.

Saraco, Alessandro. *Discernement et accompagnement spirituel dans les écrits d'André Louf*. Nouan-le-Fuzelier: Éditions des Béatitudes, 2016.

Saraco, Alessandro. *La grâce dans la faiblesse: L'expérience spirituelle d'André Louf*. Nouan-le-Fuzelier: Éditions des Béatitudes, 2013.

Scrima, André. "La tradition du père spirituel dans l'Église d'Orient." *Hermès* 4 (1967): 79–94.

Scrima, André. "L'avènement philocalique dans l'orthodoxie roumaine." *Istina* 5 (1958): 295–328.

Six, Jean–François. "De l'hagiographie à la biographie." *Vie spirituelle* Nov.–Dec. 1989: 713–26.

Standaert, Benoît. "In Memoriam André Louf, OCSO (1929–2010)." Unedited. 2010.

Trinchero, Federico. "Optanda infirmitas: L'esperienza spirituale secondo André Louf." *Rivista di vita spirituale* 62 (2008).

Verdeyen, Paul. *Ruusbroec L'admirable*. Paris: Cerf, 1990.

Vos, Louis, and Lieve Gevers. "The Catholic Flemish Student Movement 1875–1935. Emergence and Decline of a Unique Youth Movement." In *The History of Youth Work in Europe. Relevance for Today's Youth Work Policy*, edited by Griet Verschelden, Filip Coussée, Tineke Van de Walle, and Howard Williamson. Strasbourg: Éditions du Conseil de l'Europe, 2009. 29–44.

Vos, Louis, and Lieve Gevers. "Youth Movements in Flanders: A Short History." In *The History of Youth Work in Europe. Rele-*

vance for Today's Youth Work Policy, edited by Griet Verschelden, Filip Coussée, Tineke Van de Walle, and Howard Williamson. Strasbourg: Éditions du Conseil de l'Europe, 2009. 167–76.

William of St. Thierry. *The Golden Epistle: A Letter to the Brethren at Mont Dieu*. Translated by Theodore Berkeley. The Works of William of St. Thierry. Cistercian Fathers series 12. Kalamazoo, MI: Cistercian Publications, 1980.

Yourcenar, Marguerite. *Archives du nord (1977)*. Paris: Folio-Gallimard, 2015.

Notes of Gratitude

I wish first to thank Père Marc-André Di Péa, the abbot of Mont-des-Cats during the time I was writing this book, at the close of Summer 2016; he opened the Mont-des-Cats archives to me with a confidence that honors me. I also thank the entire community for bearing with my presence there during that time.

Dom Guillaume Jedrzejczak, who succeeded Dom Louf as abbot of Mont-des-Cats, was a valuable guide at the beginning of my research.

Mère Elaié Bollen, abbess of Sainte-Lioba, received me like a prince at Simiane. Along with so much else, I owe her the ability to have understood better the "poor" and the "lowly" person that Dom André became at the end of his life. I also thank the group of witnesses who agreed to meet me or to write to me, in any case to devote time to me, in order to explain episodes in Dom André's life or aspects of his personality or of his ministry. I lack room and possibility to mention all their names, although I have sometimes done so in the course of the work. Without their remembrances or their avowals, this book would not have the same interest or the same savor.

The Carthusian fathers who were contacted in the course of my research were true to their reputation for discretion. In acting thus they honored the memory of their friend André, who devoted an unconditional love to the Carthusian tradition.

It has not been the least of the graces of this work that I was able to meet the family of Dom Louf, particularly his sister Lieve and his brother-in-law Willy de Smedt.

My gratitude also goes out to all those persons who had the kindness to send me rare documents, archives, and unobtainable articles: Soeur Marie-David Weill of the review *Vie Consacrée*, Frère Jean-Baptiste, in charge of *Renaissance de Fleury*, at the abbey of Saint-Benoît-sur-Loire, Sabino Chiala of the monastery of Bose, Elisa of the Italian publishing company Qiqajon, Soeur Marie-Aimée de Jesus of the monastery of Sainte Claire à Paray-le-Monial, the university library at the Catholic University of Louvain, Carlo Valentino, secretary general of the Pontifical Biblical Institute at Rome, Frère Gérard Joyau at *Collectanea Cisterciensia*, Frère Giulio Meiattini of the Benedictine Abbey of La Scala in Italy, Marc C. Meade of the Thomas Merton Center at Bellarmine College in Louisville, Kentucky, Dimitris Kaimakis of the University of Thessaloniki, and not forgetting Laurence Mellerin, of the staff of Sources Chrétiennes, and the family of Dr. Hubert Ronse de Craene, who sent me some personal archives. I owe Louis Vos, historian emeritus of the Catholic University of Louvain, and Éric Colenbier, archivist at the Katholiek Studentenactie of the diocese of Bruges, for guiding me in the abundant history of the Flemish youth movements.

My requirements and indecisiveness have tried the patience of my editor, Michel Cool, with rude trials. May his confidence be rewarded.

Without the unfailing love of Julie Quaillet and Laura Sainton, I could not have brought this research to its end.

Finally I thank Dom Louf himself, who has watched over this work and its author like a she-wolf over her pups.